DATE DUE

NOV 29 '89		MAY 17 '91
DEC 01		MAY 1 7
MAY 21 '90 MAY 10		

THOSE WHO FALL

THOSE WHO FALL

JOHN MUIRHEAD

Random House New York

Grateful acknowledgment is made to the following for permission to reprint previously published material:

Henry Holt and Company: Excerpts from "A Shropshire Lad," Authorized Edition, by A. E. Housman, from *The Collected Poems of A. E. Housman*. Copyright 1939, 1940, © 1965 by Holt, Rinehart and Winston. Copyright © 1967, 1968 by Robert E. Symons. Canadian and Open Market rights administered by The Society of Authors as the literary representative of the Estate of A. E. Housman and Jonathan Cape Ltd., publishers of A. E. Housman's *Collected Poems*. Reprinted by permission.

Macmillan Publishers Ltd. (London): Excerpt from "The Man He Killed" by Thomas Hardy, in *Collected Poems*.

New Directions Publishing Corporation: Excerpts from "Futility" and "Anthem for Doomed Youth" by Wilfred Owen, from *Collected Poems of Wilfred Owen*, edited by C. Day Lewis. Copyright © 1963 by Chatto & Windus Ltd. World rights in the English language excluding the United States administered by Chatto & Windus Ltd. Excerpts from "Twenty Two" and "XIII" by Dylan Thomas, from *The Notebooks of Dylan Thomas*. Copyright © 1967 by the Trustees for the Copyrights of Dylan Thomas. World rights in the English language excluding the United States administered by David Higham Associates Limited (London). Reprinted by permission.

The Society of Authors: Excerpt from "Peace" by Walter de la Mare. Reprinted by permission of The Literary Trustees of Walter de la Mare and The Society of Authors as their representative.

Estate of Arthur Symons: Excerpt from "In the Wood of Finvara" by Arthur Symons. Reprinted by permission of the Literary Estate of Arthur Symons.

Viking Penguin Inc.: Excerpt from "Dreamers" by Siegfried Sassoon, from *Collected Poems* by Siegfried Sassoon. Copyright 1918 by E. P. Dutton & Co. Copyright renewed 1946 by Siegfried Sassoon. Canadian and Open Market rights administered by George Sassoon. Reprinted by permission.

Library of Congress Cataloging-in-Publication Data
Muirhead, John.
Those who fall.

1. Muirhead, John.   2. World War, 1939–1945—
Personal narratives, American.   3. Air pilots, Military
—United States—Biography.   4. World War, 1939–1945—
Aerial operations, American.   5. World War, 1939–1945—
Campaigns—Italy.   6. B-17 bomber.   I. Title.
D811.M795   1986   940.54'4945   86-5411
ISBN 0-394-54983-X

Manufactured in the United States of America

2 3 4 5 6 7 8 9
First edition

TO JEAN

Go from me: I am one of those who fall.
What! hath no cold wind swept your heart at all,
In my sad company? Before the end,
    Go from me. . . .

—LIONEL JOHNSON

Contents

THOSE WHO FALL

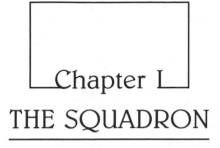

Chapter 1

THE SQUADRON

From far, from eve and morning
And yon twelve-winded sky,
The stuff of life to knit me
Blew hither: here am I.

—A. E. HOUSMAN

I suppose I am like most men who soldiered for a time. I think that something unusual happened to me; some particular meaning was revealed to me so I should set it down. Men have been boring their wives, their children, and other men with these kind of stories from Marathon through Chickamauga, and I'm no different from the lot. Having survived it all, I can't leave well enough alone, but must ponder on it and remember and talk at least about one part of it that was, I think, a kind of glory.

On the twenty-third of June, 1944, I ended my time as a bomber pilot flying out of Italy with the 301st Bomb Group, and became a prisoner of war in Bulgaria. My last mission was to Ploesti. Although that name had its own dreadful sound, the other places and other names all took their toll whether you feared them or not. It mattered very little when you finally bought it. The odds were, one always knew, that something was going to happen. It was not felt in any desperate way, but rather it came as a difference in consciousness without one's being aware of the change. In the squadron we learned to live as perhaps once we were long ago, as simple as animals without hope for ourselves or pity for one another. Completing fifty missions was too implausible to even consider. An alternative, in whatever form it might come, was the only chance. Death was the most severe alternative. It was as near as the next mission, although we would not yield to the thought of it. We would get through somehow: maybe a good wound, or a bail-out over Yugoslavia or northern Italy; the second front might open up, and the Germans might shift all their fighters to the French coast. We might even make it through fifty missions— a few did. But such fantasies didn't really persuade us, not with our sure knowledge that we were caught in a bad twist of time with little chance we would go beyond it. Our lives were defined by a line from the present to a violent moment that must come for each of us. The missions we flew were the years we measured to that end, passing by no different from any man's except we became old and died soon.

The 301st, one of five B-17 groups that made up the Fifth Wing, occupied a share of hard-won acreage on the Foggia Plains, and it included in its suzerainty a road that stretched for twelve miles between the towns of Foggia and Lucera. The airfield that served the four squadrons of the 301st was code-named Longskirt; it was three miles from Lucera, and access to it was on a rough dirt track that led from the highway to a six-thousand-foot runway, a collection of shacks and Quonset huts and a surrounding taxi strip with thirty or more hardstands where our B-17s waited, brooding under the low, gray skies of winter.

My squadron was bivouacked near the road in a grove of olive trees. We were closer to Lucera than we were to Foggia, and the entrance to Longskirt was only a short distance from us, a mile or so as I remember. Our squadron area was usually quiet except on mornings when we were preparing for a mission or when, on rare occasions, units of the British Eighth Army moved by our camp. A ruddy-faced sergeant major always led the column and always there was a piper right behind him. The English were old hands at this. Their armies had marched these roads before in other wars in other years. We were new, self-conscious with our destiny, and never would manage to be like them. Even the music of the piper was primitive, calling glory from ancient battles to echo courage in their hearts. As they passed by they would always salute our colors. The sergeant-major's yell of command would come clear to us, through the crashing rumble of their tanks, through the din of hundreds of boots battering the dusty road, through the air swirling in movement as this melee of men and machines moved by. His shout touched us with tribute and at last made us one.

I never did find out where the other three squadrons in our bomb group were located. The only comradeship with them was in the air. Our squadron was a world apart, a casual village of tents and small gnarled trees. The tents, like houses in a village, varied in style and elegance. Some were models of good labor. They put up a brave front of secure comfort with wood floors made from bomb crates and crude furniture made from the same material. A few even had flowerpots hung from the doorframes to catch the light. But the plants didn't grow. Indifferent gardeners gave them little care, and the wisps of pale greenery struggled against the sunless days. There were other tents beyond redemption, erected in contempt of any acknowledgment of permanence. Their poles were awry; their lines slack and poorly pegged. They shuddered, flapping in the cold February winds, like the tattered pennants of desperate men.

I moved into an already erected tent with three new comrades in February of 1944, having been transferred out of a B-24 outfit farther south after nine missions. The previous tenants were gone and lost. The reason for my transfer was that I had B-17 time and the 301st, a B-17 group, was in need of pilot replacements. I regretted leaving my original crew back in Cerignola, although my disappointment was

reconciled by a kind of relief. Anonymity had its advantages. Camaraderie among crews that had been together a long time made each
member vulnerable and was a burden of love that couldn't flourish.
It was better to be alone.

The tent fell somewhere in the middle-class bracket, not fancy, but
comfortable. There was a wood floor and, best of all, a stove that
worked. A good stove that didn't blow up when igniting it or during
operation was a prized possession. The installation was always the
same, yet some worked well and others didn't. This stove was a good
one. Like all the others, it consisted of a glycol tank that had been
removed from an aircraft's de-icing system. The tank was mounted on
a stand outside the tent and filled with one-hundred-octane fuel. The
gas was then piped into the tent and was allowed to drip through a
small petcock onto a bed of small stones. If all went well, the vaporizing
gas would be ignited and would burn steadily. A split half of a fifty-
gallon drum would then be placed over the burning gas to contain
the heat and radiate a comforting glow. This was the way it was
supposed to work. When success wasn't achieved, the results could be
dramatic.

Rich Egan was a madman and his tank was a menace; his piping
was a disgrace; his joints weren't sealed; this was the third tent he had
blown up; it was a better fire than the last one; when I was in his tent
there was octane all over the bloody floor. Why didn't he let someone
who knew what he was doing fix the goddamn thing? Did you see the
crazy son-of-a-bitch run when it went up? I never put Egan down
myself because I knew if I hadn't moved into a tent that had a stove
already installed, I'd have botched up the job much worse than he;
besides, I liked the man. There was a passion in his ineptness, and
his pyrotechnics were the talk of the group. No doubt about it, Rich
added to our reputation. He gave us style.

There were other originals too. Art Dillman, for one, was secretive
and gentle as Egan was precipitous and violent. Art disregarded the
war as much as possible and concerned himself only with his dogs: a
dachshund bitch and three pups. Where he got them no one knew.
None of us ever saw dogs, or cats for that matter, in this poor battered
part of Italy. They had all perished or gone into the soup long ago.
Art lived alone in his tent with his canine family. No one knew how
he managed that with the C.O. either. I remember the grooming days
that always preceded Art's occasional trips to Foggia. It had to be a
sunny and mild day. He would sit outside of his tent on a small stool,
naked as he was born except for sloppy combat boots on his feet and

a baseball cap tipped forward on his head shielding his eyes. He would concentrate on his task, cleaning and brushing each dog in turn until its coat gleamed in the sun. Only after each dog passed his critical inspection and was perfectly groomed and secured inside the tent would he leave for the shower stalls, about one quarter of a mile away, to perform his own toilet.

The final appearance of the family ready for town was a picture of true elegance. Art would be dressed in full uniform: green blouse, tie, gray trousers, and tan boots, with the bitch and the three pups on a single leather leash with four braided leads to each animal. He also toted a musette bag over his shoulder, well provisioned with the tools of seduction: cigarettes, soap, chocolate and various candy bars, and, of course, silk stockings. The promenade through the squadron area to where Art took possession of Major Devereaux's jeep we always viewed with satisfaction. The return later was something else. Art would be quite drunk, carrying the three exhausted puppies in his

arms with the bitch staggering along behind. And although we never knew where they went or to what caprice they had lent themselves, we were sure that they had accomplished their wanton task. Art never told us anything. We figured that it was at least a countess.

Then there was Willie Balcom, a tough, scrawny tail gunner from New Jersey. He was thin and pinch-shouldered with a narrow, hungry face and pale gray eyes. Willie, too, had another world apart from us. He slipped in and out of the squadron area, and we rarely saw him except at briefings. He made his missions. Somehow he always knew when he was posted on the battle orders. His real life was with a farm family up in the hills, where he spent every free moment. He learned to milk goats, acquired a taste for the sour red wine and smelled it. He amazed us all with his quickness in picking up the language. One of the Italian boys who worked for us in the area digging slit trenches and maintaining the latrine pits told me Willie's Italian was almost perfect except for a slight nasal inflection and a persistence in the use of the obscenity *fuckin'* as an essential addition to the Italian language. Willie really loved that family. It was probably the only one he'd ever had. He finally purchased the farm for the old man. It probably cost Willie no more than what he might have lost in one or two nights at the craps table. And Willie always had bad nights.

My new tentmates in the 301st were run-of-the-mill, ordinary types who endlessly complained about trifles but reasonably endured the moments of terror and the interminable boredom between as measures of luck that men must expect to encounter at one time or another. McCarthy, a navigator, was a heavyset man with a round face and small eyes and close-cropped hair. He was friendly but often tentatively aggressive, the kind of fellow who would never quite outgrow a boyhood of successful bullying. Paul Leigh, a copilot, was gentle, incredibly naïve, a perfect foil for McCarthy. He was born to be had by almost anybody. The third man, Harold Kourtz, another navigator, was a thin, tense individual, prematurely bald and a chronic bitcher. It wasn't the best possible draw for tentmates, but it could have been worse. And then I was something of a case to them too; more often than not silent and moody with a bleak humor that sometimes, I think, seemed arrogant. But we managed and a bond grew between us. We considered ourselves to be much better off than many of the others. We even learned in some ways to help each other. I arbitrated between Mac and Paul to try to ease the effect of Mac's constant baiting. We all tried to pick up Harold's spirits when we could. Paul's confidence grew, and he even got up enough nerve to kid me about my reading.

He said I was a Boston snob and, if I ever got to South Carolina, he would teach me some manners. No, Mac, Leigh, and Kourtz weren't bad at all, and they allowed me a certain deference because I was a pilot and a plane commander with nine missions. The last attribute was the most important one. Prestige was somehow linked to the mystery of survival. Nine missions was maturity; up to fifteen or more was to be regarded with awe; beyond that was magic, luck to be touched, to be near and favored beyond everything else.

Through the cold days of February with the weather bad most of the time, it was all a matter of waiting. Few missions were flown, although many were attempted. We were sent up again and again on the slim opportunities the weather would give us. Always hunting for a wedge of clear air, our squadrons would rise into the mist to flounder through the darkness and rain in search of it.

There were terrible hours of tension. The pilots, soaked with perspiration, strained by hours of concentration, held their planes in tight formation to keep visual contact. To lose sight of a wingman or a flight leader, even for an instant, to be alone in the gray mountains of clouds, meant almost inevitable collision. We would know when it happened by a reverberating shudder of air against our planes and a glow of brief light illuminating the darkness. Then there would be a different rain making its journey to the wet earth, and wisps of vapor would rise from the things on the ground.

When there was no chance of flying, the men filled the time without purpose or care. Endless bridge and poker games became a total occupation for some. Letter writers grimly sucked their pens not knowing what to say except the trite things they finally put down. There was always a craps game: an intense, passionate, vocal exchange of dollars, pounds, francs, lire, rings, watches, and vouchers for future pay. Some read. Some slept. The sound of Art's clarinet often trilled "The Muskat Ramble" in obbligato to the shouts of the craps players. Some wandered away to sit mindless in the Red Cross canteen, sipping coffee while gossiping about missions and exchanging rumors.

It seems strange to remember that we found this way of living natural. We went from the unforgiving discipline of the air to a casual apathy on the ground as soon as we left the one for the other. The sky filled our senses beyond anything we had ever come upon. In that blue crucible our youth had at last reached the place to spend itself. On the ground there was only waiting as the long minutes emptied into hours untended by fear.

Chapter II

A STRANGE RENDEZVOUS

I fled the earth, and naked, climbed the weather,
reached a second ground far from the stars:
And there we wept, I and a ghostly other . . .

—DYLAN THOMAS

My first time up with the squadron was a sweep, a tactic that was supposed to flush out enemy fighters by sending one or more squadrons of bombers ahead of the main effort and somewhat off the heading of the group and wing formations. The job was to get enemy fighters in the air so that they would burn up fuel, committing themselves to us. If the stratagem worked, they would be on the ground refueling when the real attack penetrated their area. Like most military plans, it sounded good; but the execution, more often than not, revealed that it was a waste. The German fighter groups had excellent intelligence and wouldn't be suckered. Those of us who had to fly these sorties knew that they would predictably ignore us. They would be aware of the bomber formations behind us and the urgent flow of fighters moving north to cover the real target. Our squadron would be watched for any excessive penetration, but they would more than likely leave us alone. The transparency of this sweep strategy inevitably caused it to be abandoned. Everybody knew where we were going anyway.

Takeoff was at first light, about six. I dressed at four in a dark tent, trying not to wake my sleeping comrades. They had not been listed on the battle orders for today's mission; they would enjoy the luxury of idleness. Mac stirred, murmured a good luck, and went back to sleep. Dressing was a quick business of only slipping on a flight suit over my heavy underwear and putting on boots and a jacket. The rest of my gear I'd pick up at briefing. I left the tent to make my way toward the mess, stopping to urinate on a tree, a spot I shared with Art's dachshunds. A few other ghosts moved through the woods, silent except for a softly muttered curse as someone caught a branch or stumbled on a tent line. Breakfast was good: a large hot mug of coffee with some scrambled eggs that were a minor miracle made from dehydrated eggs by our mess sergeant. A great man, our mess sergeant Rogers, a genius and an ugly mother to us all. Thick toast and jam finished it off with another mug of coffee to take care of the time until the trucks came. The mess was quiet. Men ate in the dim light and said little. One of the black mess men moved among us pouring hot coffee, a cigarette hanging from his lips, and he sang softly:

> I've been around the world in a plane.
> I've settled revolutions in Spain.
> But now I'm broken-hearted,
> 'Cause I can't get started with you.

I felt chilled, but it wasn't that cold. I was remembering my old B-24 squadron. I was remembering trying to land a shot-up plane at Cerignola with one dead man and two wounded on board. Number-three engine had been shot out along with the hydraulic system. No brakes landing. The ball turret wouldn't retract, and we tore it off when we hit the runway. I remembered the dead waist gunner lying in a bed of empty shell casings, the back of his head blown off. I remembered the tail gunner propped up against the fuselage, dazed and bleeding all over everything. Burning with shame, I remembered that I had no pity, that I had cursed them all, hating them for failing me, for their guns going silent during the fight.

There was a roaring racket of engines and the clatter of dropping tailboards outside. The trucks had come.

Briefing was in a large Quonset hut that was set up like a theater. There was a stage and a slightly sloping floor with fixed seats. The centerpiece of the stage was a large wooden frame now covered, appropriately enough, by a black cloth. The frame would eventually be uncovered to display a map of the day's mission with a black tape marking the route from Longskirt to the target. The end of that tape was the first terror of the day.

Farther back on the stage there was a screen for projecting aerial photographs of the target area; data furnished by the blue P-38s that flew alone and unarmed to get this data. That kind of lone reconnaissance appealed to me. There was a cavalier aspect to it, the gallant insouciance of a brave man daring his foe to catch-me-if-you-can. They always took off before dawn, stretching their climb as they traveled north or east over the Adriatic. Their landfalls varied between Trieste and Venice on their northern treks and in the vicinity of Split on the coast of Yugoslavia when they headed east toward the oil fields of Rumania. Their bright blue color made them very difficult to spot in the early morning light. Their speed, maneuverability, and the extreme altitude at which they operated, made flak little more than a nuisance to them. Unless enemy fighters were alerted early, they could rarely climb fast enough to get to the P-38s and, even if they reached them, when the 38s nosed down to run, without guns or armor weighing them down, nothing could catch them. But, like any quarry, if their habits became predictable and the Germans sensed they would be sniffing out one particular target area, the German fighters would be up before them, waiting in the sun.

The briefing officers came in and took their seats on the stage. The map was uncovered and, to no one's surprise, the tape led to the Udine area, a major fighter belt that guarded the southeast approaches to Europe. We were to fly up the Adriatic, penetrating the mainland west of Trieste, and head for Udine. Twenty minutes on this course, then head for home unless fighters came at us. In which case, we would not engage them, but run.

The bland statements that were made by Intelligence always stunned us. The vision of a squadron of B-17s plodding along at one fifty indicated, running from a pack of ME-109s, demonstrated that the briefing officer was ignorant beyond belief or he didn't know what to tell us to do if they really took the bait. So, he said simply—run. We couldn't run. We would be too deep in their area, and we were too slow to get out. We would have to dance to their tune if it came to that and fight them for as long as they wanted. The weather officer droned on about high cirrus formations with broken clouds at five thousand feet. Communications gave us our frequencies: Big Fence, Channel One; Longskirt, Channel Two; Mayday, Channel Three; Air Sea Rescue, Channel Four; Squadron, Five. No fighter escort today. No bombs, no propaganda leaflets. We were warned to watch for our fighters, who would be flying north along our track as we were returning. There were snickers from the crews. We fired at anything that pointed its nose at us, even if it were a sea gull or an angel of God. The chief armorer told us we had seven hundred rounds per gun and gave us the latest on the power of the fighters we might be meeting. The projector clicked on and the squadron formation was flashed on the screen. Captain Coursey was leading in 347. I had 725 and was leading the second flight. I jotted down the information I needed on a small piece of paper that I would tape to my upper leg when I was seated in my plane. The navigation officer briefed us in detail on our course, airspeed, altitude, and alternates. The briefing was about over. We hacked our watches against the master chronometer. Takeoff was at 0645.

We moved out of the briefing room to pick up our flight gear, which was in a smaller Quonset hut nearby. I felt a desire for coffee, a large mug of hot coffee, even a cup of my mother's coffee. The thought of home and my mother's kitchen with that black brew sitting in the enameled pot on the stove made me smile. No insipid, thin amber liquid for my mother. Her coffee was black, thick, and unmercifully strong. I think the pot went on the stove the day she moved into the house, and from that day on it only moved to pour a cup or two, then returned to the stove to brew through all eternity. Occasionally the pot would receive some fresh water, occasionally a sprinkle of fresh grounds, occasionally a few of the old grounds would be removed; but a fresh pot, never. My two older brothers and I considered it a test of our young manhood. My young sister sensibly avoided it altogether. My father, who was a man reared in the hard traditions of the sea, sipped the stuff dutifully; as he endured all things, this was the coffee served to him; this was the coffee he drank.

"Hey, Lieutenant, are you with us?" The supply sergeant was slamming my gear on the counter. He pushed a list in front of me that itemized the equipment issued for the mission. I signed it. It was all there: flak vest, helmet, oxygen mask, parachute, harness, medical kit, binoculars, Benzedrine pills, package of morphine tubes, inflatable vest, flare gun, flare cartridges, two quarts of coffee, one of tomato juice, escape purse, ten Wing cigarettes, headset, throat mike, and a package of Spam sandwiches that would turn to concrete at twenty-five thousand feet. I started to jam everything into a B-5 bag the sergeant gave me. "Wait a minute," he said. He reached under the counter and came up with a Thermos of coffee. He unscrewed the cap and poured a cup of the steaming dark liquid. Handing it to me, he smiled, "You're the pilot, right? You'd better wake up." I mumbled a thanks and took a sip. It was delicious; not at all like my mother's.

The dirt road was bumpy and the benches were wet. I checked my briefing notes half listening to the crashing noises of the truck as we made our way toward the field. The early light of morning gave us our first good look at the sky. There would be a mission. There was

:e of low scud and that was blowing out. The sky was clear
high cirrus in the east. It was cool, but not the piercing
l been. Along the dirt road brown clumps of winter grass
glistened with dew. A stand of poplars flashed by, jeweled
with moisture, swaying in the cool morning light. There was a faint
fragrance in the air, a promise maybe of an early spring.

The truck rattled on and the flight line came in view. I saw the tail-
low profile of my plane. She seemed poised, thrusting forward, leaning
breathless toward the sky. She was waiting with the grace of a good

creature to do my will. One who could not understand her divinity
might say she was only dirt out of the ground except for the mind of
man; that she was a machine and not a valiant steed; that life would
never touch her; that she was as indifferent to her creation as she would
be to her death; that she was without soul or spirit. But there was
something else, a mystery pilots knew of her great beating heart, and
a sacred vow she made to me: that she would put her strength in my
hands; that she would bear me to the end; that she would give herself

to my mad purpose with perfect courage and beyond all human love. And so I approached her, my noble friend, to do this day's work.

The crew chief was waiting with the engineering report in his hand. He was a big man with shaggy black hair and a cigar clamped in the corner of his mouth. He smelled of sweat, oil, and fatigue. He told me everything was all right. She was on a red diagonal, which flagged a write-up in the Engineering Report regarding two minor instrument deficiencies, but nothing serious enough to keep her on the ground. The carburetor air temperature on number four was out. The cylinder-head temperatures should have been calibrated, but the instrument man hadn't shown.

The chief paused, thought about it, and nagged me anyway. "For Chrissake, Lieutenant, keep that inside wheel moving when you turn her around. These steel mats are chewing the hell out of the tires. The captain told me the tires we were supposed to get are down the bottom of the fuckin' Atlantic Ocean so we gotta make these ones last. So—okay, Lieutenant?" He talked on as we walked around the aircraft and I made my preflight inspection. He pointed to two riveted patches on the fuselage. "Just finished those this morning. I'm no fuckin' seamstress, but that's a pretty good job, huh? I'm supposed to have a guy to do that kind of stuff, but they don't give me nobody. I got two guys and I get an extra one when I change an engine. Ever try and change an engine with a crummy A-frame and three dummies?" We were behind the tail when he put his hand on my arm and turned me toward him. He stared straight into my eyes and then made a sign over me and murmured something that, I guessed, was a blessing. Then, as though nothing had passed between us, he continued his monologue. "You guys are going to sweep Udine today, huh? I hope nobody shows. I don't want no more fuckin' holes in this airplane." We had almost completed our circuit when abruptly he walked away to pick up the extinguisher he would hold as I started each engine.

I talked for a few moments with the crew to confirm our standard procedures before we entered the plane. The crew members were strangers to me, as I was a stranger to them, and this was to be the situation, with occasional exceptions, on future misions. The squadron did not subscribe to the policy of trying to keep original crew members together; it was considered inefficient and contributed to morale problems when men were killed or wounded. It was a matter of depressing the incidence of crew overidentification I think they called it. The sad realitites of combat had to be accommodated: crew members had to be replaced, and this attrition contributed to the squadron's decision that it was not possible to retain discrete elements of air crew. We were pilots, navigators, bombardiers, and gunners, and, as squadron operations saw it, we need not know the other men in order to function as a crew. A B-17 required the hands and minds of ten men; ten men were provided. Neither the plane nor the mission needed anything else.

I had some trouble with my chute harness. The leg straps were tight, as they should be, and it took a few moments to snap the hooks. I went through the nose hatch, as the copilot and I usually did, by grasping the hatch edge over my head, lifting my weight, and swinging my legs up and through, like a boy climbing a tree.

I kept the inside wheel turning. The trick was not to use the brakes, but start the one-hundred-eighty-degree turn by gunning the inboard engine that was closest to the inside wheel and getting that wheel to start rolling very slowly; then cutting that engine back to almost idle, gun the outboard to make a tight turn, easing on power as I had to on the inboard to keep the wheel pivoting. There was little room on the steel parking mat to make the maneuver. It was much easier simply to gun the outboard engine and spin her around, grinding the inside wheel into the mat; but my pride was at stake, and I could see the crew chief standing at the end of the grass watching every move. His face broke into a grin as I completed the turn, and he made a thumbs-up gesture of approval. I started to taxi out, returning his salute with an obscene finger motion. His grin got broader. I stopped at the periphery strip to let Coursey and his wingmen go by and moved out behind them. I picked up my wingmen and tail-end Charlie at their front door, and the seven planes taxied slowly in a clumsy line toward the runway.

Coursey's second wingman was twenty seconds down the runway when I started to roll. Without the usual bomb load she responded quickly to the advancing throttles. We were a third down the runway and were at eighty. As I came back easy on the wheel I felt a slushy, responding pressure from the elevator surface; the nose raised and I held her gently, ready to ease off if she didn't want to hold it. At one hundred she wanted to go. I let off a little back pressure on the wheel and set the elevator trim. At one hundred and ten she left the ground, and the throbbing of the four engines was our pulse and heartbeat now. The earth dropped away. With her wheels tucked neatly up in the engine wells and the wings clean of trailing flaps, we banked in a shallow climbing turn over the old walls of Lucera. My wingmen were now clear and turning inside of me. We all aimed inside of the lead plane to join the formation as quickly as possible. At the end of the downwind leg, I was sliding in under Coursey's flight at the same time my wingmen were easing in on me. Tail-end Charlie was already in his position, slightly behind and below, his nose almost nudging my tail guns. The air was smooth as the squadron turned east in a slow climb over Lake Lesina and headed for the Adriatic.

Once well over the water, we opened the formation to test-fire the guns. The arrows of tracers sped through the morning light as the guns chattered briefly and were silent. The sea now stretched endlessly below us. The sky was blue and clear except for a few stratus clouds scattered like pink-and-orange ribbons across the sunrise. Today there were no concerns for rendezvous with wing-formation or with fighter escorts. We were alone and on our own. The steady sound of engines and the intermittent whir of the tracking top turret behind me were comforting, easing my consciousness to lay a calm hand on the fear inside me. In about an hour, we would make our landfall. Coursey's lead was good and the seven planes flew as one.

At twenty-one thousand feet we leveled off. We were suspended there, fixed in this place. Seven gleaming machines hung like a mobile in a vault of perfect sky. This was our purpose, to be simply here, to touch only this part of space and air with presence. We would never be beyond this, never to new battles nor back to old friends and time, but always here. Slender white streamers left our wingtips to mark our passing. The propeller blades hardly seemed to turn, and I lazily tried to count the spinning tips. Oxygen flowed cool over my mouth; I yearned for a cigarette. Away from the earth and things to measure by, the seven planes were seven crystals, delicate and shining in the sun. The moment was not to be held, but, as briefly found and almost entered, it passed. The copilot touched my shoulder pointing to the horizon, where I could see a bank of low cumulus and knew that land was down under there somewhere. It was thirty minutes to our landfall.

The coastline became visible below the clouds, and I could make out the islands that fronted the mainland. Grado was dead ahead; the peninsula of Bibare was off to the left. We were exactly on course, penetrating toward Udine in a line parallel to the highway that connected Udine to the town of Aquilera. As we passed over Grado, the ball turret called out two errant bursts of flak that fell about five hundred feet under us, probably marking bursts from German observers; and for a little while anyway, even if we didn't flush a fighter, we would be the center of some attention. The long slender snouts of the 88s would be pointed toward us—out of range, but patient. The train and elevation gears of the batteries would be meshed and moving, just waiting for that final signal from the careful eyes that watched the scopes, where we appeared as a pulsing yellow beetle crawling across a dark surface. Alarms and sirens would be screaming in the towns; and the people, crouched in horror in whatever shelter they could find, could not be told by us it was only a game today.

Our gunners were tracking intently. The whining of the searching turrets and the occasional clang as they hit the stops was an endless nervous sound as they picked at every inch of the sky looking for specks of black that could, in seconds, be what we hoped would never come: attacking fighters slashing at the formation with blinking guns and the closing venom of twenty-millimeter cannon shells, their last and best weapon, spitting at us in final hate as they hurled themselves against our guns. The sky was still empty. Even the intensity of our fear and watching couldn't summon them.

Three bursts of flak blossomed to our right, then collapsed into wisps of greasy haze. We were nearing Udine. At last, Coursey's left wing dipped and the formation wheeled back toward the sea. We hadn't raised a single fighter. The few bursts of ground fire were only contemptuous acknowledgments that they knew we were there. We had no importance. They weren't going to waste a thing on us.

In the safer air over the sea, the squadron trimmed for a slow descent. Manifold pressures were reduced, and the engine speeds came back to seventeen hundred. Fuel mixtures were leaned out as we settled down for the journey home. My throat was still very dry. The dreaded thing hadn't come this time.

"Bogey at six o'clock." The gunner's voice was calm. "It's only one. Christ, it looks like a P-38. Yeah, that's affirmative. It's a Little Friend. He's smoking." Every gun on the ship spun toward the tail, but no one fired. There had been no time. The tension had only hit us when the relief at the gunner's identification wiped out the fear that should have followed. "He's heading right at us. No, he'll pass to the left. Top turret, do you have him?" The tail kept talking, keeping the other gunners alert on the exact position of the approaching fighter. He had a good voice, Southwest, but not a drawl. Maybe California. I wondered who he was. "Jesus, he's all shot up. Hey, it's a recon job! Baby, he bought it today." I reached under my seat for my binoculars, motioning to the copilot to take over. "Left waist, he's closing. Track him. Do you have him? He's leaving my zone." I pressed the glasses against my window and looked aft. There he was, a reconnaissance P-38, smoking and burning. He was slanting by us in a shallow dive.

I tried to hold the binoculars steady. His canopy was shattered and there were jagged holes strung out along his fuselage. I could make out the pilot's form, still strapped in his seat. He had to be dead and probably never knew what hit him. The starboard engine was an inferno of orange flame. Smoke poured into his slipstream, leaving a trailing wake of broadening black that stained the sky for miles behind him. He was in my sight for only a moment and then he was gone, his dive carrying him down in a sloping, inevitable line to the sea.

The doomed plane wouldn't leave my mind. Threads of his smoke could still be seen and flecks of it whipped across my windshield. We had done their will and flushed a fighter, a poor wanderer of our own who came to us too late. The smoke was almost gone now. He was ending his journey. The blue water far below us waited to embrace him and hold him forever.

The formation held steady, slowly losing altitude. I didn't like our heading. We were going straight for Ravenna. At thirteen thousand feet we came off oxygen, and I had some juice and lit a cigarette. Fighters had caught him. He had probably been nosing up around Regensburg, where they were waiting with the sun at their backs. There was heavy reconnaissance in that area, and we were hearing rumors. It would be a tough target. Coursey finally corrected away from Ravenna. If he had got to us sooner, when he was making his run for it, maybe we could have helped him. Damaged fighters sometimes joined the bomber formations and limped home under the shield of their guns. Coursey broke in on me on the command frequency. "This is Red Squadron Leader. My navigator will make his splash. Pilots, don't let your gunners relax. Keep your eyes open. We're still in their backyard. Out." Coursey was not much for epitaphs.

Chapter III

R & R IN BARI

Now to your grave shall friend and stranger
  With ruth and some envy come:
Undishonored, clear of danger
  Clean of guilt, pass hence and home.

—A. E. HOUSMAN

I don't know whether any of this is true or not. Everything happened
that I have said happened, but it's memory now, the shadow of things.
The truth lives in its own time, recall is not the reality of the past.
When friends depart, one remembers them but they are changed; we
hold only the fragment of them that touched us and our idea of them,
which is now a part of us. Their reality is gone, intact but irretrievable,
in another place through which we passed and can never enter again.
I cannot go back nor can I bring them to me; so I must pursue the
shadows to some middle ground, for I am strangely bound to all that
happened then. We broke hard bread together and I can't forget:
Breslau, Steyr, Regensburg, Ploesti, Vienna, Munich, Graz, and all
the others; not cities, but battlegrounds five miles above them where
we made our brotherhood. It's gone and long ago; swept clean by the
wind, only some stayed. Part of me lives there still, tracing a course
through all the names. I don't know why. What is it that memory
wants that it goes through it all again? Was there something I should
have recognized? Some terrible wisdom? The kind of awful knowledge
that stares out of the eyes of a dying man? I was at the edge then and
almost grasped the meaning, but I lived and failed the final lesson and
came safe home. I linger now, looking back for them, the best ones
who stayed and learned it all.

Mac and I decided to go to Bari. All of southern Italy was under a
huge front. Bad weather was forecast for at least three days. The group

was going to stand down, and Major Devereaux, our squadron commander, gave out a few leaves. Mac persuaded me that Bari was the place to go. At that point, I was willing to go anywhere to get out of that tent to get away from Kourtz. Harry was in a bad way, being overcome by the worst kind of sickness, fear. We tried to rationalize it as an attack of ulcers and complained that X rays didn't mean a thing, that the flight surgeon, Doc Javit, was drunk all the time and didn't know what he was talking about. It was true Doc was always a little drunk, but Harry's problem wasn't ulcers.

Every mission he flew became more of an agony for him. He had only got in three; on two more he should have flown, he somehow got himself off the plane before takeoff. The last one he completed was a milk run up to the rail yards in Milan, and he was so bad afterward we didn't think he'd make it through the night. He vomited violently. We covered him with five blankets, and still he trembled. During brief spells when he slept, he perspired heavily, and twice, in the convulsive spasms of his fear-filled dreams, he soiled himself. As we washed him, his moans of apology were worse for us to hear than for him to say. He was possessed by a primal hell we could not exorcise. Doc helped by giving him some medication to sedate him, but he warned us: Harry's condition was serious and our efforts to cover it up must end. We didn't know what to do. We couldn't make a direct appeal for somebody to do more than what we were doing for fear that, in acknowledging Harry's condition, we would be abandoning him to the harsh judgment of a court martial. He couldn't fly, but Devereaux, the C.O., had to know and probably did. Harry's frail physique could not stand much more. If combat couldn't be borne, most men's minds would preserve at least the physical part of them by an escape through illusion and madness. Harry's mind accepted the shock and would not take refuge. His body fought alone to reject what it sensibly concluded was an assault that couldn't be endured. He was ravaged by his will to do what he thought he must, and the rebellion of his flesh that refused to submit to it. His struggle was hopeless.

In the morning, Harry was able to sit up on the side of his cot. Paul made some chocolate, and Harry tried to sip it. He couldn't get it down. Mac paced about like a bull. "For Chrissake, Leigh! How can you expect anyone to drink that piss? Give him somethin' he can drink, for Chrissake. Get some whiskey from the Doc. Hot whiskey would go down okay, wouldn't it, Harry?" Harry didn't respond. His pale eyes were fixed, concentrating on some inner vision of despair. "Couple of good shots and you'd feel the old guts warm right up. Isn't that right, Jack?" I told Mac to shut up. "Okay, okay. You guys know everything. To hell with you." He stormed out of the tent, which is what he wanted to do in the first place. I draped a blanket over Harry's shoulders. He was so fragile I was careful when I touched him. Even a gentle hand could shatter him now.

It was at this low ebb of our fortunes that Major Billings asked to see me. Billings was our operations officer, an exceptional man with the earned reputation as the best pilot in the squadron. I didn't want the confrontation. How could one explain Kourtz to a man like Billings? I walked slowly through the trees to the operations shack. The day was bleak with a steady, wet drizzle soaking everything. Card and craps games were in full swing, and the letter writers were sitting by themselves, puzzled over the white paper in front of them. Billings was alone. There was nothing forbidding about him, yet I wasn't at ease. He was the kind of man who put you off. He was deceptively ordinary in his appearance, slightly built with dark hair cut very short. His face was thin with a somewhat long nose. His eyes were dark brown, and when they looked at you, they held you with an unrelenting intensity. Today he looked old, like a disconsolate monk harassed by the failing virtue of his flock. The brown sweater he had on was too big for him, and there was a hole in its right elbow. He didn't say anything for a moment, but motioned to a coffeepot on his desk. I poured myself half a cup.

"How's McCarthy and Leigh?" I said they were all right. "Leigh's got a lousy efficiency rating. What's the matter with him? No, scratch that. I'm going to assign him to you on your next operational. If there's anything wrong, you'd better find out. By the way, you've got an additional assignment. I want you to report to engineering and give them some help. They need someone to slow-time engines. I'll square it with you later." He paused, sipped his coffee, and fumbled under his sweater with his free hand for one of his small cigars. "Want one of these?" I shook my head. The cigars were vile, twisted black things that smelled worse than they looked. "I'm going to send Kourtz to Foggia for a complete physical examination. It may take some time. In fact, it will take a helluva long time. Do you read me, Muirhead?" I said I read him okay. "He might as well be useful while he's there, so we're cutting paper to transfer him temporarily to the quartermaster."

So, we were off the hook. There would be no court-martial for Harry. He would be eased out quietly to be abandoned in some warehouse in Foggia. A feeling of relief came over me that was immediately displaced by a rising resentment. Billings had obviously been aware of what was going on with Harry. Why had he made us struggle with it and keep up the pretense? I apparently didn't mask my indignation very well because Billings came right at me. "Come on, Muirhead. Kourtz is lucky. I could have thrown the book at him. Look, there was nothing else I could do. I had to know. I had to let him go as far as he could. Doc kept me posted." He was right, of course. I poured some coffee into my cup. The rain was coming down heavy. Strong gusts of wind sent swirling streams of mist racing through the trees, striking the tents into a violent flapping response against the attack. Small rivers of water hurried through the area with the urgency of the foolish. Shallow pools were forming everywhere. All the glistening surfaces of water danced with broadening, bursting targets of rain.

It didn't seem there was anything more to say, and I started to leave. Billings called me back. "Hold it, for Chrissake. What's your hurry." He motioned to a chair beside his desk. I got the feeling I was about to be had, a feeling that was reinforced when he reached into a drawer and pulled out a bottle of Old Overholt. "You've been around, Muirhead. I need your help." He poured about four fingers of whiskey into two glasses, and pushed one toward me. "I'm worried; it's the copilots we're getting with the replacement crews. They're bloody awful. Have you noticed it? You had one on your last operational."

As usual, Billings was right on the money. The new copilots were not simply bad; they were an absolute hazard. On my last mission, I had to fly for seven hours without relief. The copilot, a boy named Joe Carlson, could not hold the plane steady in formation; in fact, he had scared the shit out of me each time I had tried to get him to take the controls. Being killed by the krauts went with the job; being killed by an untrained copilot was an obscene stupidity.

"It's the pilots," I said.

"Oh? How do you come up with that?" Billings asked.

"The pilots receive their copilots direct from cadet school. The copilots are supposed to be instructed, by the pilots, during the three phases of operational training. In too many cases, it doesn't happen. The goddamn pilots are so ego ridden, so in love with their image in that left seat, they won't let the copilot touch anything but the fuckin' wheels and flaps."

"And so we're stuck with them," Billings prodded.

I could see it coming, another assignment. I took a large gulp of my whiskey, which went down as smooth as silk and then gently exploded with a delicious warmth in my throat and chest. "Yeah, I guess we're stuck with them," I said.

"The hell we are." Billings was apparently satisfied with my analysis of the problem if not with my indifference to it. "You and Captain Ewell will stand down from all operations for a week, maybe more. If your name gets on the battle orders, let me know. You'll work with the new copilots; routine transition training, with emphasis on formation flying. Okay?" He didn't wait for my answer. "I'll set up a schedule, and I'll check-ride each man when you think he's ready. Let's see, you're on leave for two days, right? Okay. I've got two aircraft that will take at least two days to get ready." He gave me an evil smile. "They're real crates, but that won't bother a hotshot like you. Right?"

Having saddled me with the role of Paul Leigh's surrogate mother, the boring task of slow-timing new engines, and only a week's time to qualify some very green pilots, Billings now generously invited me to

work on the quart. We drank and talked about many things: the weather, when it would lift; books we read; hometowns; would Doc ever dry out; was the world safe with Egan in it; and on through the hours of pleasant discovery that mark the beginning of friendship. When I left Billings's tent late in the afternoon, the weather had eased from heavy rain to soaking drizzle. His parting words to me, although somewhat slurred, made me sure we had become real friends indeed. "Jack, my boy, if you aren't back here in two days, clean and sober, I'll bust your ass."

Mac and I started on the road the next morning after breakfast. When I said good-bye to Harry, I tried to be casual, telling him to rest and be sure to take the medicine Doc had given him. Mac was more truculent than usual. I was afraid he would blurt out something stupid, but he seemed content to badger Leigh, shocking him with explicit descriptions of the vice dens of Bari in which we planned to wallow for the next two days. Poor Paul took it all in, probably half believing it. I watched his young face frown at everything Mac was saying. What could it be about him that was troubling Billings? It would have to wait until we got back. We finally made it out of the tent with even Harry managing a weak grin at our folly.

The sky was still overcast when we left our warm stove and headed for the road. Occasional blustery showers pushed us reeling toward the highway like children being driven by an angry parent. We had good luck and picked up a ride almost immediately, except it didn't get us very far. After less than an hour, the English sergeant, who was driving the lorry and who was silent the whole time, cheerfully ended his reticence by telling us he was heading south only as far as Trinitapoli.

We were stranded. The landscape was cheerless and empty. There were no farmhouses; there was only undulating land streaked by the rainy winds. Away from the squadron where we lived, sealed from any intrusion, this sudden abandonment into the midst of an indifferent land left us uncertain. We stood mindless as browsing cattle, listening to the flap of our coats against our legs. We could have been the only two men in the world caught in some labyrinth of time where the wind would swirl about us always or until some forgiving grace would let us continue our journey and put other sentinels in our place. We didn't consult each other. It was all too melancholy to discuss. We started to walk. In three hours, five Army trucks passed without even a glance at our frantic waves for a ride. It could have been that we looked suspicious. Truck hijacking was common on these remote roads,

and our Air Force uniforms must have looked too unlikely for any
driver to take a chance.

The afternoon light was fading, darkness would be on us soon. Mac's
bulky form plodded on ahead of me. Good old steadfast Mac; he was
still determined that we would get to Bari and would have a good time.
He sustained himself with complaints, and obscenities were flung over
his shoulder for my edification with reference to everything Italian and
truck drivers in particular. I didn't share Mac's energetic commitment
to this enterprise, but now there was no choice. I followed dutifully
along, wondering where we'd sleep. The prospect of a night on the
road without shelter or food was a dismal one. We'd have to pick a
spot soon, before it got completely dark.

Night is a time to withdraw from all labor, a time to seek friends
and family for the pleasure of peace and love. Night is a time of warm
fires, a time of food and drink, a time that ends the hardship of days
without honor or hope. Night is a goal we must reach, the sweetness
of a little death we must come upon before we begin the travail of
another day.

We could find neither day nor night. We were lost in a world the
color of old gray stones, where the silence was broken only by the
sound of the wind rushing by us. The road had disappeared; we could
see nothing but the wet silt under our feet. A feeling of complete
discouragement came over us. Our need was not even to be warm and
dry, but to be in the company of other men; to be reassured that we
belonged to some companionship, to some better community than
this miserable destination we had come upon. We tried to brazen it
out and talked hopefully as we could: trucks would be coming along;
they moved more at night anyway. Mac hummed tunelessly; and I
found myself getting more and more irritated with him, silently cursing
myself for being persuaded to accompany him anywhere. The sky and
all the contours of the land were now consumed by the darkness. But
it wasn't night; it was like a sorrow, the sorrow of the final tired day
of a ruined world. And the last to perish before us was Mac's cigarette,
which he flipped away in an arc of brave contempt that died in a tiny
spit of anger on the muddy road.

"Hey, Joe!" The young voice came out of the darkness. We were
startled. We wanted to be rescued, but were wary of this sudden
contact, this intervention that callously entered our dilemma. There
should have been some concern or acknowledgment in the greeting
that there was something unusual about our plight. "Hey, Joe." The
voice was undisturbed by our silence. "You wanna eat? Come on,

Joe. You eat, you drink. Mama fix you up." He appeared out of nowhere. He was indistinct, a boy-shadow of some age and form. We were so surprised we couldn't respond and held on to our misery with the perverse sullenness of the defeated. He pointed into the gloom then, impatient with our stupidity, grasped my hand and began to pull me in the direction he wanted us to go. There was no decision to make. We stumbled after him, resigning ourselves to his care. Anything would be better than our present circumstance.

He took us to a small farmhouse that was hidden from the road by only a slight curve of the land. It couldn't have been more than two hundred yards from where we had been standing. It hadn't occurred to me to go to a high point and survey the countryside for shelter. My lack of any kind of sense embarrassed me so I didn't comment on the obvious. Another time I would be more observing, was a thought that came to me then and has never come true. I am still a confused traveler. I understand little of what I have seen and am still surprised to find myself where I am. As I followed my fateful boy on that dreary night, I have drifted after other guides no clearer to me than his slight figure moving in and out of the rainy mists. I have never found my way with any certainty.

It was a large room dimly lighted by candles. There were three tables against the wall on one side and one longer table in the center of the room. One of the tables was occupied by two soldiers and two girls. They were all in English uniforms. Another uniformed couple sat at an adjacent table oblivious to the world, clinging to each other in an embrace that excluded everyone. We felt no envy for the lovers. We were happy to be inside and out of the wet.

On the opposite side of the room, a large Italian woman worked over a black wood stove. There was a smell of cooking oil accompanied by the wonderful sound of eggs frying in a pan. The boy pulled us to the center table, yelling loudly at his mother, probably describing our rescue and the good fortune that would bring a few more lire into the house. He turned his attention to us, making motions of eating and drinking. Mac and I nodded eagerly. I reached in my pocket and gave him a handful of notes. It msut have been a large sum to him for he stared at it unbelievingly and then ran happily to his mother. He waved the bills at her, laughing and gesturing back at us. Then, with a mischievous motion, he attempted to thrust the money down the front of her dress. She roared with laughter and with mock anger she pushed his hand away, grabbing the money with the same motion. It went where he knew it would, between her deep, full breasts, with a quick

shy move that ended the game, if not the knowledge between them
that they had made their needs for another few days.

Hunger is a rare seasoning that makes a banquet of any meal. Three
eggs fried in olive oil, stiff as parchment, with coarse bread and cheese,
washed down with the ubiquitous combination of American grapefruit
juice and English gin, tasted so good to me I couldn't imagine anything
better. The boy attended us as though we were kings. His dark eyes
gleamed with pleasure at our ravenous appetites. He kept motioning
for us to eat more and brought fresh drinks before us. I had two more
eggs while sipping my third drink. Mac was halfway through his fourth.

The room was more attractive than I thought. The pleasant warmth
of the wood stove and the wavering light from the candles, kindly to
this poor house, revealed little of its bare poverty. But it seemed splendid to us, like a favorite inn where good friends met to be together for
a while. Our English companions were subject to its spell too, chatting
with us as if we had seen each other only yesterday. The girls were
nurses from a nearby hospital. The men were P.T. boat officers from
Air Rescue in Bari. Mac and I were quick to take advantage of this
opportunity and asked for a ride. It was all agreed. At the end of the
evening and, of course, after they had made a proper good-bye to the
girls, they would take us to Bari in their truck. Things were looking
better every minute. Perhaps it was the gin, but Mac's small eyes
seemed to be getting smaller. He grinned at me as if to tell me what
a clever fellow he was to plan this grand adventure. The English
foursome attempted to sing "Roll Me Over," with Mac and me joining
in on each chorus to contribute our share of the noise.

The dissonance was mercifully ending when the boy, caught up in
the celebration, began to sing. His voice surprised us with its clear,
high strength. It didn't seem possible that this slender instrument could
hold the sound that burst into the room; a passion that made us submit
as lesser men in the presence of a ragged prince who now led us again
to another fire and another feast. His song was a sentimental Italian
ballad, full of sobs and despairing complaints of lost love, to which
his mother responded in a strong mezzo voice, a vibrant and yearning
counterpoint which left no doubt that indeed it was a very sad song.

We all applauded wildly and the lovers at last joined us, leaving
each other's comfort for a moment to cheer for more. He made a bow
like a great professional performer, but, because he was a boy, he
couldn't hold the pose and broke into delighted laughter at our enthusiasm. He sang more for us that night. Sometimes his mother joined
in, but mostly he sang alone. Even now I can hear the sound of his

young spirit caught in the tragedy of Tosca, his head thrown back in the climax of the aria while we sat breathless to the end. We had many more drinks with bits of cheese, which we delicately balanced on the last scraps of hard bread. The boy, exhausted, finally fell asleep at our table, his dark, curly head resting on his arms.

As we prepared to leave, we all kissed the woman, promising her we would be back again. The English girls embraced Mac and me with the smiling patronage of their men. Each of us gave the other his name and base and solemnly wrote it down. We put the slips of paper carefully in our wallets. The boy didn't stir as we left. There was nothing more he could do than what he had: making a bright new thread in our poor fabrics that would always hold us to him. It has held for me. I wonder if the others remember.

We slept that night in the wheelhouse of the P.T. boat in the Bari harbor. The slap of the water against the hull was the last thing I heard before the gin and the fatigue of the long, long day took its full measure of me. I had only closed my eyes when morning came into my oblivion with a shake from a British sailor who gave us two strong mugs of tea and then went about his work. Our friends from last night were gone. They had a mission briefing, and we were to get off the boat as quickly as possible. They were to be under way in an hour. Mac and I tried to clean up in the small head, taking turns nagging each other about hurrying up. By this time, we were in poor shape. Our uniforms were still wet and stained from the grime in the truck. We were shaved at least when we left the dock for the center of town, which was only a few blocks from the harbor.

We needn't have concerned ourselves about our appearance. No one paid any attention to us as we wandered aimlessly around the streets in the midst of all kinds of uniforms of rear echelon personnel and British Navy types, who seemed to be the main occupants of the town. We were at a loss as to what to do. Everyone else was so busy going from one place to the other, so intent and occupied, it made us feel uncertain.

But the city, being the same in Italy as everywhere else, sensed us as lost ones and the tendrils of caring reached out: we were accosted by two sad-looking whores who promised to bring us joy for a reasonable sum. This encounter would have added to our depression if Mac hadn't rallied and begun to haggle, performing a pantomime that conveyed that they should pay us. This proposition, in defiance of tradition, struck us all as hilarious, a point of view which was not shared by the M.P. who joined the scene and motioned for the girls to be on their

way before he asked for our identification. He wasn't a bad sort once
he learned we were harmless, although he couldn't understand why
anyone would want to come to Bari for a two-day pass. The city was
jammed with all kinds of servicemen, and what meager facilities there
were certainly were not available for the likes of us. Transient combat
air crew or infantrymen were the least of the social structure. Their
presence was endured, but not encouraged. The M.P. told us a few
other things about hotels, places to eat, off-limits bistros, whorehouses,
curfew, and spots around the dock where one could get one's throat
cut. It was a discouraging recital. He ended it with a lame recom-
mendation that we perhaps should go to the USO; at least there we
could get a shower and a decent cup of coffee. It wasn't the kind of
holiday we had in mind. Certainly not anything we could brag about
when we got back to the squadron. We would have to lie a little.

We found the USO. I didn't like it, not the saccharine patronage
nor the admission that we had to go there at all. The girl at the desk
was condescending, wary of us, but still managing to tell us what
services were available with a cold, distant manner that was less than
inviting. It was a stand-off. We were not pleased to be in the place;
and she, obviously, regarded us with distaste, like two pieces of lint
she couldn't wait to remove from her tidy carpet. We did not belong
here. Our awkwardness was an acknowledgment of distance from this
world of comfortable liaisons and little pleasures. It was an obscenity
to us. What were we doing here? The girl stared at us, waiting for us
to say something. Mac shuffled about uneasily and then incredibly
blurted out, "How about girls? How does a guy get laid around here?"
To her credit, she accepted Mac's question as though he had asked
her the time of day. She watched us leave without saying a word.

We walked back toward the docks. I half-heartedly bawled at Mac.
"You stupid bastard. She could have called the M.P.s. Then we really
would have had it." It was useless. Mac beamed with satisfaction. He
had struck a blow for all of us, and left some of our bitter stain on
her. She would remember his lewd, ugly face staring into hers the
next time she told a G.I. about the duplicate bridge games or the
schedule for the availability of the Ping-Pong table. I had to grin at
him finally. He was as happy as a pup that had pissed on the floor
and had got away with it.

A few blocks away from the USO our luck began to change. We
found a small hotel that took us in; better still, the woman who owned
the place spoke English with only a slight Italian accent, and she
treated us with exceptional kindness. Like most of the houses in Italy,

it showed neglect and wear. The rooms were bare cells; the toilet at the end of our hall was primitive beyond belief; it was damp; there was a pervasive odor of wet plaster and cooking oil: none of which discouraged us. We needed nothing more than a place to sleep at the end of the day. It was perfect.

She was cook, maid, concierge, manager, owner, and total mistress; her name was Maria Cardimona. She was probably in her late thirties, a woman who was neither plain nor beautiful but who seemed able to be either if she chose. There was a trace of elegance in her slight figure, elegance worn thin by hardship. She was married to a British merchant marine officer, and had been stranded in Italy when the war broke out. She showed us pictures of her husband, and pictures of their home in a suburb outside of London. She was particularly apologetic about the state of things in Bari, punctuating her remarks by waving her arms and exclaiming, "It's the goddamn war. Ah, it's all the goddamn war." She took us over completely, opening her campaign for our improvement by telling us we looked like hell; then she gave us explicit directions to a public bath where we could get properly cleaned. She also told us that for a few extra lire we could get a fast cleaning job on our uniforms. If we could get her some soap and cigarettes, we would not have to pay for our rooms and she would fix us some spaghetti with bread and a bottle of wine. Then after supper, we could go to the opera.

"What opera?" I asked.

"Oh, it's not real opera." She grabbed my arm, laughing. "It's light opera; Victor Herbert or Rudolph Friml or some goddamn thing like that. You go to it. It is better for you than getting drunk."

Everything was as she said it would be: there were steam baths, tubs and showers, and the cleaning shop near the baths did a fair job on our uniforms. There was even an exchange for British and American military personnel where I bought six bars of Palmolive soap, two cartons of Chesterfields, and a box of Hershey chocolate bars. The gifts must have pleased Maria for she did better than just spaghetti. We had green peppers and onions, a mountain of spaghetti, one sweet sausage for each of us, bread, cheese, and a large bottle of red wine. We ate in her small kitchen like a family, listening to her wonderful stories about Italy, her girlhood in Taranto, how she met her husband, and what she was going to do after the war. Mac seemed to have caught her fancy, for she directed most of her intensity at him. When I complained that she was not paying any attention to me, she scoffed, "You? You're a skinny cold goddamn fish. Now, Mac, he's got some meat on him. He's gonna stay right here with me until my Roberto gets back."

The mention of her husband's name must have touched her heart; perhaps it was more than she should have tried to share with us, for her bravado suddenly crumbled. Her eyes filled and she moaned, "Oh, my God. Will I ever see him again?" Mac moved quickly from his chair and stood beside her, placing his hands on her shoulders. She reached back and patted his hand. "Please," she said. "Please, please go away. Go to the goddamn opera, please." When we left, she was staring at the wall, trying to control her tears.

We walked toward the opera house in silence. Mac seemed particularly distraught; and this was a new side of him to me. It would never have occurred to me to think he could display concern for anyone. His unrelenting belligerence, his scorn of any manifestation of sentimentality had, until a few moments ago, convinced me that he was beyond the persuasion of any tenderness; in fact, I had always thought of Mac approaching even heaven with undiminished irascibility, snarling at the gentle angel at the gate, "Never mind the shit about sin. Just open the fuckin' door." Maria must have made a strong impression on him.

The opera house was a pleasant surprise: it was a large, imposing structure in good repair with well-kept grounds. Inside, the carpeted lobby was bathed in a soft light that discreetly revealed the gambols of sculptured fauns and maidens in a verdure provided by large potted plants and vines. There were portraits on the walls of artists who had performed there; comfortable chairs were arranged in a way that did not intrude on the main space of the lobby, where the uniformed guests talked quietly and waited for the curtain bell that would summon them to the first act.

It was as Maria had said, not real opera; it was *The Merry Widow*. The performance was by a British company. Although I was not generally fond of light opera, perhaps because I always associated it with Nelson Eddy and Jeanette MacDonald yelling into each other's face, I enjoyed this performance. It was melodic and the singers' voices were pleasing; but what gave me the greatest pleasure was the extraordinary color on the stage. The sets were splendid and the vivid hues of the costumes contrasted brilliantly as the players moved through the enchanting nonsense of the story. Each time the curtain parted for a new act or scene, I found myself applauding like a boy at a circus. It was an evening of delightful illusion, a fulfillment of a need I had nearly forgotten. Leaving the theater, I whistled the waltz and imagined

myself in one of those uniforms with the high black boots, the blue
sash, and a saber dangling at my side; and for good measure, that
beautiful young lady on my arm, singing of her ardent love for me
alone.

"Christ, that was lousy." Mac had returned to the world. We walked
back to the hotel without much further conversation except for Mac's
complaints about being cold.

Morning came in my small room with a faint light revealing a patch
of unswept floor. It was early, six o'clock. There were sounds from
the street: a rattle of a hand-pushed cart, the whine of a truck in low
gear in the narrow street, a man's voice, then a silence followed by
the sound of a metal gate being opened. It was the last sound that
brought me wide awake; perhaps it was a coffee shop opening its door.
I dressed except for my shirt, gathered my shaving gear, and headed
for the bathroom at the end of the hall. As I passed Mac's door, I was
tempted to knock to wake him but changed my mind. After a wash
and a shave I would be better prepared to put up with his usual bad
humor. I was almost past his door when I heard Maria's voice. It was
too much to resist; I paused and listened. The voice was unmistakably
Maria's, and it was definitely from Mac's room. Her words were blurred,
but the fact of the liaison was confirmed by the gruff tones of Mac's
bellow rumbling through the thin partition between them and me.
"Hon, there's another carton of butts in my bag, on the floor over
there by the wall." I continued on my trip to the head as quietly as
possible.

Back in my room, I dressed quickly and stuffed my gear into my
bag, but not before leaving my extra soap and cigarettes on the bed
for Maria, a gift to celebrate the joining of Beauty and the Beast. I
was as titillated as a schoolgirl, giggling to myself as I went down the
stairs to the street: Mac, who had the charm of wet steel wool, and
Maria, the sad housewife—God Almighty! Incredible!

The street was quiet. A horse-drawn wagon moved past me, the
driver half asleep munching on a piece of bread. I walked in the
direction where I thought I had heard the sound of the opening gate.
After almost an hour of exploring the streets and alleys around the
hotel, I found nothing that resembled a coffee shop. Reluctantly, still
lusting for coffee, I made my way back to the hotel.

I had just passed through the door and was about to start up the
stairs when I heard Maria, "Where the hell have you been? Get in
here." She was yelling at me from the kitchen. "I fix you some breakfast
and you're out wandering around some goddamn place. Come in

here." Maria was standing at the stove pouring coffee into a cup. She placed it on the table, impatiently motioning me to sit down. Mac was sitting there dressed and ready to go, grinning like a damn fool. Maria opened the oven door and removed what looked like a small turnover, which she placed, with a slam, beside my coffee. "Hurry up. Eat and get out of here. Mac says you're supposed to be back early." The pastry was good, warm with a cheese filling; the liquid in my cup was a thin bitter brew, something like coffee. Maria gave me a smile. "Thanks for the extra cigarettes and the soap. It helps."

I was amazed at the smile, and the softening of her manner toward me. I said, "Maria, love, we should really pay you some lire for all you've done for us."

She drove her small fist against my shoulder, "Don't you Maria me. You keep your damn lire. It's no goddamn good; you know that." I waved my arms in surrender and she laughed, patting my cheek. "No, you've given me plenty. You're a good boy, Jack, but you're too damn skinny."

As I finished my breakfast, I tried to tell her about the opera: the fine voices, the color on the stage, the elegance of the theater, and all the things that had pleased me; but she was not interested. She brushed my account of the evening aside with a contemptuous wave of her hand. "Mac said it stunk."

"Yes," I said, "Mac is usually very perceptive about such things." My sarcasm was wasted; Maria was aware only of Mac and didn't appear to have heard me. I put on my coat, said a perfunctory good-bye, which she acknowledged with an impatient grimace, and I started for the door. Before I left, I made it a point to get Mac's attention. "I'll see you outside." His eyes didn't leave Maria's. He did manage to nod, so I knew he had at least a minimal level of consciousness that would soon return him to me and the despised reality I must have been for both of them.

Another time I would have been pleased to have Mac silent, not bad-mouthing everything in or out of sight, not telling me Paul Leigh was a weak sister or Harry had no guts, not bitching about the weather, the limeys, the wops, the frogs, the krauts, the bastards back in the States, and endlessly on through all the subjects he considered worthy of his malevolence. His brooding silence now was worse; it was the sullen petulance of a child. He had been deprived of his goody. I had taken away his comfortable woolly blanket of love and, by God, he was going to sulk.

At the loading docks I checked the trucks that were ready to pull

out, and I found an agreeable English driver who, after thinking it
over, finally grinned and said, "Okay, mate. I can drop you off at
Foggia. Pile in the back. Two other blokes back there—bleedin' Indians
they are. Watch out for 'em. They'll cut your fuckin' ears off if you
don't watch 'em." I laughed with him and went around to the back
of the truck. As I started to pull myself over the tailgate, a strong brown
arm reached down to help me. I took hold of the extended hand and
looked up into a dark, handsome, bearded face smiling in amusement
at my awkwardness. He was a big man of forbidding presence, an
exotic noble from some cruel darkness I would never dare to know.
He pulled me up with extraordinary ease, as if I were a mildly interesting trifle to be examined for a while, then put aside.

The truck was full of long boxes that were securely lashed, leaving
about three feet between the tailgate and the last tier of boxes. I settled
in as best I could by jamming my back against a box with my feet
pressing against the gate. The other Indian soldier looked just as fierce
as his companion. I offered him one of my Chesterfields, which he
accepted with a smile, offering me one of his Players in return. I lit
his, then my own. He continued to smile at me, then made a puzzling
gesture, putting his finger to his lips, saying, "Ssh. Ssh." I looked at
Mac. What was going on? The Indian soldier repeated the motion
with his finger across his lips warning me to be quiet. As he pointed
to the boxes, his smile got broader, and he was obviously amused at
my puzzlement. "For soljas sleeping," he said. His friend was watching
me too, waiting for me to understand the joke.

Suddenly I knew. Of course, they were coffins. We were riding with
what would be the sad trophies of some victory or some defeat. It
wouldn't matter to the men who would finally sleep in them. I nodded
at the Indian soldier who had helped me into the truck, to let him
know that now I understood the joke. His dark eyes held mine for a
moment, as though there was something he wanted to say to me,
perhaps from a wisdom greater than mine: of Brahma, the creator; of
Vishnu, the preserver; and of the wisdom of death, of Shiva, the
destroyer. At last he withdrew from me, and returned his gaze to the
docks and the sea beyond. The truck started with a jolt. I reached out
and touched his arm, pointing to Mac who had already managed to
curl up in the cramped space and fall asleep. The Indian smiled again,
then touched the box behind him, and nodding toward Mac he said,
"For solja sleeping."

Chapter IV

SQUADRON CHORES

What is this life if, full of care,
We have no time to stand and stare.

—WILLIAM HENRY DAVIS

We were back in the squadron before noon. Nothing had changed except Paul was alone; in our absence Harry Kourtz had been spirited off to his new life with the quartermaster. In his shy way, Paul was happy to see us and, thanks to Mac's melancholy, he didn't have to listen to Mac's usual ration of crap. Major Billings had left a message: I was to report to the flight line as soon as I got back. I took this to mean after I had showered, changed to clean suntans, had something to eat, and checked my mail—especially my mail. Letters from home, to me and to everyone else, were the most important event of any day. They were our communion with our past, our sacred past; they were our confirmation of life expressed in simple words of love so eloquent we could not deny them: not their hope, nor their prayers for our safe return, nor their reminder that we were theirs and could not be taken from them; nor could we deny their reminder of days without care, of things we must do when we returned home, of promises we must make to be careful and not take chances; as if all their passion and all their love could change the mindless fate that held us.

At two o'clock, I talked the officer of the day into giving me a ride to the flight line. When we arrived at the field, I tried to guess where Billings might be; he covered a large territory in the course of a day. He could be in any one of a number of places: the weather shack, Ordnance, Engineering, at any one of the hardstands where the planes were parked, the tower, or even in the briefing hut, the home of

Intelligence, our local arseholes who, combined with their counterparts in group, would inevitably kill us all. Since his concern, when
I last saw him, was for the condition of the two aircraft we were to
use for transition training, I tried Engineering first.

Engineering was administered out of a small office that was an
appendage to a large but flimsy structure used to house battle-damaged
aircraft. These planes were beyond repair and would never fly again;
they were strictly for spare parts and were now in various stages of
planned destruction. I was not familiar with these techniques of in-
ventive maintenance, and the scene in the hangar appeared to be utter
chaos to me: a junkyard of machinery, cable, sheet-metal ducts, tubes,
tires, pipe, parts of wings, fuel cells, lengths of longerons, spars, tail
assemblies, nose assemblies, gun turrets, bomb racks, sections of Plexiglas, hatches, wheels, flaps, radios, piles of instruments, seats, slabs
of armor, and a hundred other parts of what had once been several
splendid machines. Maintenance personnel wandered through the hangar
with their clipboards, occasionally signaling a chainfall operator to
pick up this part or that and move it to here or there. Out of this
carnage, Engineering and the line crews salvaged what could be used
again to keep us in the air. Their war, which they fought with inge-
nuity, intelligence, and interminable hours of hard work, was a war
against the attrition of battle, against the wear of time and exposure,
against shortage of material, and, most of all, against the ruthless
demands we pilots had to make on these machines. Without the quiet
valor of these men, the sky belonged to the enemy, and we were
impotent warriors who could do no more than shake our fists at heaven.

As I approached the office door, I heard Billings's voice, loud and
impatient. "You told me they'd be ready today. Goddamn it, Mike,
I haven't got that much time."

Captain Salinas's response was just as loud, or maybe a shade louder.
"Listen, Major, I'm no miracle worker. I've cannibalized everything
around here and I'll have them ready by ten tomorrow. There's only
so much you can do with fuckin' spit and glue. Now if you'll get the
fuck out of here, I'll go back to work."

Opening the door, I played the cheerful innocent, "Hello, Major.
Hi, Mike."

Billings turned to me, pleased no doubt to get out from under Mike's
anger. "Where the hell have you been? You were supposed to be back
this morning."

Salinas laughed. "He was probably shacked up with a bloody duch-
ess, and she couldn't bear to let go of his goddamn great cod."

"You got that exactly right, Mike," I said.

Billings wasn't amused. "You get your ass down to the west strip. You can get at least two hours on 837. Number-three engine has zero hours. If you can't get a clearance from weather to get out of the local area, fly the goddamn traffic pattern."

I started to leave when Captain Salinas stopped me. "Wait a minute; you'll need this." He took a form from his desk and handed it to me. "If everything's normal, just fill in the entries every twenty minutes. If you have any problems, I'll be in the tower."

When a new engine was installed in a plane, it had to be what we called slow-timed; that is, it had to be operated at a low manifold pressure and engine speed until it could be assured that the temperatures and pressures were normal. The break-in period was about twelve hours, which was not done in one run-up but in a series of shorter runs of four hours or less. The plane had to be flown when the new engine was running; we had no other way of keeping it cool. In flight, the new engine's power setting was, in terms of thrust and drag, equivalent to a shut-down engine with the prop feathered.

For the pilot, flying a slow-time was mostly a bore except for takeoff and landing. During takeoff, the pilot had three engines, not four; during landing, he had to move quickly to correct his trim as he reduced power on his final approach. Today with 837, I didn't have much of a problem: the new engine was an inboard, which had minimal effect on the plane's yaw. Taking off with a new outboard on our short runway at Longskirt would be more difficult; the tendency of the plane to yaw toward the slow engine would be severe and a challenge to the pilot's skill—or luck.

I managed to log over two hours on the new engine before the tower called me in from circling the traffic pattern. The weather was still very thick, and I had not been able to fly over seven hundred feet. The afternoon light, what little there was of it, had faded swiftly; on my final approach I could barely see the runway. The flight engineer had recorded the engine data on the form Captain Salinas had given me; there were no significant anomalies. Mike should be happy; it was a good engine.

Rather than going back to the Engineering Office to pick up a ride to the squadron area, I decided to walk. Perhaps it was the tedium of three days in Mac's company or the irritating intensity of Billings's dedication to every bloody thing in the squadron, or perhaps it was the cramped monotony of over two hours of flying the traffic pattern: whatever the reason, I felt a need to be by myself.

This need for occasional solitude was never addressed in any military manual. Maybe solitude was considered counter to the we-band-of-brothers camaraderie encouraged by the Army: for it might seem to them if one had too much time to reflect, one could become bemused by the madness of war, and not be able to fight at all.

I wanted to be alone now with the same perverse desire for loneliness I had often felt when I was a young boy. Then, even at the happiest of times, I would wander off to walk through the woods across the street from my house, and make my way in a little forest of tall elms and overgrown and neglected fruit trees, to a favorite spot under a great beech tree. Beneath that giant, whose massive branches and thick red leaves shut out all but a filtered shimmering light, I would stretch out on the yielding earth to listen to the wind rustling in that vast universe above me. And I would dream of brave deeds and of slender girls with golden hair.

The dirt road from the airfield ran for about a half mile on a gentle rise until it met the main highway between Lucera and Foggia. Then I would follow this main road for a mile to the entrance of the squadron bivouac. It felt good to stretch my legs, and I was alone for the first time in weeks.

The stillness of the early night was a cool embrace of quiet, with soft mist sweetening every breath. I could have walked forever and was disappointed when I realized I was nearing the highway. Time had passed too quickly, so I slowed my pace for the last half mile. I didn't want to go through that gate; I was hungry but I dreaded entering the mess hut; I didn't want to go back to the tent, to Mac's sullen muttering or to Paul's timid friendship. I never wanted to see an airplane again nor hear the litany of a mission briefing to which I would respond like a good member of a congregation servile to a wretched God.

In the morning, after breakfast, I drove to the field in Mike's jeep with Joe Carlson and Paul Leigh in tow for their training flight. I didn't feel well. I had eaten too much of Sergeant Rogers's hash and guzzled too much coffee, all of which sat queasy on my bellyful of whiskey, a vile reminder of Billings's company last night and his warning to be on the flight line early. I had little appreciation of the day, which was fair and cloudless except for some scattered cumulus in the northeast. I wondered why the group was still standing down; maybe they were going to hold up the war until Ewell and I were operational again. A little bud of optimism tried to push through the whiskey fumes and my churning stomach: how wonderful it would be if they forgot about us.

I had just finished my preflight inspection of the plane Billings had assigned to me, a relic named *Omar the Dentmaker,* when Capt. Jim Ewell and Salinas arrived with Ewell's two copilots. Ewell didn't get out of the jeep but sat staring at my plane in disbelief. "Jesus Christ, you've got to be kidding." He turned to Mike Salinas. "Is mine as bad as that bucket? Mike, come on, cut the shit."

Mike didn't crack a smile. "Captain Ewell, you'll find your aircraft in excellent condition. If you find anything that's not to your satisfaction, write it up on the Form fuckin' One. You can fly it or stick it up your ass, it's all the same to me." I thought for a moment Salinas might be joking, but he wasn't. He looked exhausted; his face was gray with fatigue, and he had probably worked all night with his crew to bring the two planes on the line. He was, obviously, in no mood to tolerate any complaints from Ewell.

But Ewell knew, as we did, how hard Mike Salinas worked to keep our planes in the air, and he knew that he had yanked Mike's chain at the wrong time. He quickly tried to make his peace. "Mike, I'm sorry. I'm sure the planes are in fine shape. Raunchy pilots, you know, they have to pop off." He paused, and then he pointed to me. "I wasn't going to say anything, but that son of a bitch there put me up to it."

Mike grinned at me. "Did you tell this lying bastard to needle me?"

"No, Mike. I wouldn't do that. You have to realize that Captain Ewell is a lying prick from Kansas. He's just a goddamn sodbuster with no class at all. You know, Mike, he still thinks an airplane is some new kind of fuckin' mule."

Mike seemed to have regained his good humor. He pushed Ewell out of the jeep with a laugh. "Get goin', you asshole. I've got better things to do than jaw with you clowns. Hey, remember now, if you notice anything with these kites, write it up. And write so I can read it. I'll check in with you from the tower in a couple of hours."

Jim Ewell and I discussed our flight for a few moments before takeoff. We had been cleared for six hours off the coast between Manfredonia and Barletta, and we were to be careful not to approach Bari on our southern leg. We were not to intrude inland beyond the highway between Foggia and Bari. Ewell would fly lead for the first hour, and we would switch every hour after that. The copilot would work from the left seat.

We got in a first good day. Carlson and Leigh did well; they responded to instruction in an eager, intelligent way that confirmed what I had suspected: that there was nothing wrong with their basic flying skills. Their pilots had simply denied them any opportunity to learn the special characteristics of the B-17, and consequently, the copilots were awkward and without confidence. Paul Leigh's aggressive enthusiasm surprised me; even when Carlson was in the left seat, Paul stayed in the jump seat between Joe and me, and he never let his attention waver from Joe's performance or from any comment I made during the flight.

Paul also weathered my plot to test his composure; in fact, he weathered it with a quiet style that surprised and pleased me. I had been concerned about what seemed to be a certain timidity in Paul, a lack of assertiveness, so I planned to really chew his ass, if he gave me the opportunity, to see if I could destroy his concentration. I got my chance as he was taking his turn in the left seat and flying on Ewell's right wing.

During the first ten minutes of his hour, Paul had held our plane fairly steady on Ewell's wing. Everything was going well when we hit a spot of rough air, and our plane lurched toward Ewell's. Paul recovered, but he had come too close to Ewell, or at least close enough for me to fire my opening salvo. "Paul! You stupid bastard! Fly this fuckin' airplane! What the hell's the matter with you?"

"That bump caught me by surprise. The wing dropped before I could catch it."

"The wing didn't drop, for Christ's sake! You let it drop! YOU! YOU! This machine doesn't do a fuckin' thing except what you make it do. Don't ever tell me anything like that again unless you want to go back to the States and tow targets for the rest of your fuckin' life. You're flying this goddamn kite, now keep your head out of your ass and hold your goddamn position!" I was yelling as loud as I could. Carlson looked like he wanted to jump out rather than follow Paul in that left seat.

Paul kept his eyes riveted on his reference point on Ewell's plane. His face flushed, but he didn't say a word. He flew a perfect wing position for the balance of his hour, and I kept giving him sporadic blasts of criticism, well spiced with obscenities. I finally motioned to him to get out of his seat to let Carlson take over. I gave him a parting shot. "Well, Paul, I guess you did okay. By some fuckin' miracle, we're all still alive."

As he squeezed past me, he gave me a disgusted glare. "You know, Jack," he said, "I really don't mind you trying to shake me up, but I don't like swearing. You can yell all you like, but swearing is offensive to me; you know that, and you've never sworn at me before."

Paul's young face was earnest and brave. He was Robert E. Lee's subaltern incarnate, as pure as Galahad, as noble as Roland himself; his goodness was beyond me. "Is it all right if I kick your butt once in a while?"

"Absolutely," Paul said. Then he smiled. "But only when I deserve it, and when you haven't got your boots on."

In the three following days, Ewell and I flew sixteen hours of transition training, and I finished slow-timing the new engine in 837. The group had completed a mission on a tactical target in northern Italy, but had to abort an attack on a synthetics refinery near Wiener Neustadt because of bad weather in the target area. On the fourth day, Major Billings joined us for the final check rides that would release our copilots to the glories of combat or send them packing to some ignominious chore of humiliating drudgery.

How hard we all worked for the honor of combat; how bitter it was for any of us to fail, to wash out at any stage of our progress from neophyte cadets to the elitism of terror. Paul Leigh, Joe Carlson, and Captain Ewell's two copilots climbed into Billings's plane for their check ride like four trembling virgins waiting for the first touch on their flanks. Before going to our plane, Ewell and I watched them taxi out, and I know we both felt the same: if we could only have had a few more hours with them.

Jim Ewell and I flew lead, and Billings's plane flew a wing position, shifting from our right to our left wing, to satisfy himself that each copilot could fly tight formation from either the near seat or across the cockpit.

After three hours, Billings called me. "Okay. You guys go back to Longskirt—but hang around. I want to do some stalls with these boys, and then shoot a few landings. Wait for us at the strip. Out."

After landing and securing our plane at the hardstand, Jim and I began our vigil. It seemed an interminable wait before we finally saw Billings's plane on the approach. The first landing was a good one, a beauty. I was praying it was Leigh in the left seat, but we were too far away to tell who it was. The plane circled again, and made six more follow-through landings before it rolled to a stop at the end of the runway, then turned and taxied slowly toward us.

As Billings came out of the waist door, Jim and I said nothing but waited for the worst. Billings stood quietly until the four copilots were in front of him, looking a bit rough around the edges but not totally destroyed.

Major Billings's first words made my day. "Well, gentlemen, I think you're going to be okay. You gave me a good ride. You've got some work to do to smooth your techniques, but that'll come. If you have any questions at any time, talk them over with Jack or Jim here; I'm sure they'll be able to help you." He then shook hands with each of them, and added, "It's an honor to have you join the squadron."

Paul's face was radiant; he had just pulled Excalibur from the stone.

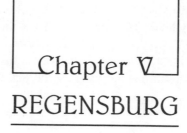

Chapter V

REGENSBURG

Conceive these images in air,
  Wrap them in flame, they're mine;
Set against granite,
  Let the two dull stones be grey—

—DYLAN THOMAS

Our fate should not surprise us. We know death is at the end for us; or, if one chooses to believe so, it is at the beginning. But these mysterious ends or beginnings are distant and not at hand. On a cold, clear morning in late February of 1944, this distance was stripped from me. I was confronted by the tape on the briefing map stretching from Longskirt to Regensburg. It was a moment of awe. It was a moment of dread. It was the terrible last moment of comprehension of the lamb in the jaws of the beast.

The longer hours of light and the steadying air masses emerging from the turbulent winter months that had sheltered us now signaled the time to measure the work and set us to it. The lid was off. We would be thrusting out all over Europe and to the oil fields in the east. Regensburg was a beginning, the first planting of our bitter season. For those of us who made it through this day there would be Ploesti, then Steyr again and Regensburg again, if we didn't do the job today. There was no way to turn away from it. This is what I said I would do, but, for the first time, I saw what lay ahead. It was not a vision of victory, but the countenance of fate, that blind and mindless brute, I saw mocking me. I had made it through nine missions only to be confronted now by the long, hard journey still before me. I had escaped nothing.

The briefing was a grim business of laying it out. It would be a maximum effort. We would put up thirty-one aircraft. Our fighter escort would be stretched very thin trying to cover all the bombers, and most of them would have to leave us before we were halfway to the target. The German fighters' first attack would force our fighters to drop their auxiliary tanks in order to maneuver. This would be the end of our cover, for their range would be cut by half and, at maximum combat power, their battle would be over in minutes. We would expect intense attacks, both going in and coming off the target. There would be heavy flak. We must make our rendezvous with the other groups. We must conserve ammunition. Short bursts only. Shoot at nothing outside of four hundred yards. Cripples must try for the sea. Air Sea Rescue would be out in full force to pick up survivors from ditching aircraft. The formations must be tight for effective firepower and a good bomb pattern over the target. Deputy squadron leaders must be ready to take over. The weather was marginal, but would hold to broken clouds over the target area. Aircraft damaged during the bomb run and unable to keep their positions must head for the deck. Each unrelenting statement blocked the paths of our twisting, despairing hopes to a final surrender of each of them as we simply listened, staring at the black tape on the map.

Major Billings had kept his promise: Paul Leigh sat beside me. He was to fly his first operational mission as my copilot. His face was serene; his composure was impeccable, as though this was to be a regular working day, and anything that might happen would be appropriately meted out by some just South Carolinian deity in gray and gold. I envied him. I put my arm around his shoulder. "Come on, Paul, let's get our gear and get down to the line. I want a little extra time on our preflight."

Her name was *Laura*. Her image stretched languorously along the forward fuselage from just above the chin turret to the leading edge of the wing. She peered at me over her wineglass with a warm smile, accepting my homage to her splendid breasts that were bravely tipped by two spinning propellers. A grease stain marred the pink roundness of her shoulder, but did not to me diminish her charm nor my admiring lust. Neither did the intrusion of the riveted edge of an access panel on the perfect curve of her buttocks seem to me to be a distraction from her invitation. The first light of the sun, now clearing the horizon, harshly revealed her imperfections where paint had flaked from her golden hair. We stared into each other's eyes sharing the beginning of the day, which she greeted unchanged and chaste, as women do, still watching me, wise and knowing, as I turned away to make my preflight. She was a gallant girl, one could tell.

I could hear Petrosky's voice from under the wing where I made the motions of checking the supercharger blades. Pete was the best top turret in the squadron. It was an omen of luck to have him today. "Never mind your tracers. You won't hit a goddamn thing if you follow them. Watch the curve of the attack. You know the right radii to lead him. Keep your eyes glued right on him. If you hit him, you'll see it. Hold the same lead and pump 'em in. Don't swing your piece fast. You'll just spray shells all over the fuckin' sky. For Chrissake, don't take a bad angle. You know your zone. It's going to be a helluva day and your balls are all up in your belly. I know it. I know all about it. But don't forget, if we give 'em a hard time, they'll try another group." He paused and the gunners waited. Even from under the wing I could picture Petrosky's ruddy face breaking into a grin. "After all, we wouldn't want to keep all those fuckin' MEs to ourselves. Share 'em with your buddies. Share 'em." He addressed his expertise to the ball turret. "Danny, you'll have to keep us clean underneath. Don't let them slide in there. Sucker them. You know how they slip in there. Let 'em come in to three hundred yards or so, then shut the fuckin' door."

I was concerned about all this close-range talk. Four hundred yards. Three hundred yards. Six hundred was the usual range to open fire. But Pete knew what he was doing so I kept my mouth shut. I suppose he figured if he said three, they'd open at five, which would be close enough. The armorer briefed me on the bomb load: one-thousand-pounders on the bottom racks, the rest five hundreds. The crew chief and I went over the Form 1. *Laura* was in good shape. Low engine hours, no problems. Her compass deviation card had not been checked, and she had a shear pin replaced in her tail wheel assembly.

All the time I was considering the odds. I had drawn a good plane and a good crew. Our position in the formation wasn't bad either. The thirty-one planes were arranged in four squadrons of seven planes: a lead squadron, a high right, a low left, and a trailing squadron filling the box. Three spares were to fly a high-right position on the trailing squadron and were to fill in for aborts or casualties. Our spot was the last plane in the high right, a good position since the fighter pressure would come from head-on attacks. The planes ahead of us would break the edge, or so I reasoned. I scavenged for any crumbs that would feed my logic that we had a better chance than the others.

Longskirt was a plain of waving grass. To the southwest, the land sloped upward to the hills. There were probably vineyards there. In the summer, the plain would be streaked with splashes of red where wild poppies grew. Now I stared through my windshield, waiting, and it was all a dark sea before me. Mists, far away, moved across the hills like ghost hounds sniffing the morning. It was old, barren land, holding to itself its stories of ancient armies when other men for other reasons might have waited here. It gave me no comfort, no kindness from all its wisdom, but held my gaze for the moment, yielding to me perhaps the only truth it could: that it was indifferent and tired of us all.

Wind buffeted the wings, and I could feel the movement from the control surfaces against my hands. She was eager to go, ready for the day and the endless sky. We were seconds away from the time to start our engines. It was now. A flare burst in the center of the perimeter, an explosive puff that resolved into a rising arc of green fire, soaring upward above us, then falling back to earth. The mission was on. My hands moved through the ritual, doing the sacred things that would bring *Laura* to life: master switch, on; generator and batteries, on; throttles, idle cut off; fuel, full rich; fuel pumps, on; boosters, on; carburator air, off; gyros, locked; tanks, cross feed; altimeter, pressure altitude set; supercharger, off; controls, free; automatic pilot, off and locked.

Paul watched me closely, his hands already on the engine switches. I gave him as good a grin as I could. "Okay, energize number one." A low whine from number one built up quickly to an almost intolerable scream. "Start one." The engine spat twice in protest as hot flame hit cold metal. Smoke belched out of the exhaust, but it caught and settled down to a steady roar. Each engine, in turn, now joined the thunder of the thirty other planes, making a holocaust of the morning's quiet. Birds flashed out of the grass in terror, breaking for space in a panic of flight.

It is routine that saves us, the details that must be served to whatever end we go: to a madness five miles above a city in Germany or to a better purpose. It's all the same. Men on their deathbed plan gardens. Women, in sorrow and pain, arrange their hair or mend children's clothes and fret that they might be hungry or that their shoes are scuffed. It is the endless weave of small cares that is the grace through which all things are endured. They are more than the events that obscure them, for they are our fragments of truth beyond which are only dreams.

And so we lost our fear to the charity of small tasks that required our attention, putting aside our dread of the coming battle as something we would take care of later when the time came. We ran up each engine, checking carefully for any malfunction. We bled warm oil through the prop feathering system, checked each magneto, checked flaps, manifold pressures, radio equipment, fuel pressures, bomb racks, oxygen systems, hydraulics, flight instruments, and all of *Laura*'s demanding needs. The gunners groomed their weapons and arranged the ammunition boxes so the belts could move freely. Turrets whined through their gears. In the nose, the navigator was poring over his maps and noting the compass deviation posted on a card on the aft bulkhead. The bombardier bent over his sight, adjusting it to store data that would save crucial seconds on the bomb run: our predicted altitude and airspeed, the interval between the bombs, and the sweep angle of the sight that would be right on target if we arrived precisely at the Initial Point, a dot on a Mercator chart from which we would assault the Messerchmitt factories of Regensburg.

Takeoff was routine by our standard, which measured any incident as routine that eluded disaster. The thirty-one overloaded planes staggered down the runway, lurching into the air from the last available inches of runway. Cyclones of dirt and grass trailed them as they desperately held their few feet of altitude until the extra miles of airspeed could be gained to increase their climb another degree. They fought for every foot to clear the walls of Lucera. *Laura* pulled forty inches of manifold pressure and waddled over the town. The church steeple serenely viewed our labored passage. I could see the bell over the wingtip and could have heard the prayers of the supplicants at the altar breeching skyward, but for the roar of our engines. Boys in the streets waved at us as though they knew where we were going and wished us well.

One hour on course and there was only one other group about two miles west of us. We had been on time for wing rendezvous, but all we could see was that one other group. There should have been three more. The wing echelon should be five groups spread across a three-mile track. There were no fighter escorts anywhere. We had sighted twelve low-flying P-47s heading north, but they probably were tactical aircraft moving in to support the infantry. Nothing was shaping up right. Three of our planes had turned back with mechanical troubles. We were thirty-nine guns weaker. The tougher the mission, the more aborts; and they would get away with it, claiming excessive engine temperatures, low oil pressures, oxygen system malfunctions, or any number of excuses. The crew chiefs back at the base would check everything and often would find nothing to confirm the pilot's claim. There would be a half-hearted investigation and a report that would end up in a file that someday should be resurrected as a monument to the contemptible. Two more peeled off and headed home. I found myself wishing that fighters would jump us early. An attack would be the one thing that would hold them; then the formation would be their refuge and they couldn't leave. The three spares that had been flying a high-right position moved in to fill three of the spots. One of the aborts had been from my squadron so I moved in on the right wing of the second flight. Things settled down as we plodded on. The sky was perfect, blue space that stretched endlessly beyond us. Bannered by white streamers of cirrus, it held us in its silence, and we breasted the winds that touched all the places on earth.

Our heading would take us east of Pola, where heavy flak concentration guarded the submarine pens. The guns had the range to pick us off if we shaved it too close. With the main peninsula to our left, we would penetrate the mainland at Fiume. From there on, it could happen anytime. The Udine fighters would have us first, then the groups around Klagenfurt would take over until we hit the main defenses or until we crossed the German border. In the next thirty minutes, five more planes aborted. We had lost a total of ten, and the group was wasted by one-third without a shot being fired. There was some comfort. I spotted another group. There was other encouraging news. The tail gunner sighted a B-24 wing behind us. We were not alone.

We edged past Pola and were saluted with a barrage of flak that for all but a few bursts fell short of the low-left squadron. Three stray shells exploded in the center of the formation. I could see the orange flame in the middle of the black puffs. Two successive bursts erupted off the tip of our right wing and magically an array of star-shaped holes appeared in our windshield. When they came close like this, they made a thumping sound like the threat of a terrible anger. It never seemed to us that the flak came from anything on the ground. Not from guns that men fired. Flak came from the sky itself; it blossomed there. In a glory of flame, the black flowers would burst among us, an evil garden whose paths we crossed in terror; whose essence was the stink of hell; and whose iron seed was spilled on us, a cruel planting we had to bear. But today we skirted Pola and its black garden, and we held our course steady for the mainland at Fiume.

As we passed the city, there was a sense of the irrevocable, like a door shut and locked behind us. Nothing would turn us back now from the long corridor to Regensburg. Resolution came to us because we had no choice. We were lost to everything but our will to do this task that was beyond all reason. Minute after minute passed as the group moved over the hostile land. Swelling cumulus towered in the east. Below us layers of broken stratus allowed the patterns of earth to reach us as changing scenes of little towns and streams and rolling hills with trees climbing the slopes. Our minds and hearts locked on our peril. Our senses submitted only to the needs of fear, to its probing search for the things that hunted us. There was not a blemish in the sky, yet we knew they were there.

The formation tightened. Dark hackles of guns raised from the gleaming metal skins. My left wing tucked in about ten feet away from the waist window of the flight leader. I could see the strange figure of his gunner swaddled in his felt heated suit crouching over his weapon. Helmeted and goggled with the dark mask covering the bottom of his face, he appeared grotesque, an inhuman creature watching for other demons. He was firing! An object came between us, hurtling over the top of my wing. A shining teardrop, a belly tank released by one of our fighters tumbled through the formation and vanished behind us.

"Bandits! Bandits! Christ, there's a million—"

"Shut up." Petrosky's voice came over the intercom, hard and flat. Then, in a calm tone, he spoke to me. "There's an awful lot of 'em, Jack. They're mostly forming up ahead. Somebody got hit up in the lead squadron. That first pass came out of nowhere. Jesus, there's more of 'em coming up over there, see around ten o'clock high—"

"Hey, Pete! Six o'clock. Comin' in, level." The tail gunner's voice was excited, but under control. I could hear the top turret turning, then the short bursts of his fire joining the tail guns and the ball turret. White lines of tracers swept by my window. A quick spread of black explosions leaping out ahead of us—

"Okay. Okay. They're breaking to three o'clock."

We had taken the first fighter attack. The gunners were silent, concentrating all of their attention on whatever part of the sky they could see. Anything they said now would be said quickly and to the point. To react, we needed to know how many were coming in and from where. Nothing else. Our survival depended on our alertness. To fail to see incoming fighters or to see them late assessed a penalty, a final one. I motioned to Paul to take over. I wanted to look around myself. Far ahead of us, an eternity of minutes away, a string of small dark shapes stretched in a slanting line across the sky: fighters climbing for position. There were more forming high on our port side. A B-17 was smoking up in the lead squadron with his number-three engine on fire. All he could do was pray that the fire would burn itself out. If he dropped out of the formation, they would be on him like wolves.

The tail gunner came back on the intercom. "There's twenty trailing us. Six o'clock low. About fifteen hundred yards."

Pete put another nail in. "There's more. Four o'clock high."

"Bandits attacking. Twelve o'clock." I took a quick last look before taking back the controls as Paul did before going back on monitoring the engine instruments. My hands soothed *Laura* to the dangers, holding her close to the flight leader; but my mind held the vision of twenty MEs boring in, and I waited for the shock.

"Jesus Christ! There goes Coursey!" Coursey was leading the low left. I couldn't look. I couldn't let my attention waver from the tip of my wing and the leader's window. Graceful streams of tracers curled by, and some metal strangely flew away from the top of the left wing. For an amazing moment, four MEs that had pressed their attack through the lead squadron were framed in the middle of the group. Every gun had them as they desperately rolled for a vertical dive toward earth. The last one didn't make it. He exploded in a geyser of flame that shot upward and made a white parasol of smoke over the empty space where he had been the instant before.

"Hey! Three o'clock! Closing. Six hundred yards."

I felt a violent impact from the back of my seat and smoke swirled through the flight deck. We had taken a hit somewhere aft. I looked for Paul. He was leaning forward like a nearsighted old man reading the paper. He waved the smoke away and wiped the glass surfaces of the instruments with the heel of his gloved hand. The guns were still firing, and *Laura* was responding to the controls.

"Right waist to pilot. Left gun is out. Twenty-millimeter hit it, I think. Marty's bought it. He's bleedin' somethin' awful."

Paul was already half out of his seat when I pushed him back. Someone else would have to go aft to help out. Paul knew better. It would take the two of us. Even if we had the luck, it would take the two of us. The radio gun was the least critical station. I held my throat mike snug with my fingers. "Pilot to radio. Go aft. See what you can do." My voice surprised me. It was calm, as though what was happening was very routine. There was no hint of the terror that raged inside of me. It was wonderful. I was playing a marvelous trick on them. They would never know.

Paul took the controls, and I peered under the flight leader. Two planes were missing from the low left. Coursey, the leader, and his right wingman were gone. The remaining planes were maneuvering to adjust the formation. The new leader was trying to hold them steady. God, they were all over the place! Too much space between them.

Too much. Close it up. Please— Oh, Jesus! Close it up. The nose must have seen what happened. "Andy, where's Coursey?"

"They took a head-on pass from twenty. First thing, Coursey's upside down all on fire. Everything— Jesus, you should have— His wing blew off and his right wingman caught most of it. They burned like— Hey! Ten o'clock! Ten o'clock! Closing."

I left Paul with the wheel. Six attacking MEs were concentrating on the shattered low left. Danny's ball turret had a good angle. The first ME flashed in low. Danny had him! His canopy blew off and flame spurted from his wingroot—

"Radio to pilot. Marty's dead, I think. The gun's gone. We took two twenty-millimeter hits. One in the bomb bay and the one that got Marty. I'm going back. Okay?"

"Okay, radio. Out." One in the bomb bay. Why hadn't we blown? Jesus, the bomb bay. Who was Marty? I couldn't remember. Up in the lead squadron, the plane that had been hit on the first pass was now beyond hope. The right wing was enveloped in flame. Banked in a sighing departure of pain and defeat, the B-17 fell slowly. The crippled wing dipped lower and lower. Some dark forms fell out. One chute. Two. Three. Two more. The doomed plane twisted down in a sickening spiral that tightened and tightened into a snapping spin. The right wing drifted away and a fountain of fire consumed the rest.

How long it was. How long, long, long it was. It never ended, but only paused, gasping for breath, to begin again. It was happening. What never could come for any of us was happening. We would never make it. Still, we held steady, giving nothing to them. We would never turn back. It was gone, everything was gone. There was no beginning, no end. We were in the heart of battle; beyond the world and beyond ourselves in this agony of striving. There was no way out. We were for it all the way or until we could reach the shelter of the flak at Regensburg because there, in that cruel furnace, the fighters would never follow.

The lead squadron and the low left were getting the worst of it. Head-on attacks and slashing passes from ten o'clock raked them again and again. Another one up in the lead was on fire. Her two starboard engines were feathered, and the wing that held them was vanishing in plumes of brown smoke. She didn't last long, staggering in her position for only a few brave moments before she left us in a wide turning dive toward earth. Two fighters followed her with exulting speed while our guns, hopelessly out of range, fired after them.

We killed and crippled them and still they came. Some lived for another day, like some of ours, drifting down under white and yellow parachutes as enemy and friend, swinging in soothing, gentle arcs, marked the sky with tiny pendulums. Burning debris fell through them, but they were untouched and continued rocking in our wake until they were gone far behind us, sinking in the blue walls of silence and lost, forever lost.

The fighters had disappeared; they were gone, we were free of them. The sky was empty, as serene as though they had never been there, as though we had awakened from a terrible dream and could rest now without fear.

Paul leaned toward me, and I switched my communication frequency from command to intercom. "Jack, there's no engine problems except number-one cylinder head is running kind of hot. I'll crack the cowl flaps. Okay?"

"Yeah, okay. If it starts to vibrate, close the flaps and richen the mixture a little."

"Want me to take it for a while?"

"Yeah, you got it."

Paul took the controls, holding *Laura* snug under the lead flight. I looked around; there were still no fighters in sight. The group was in bad shape, with the remaining seventeen planes floundering in a loose formation that was an invitation to an attack. The group leader saw our situation, too, and he broke radio silence. "This is Green Leader. Reform. Reform into three squadrons. Trailing squadron, pack it in; fill in the holes. I want six here in the lead; six in the low left; and five in the right. Hurry it up. Out."

The planes moved to his commands like giant obedient beasts, one after the other, sliding in gentle turns or urging forward to a new position. For a few desperate moments it was a melee, a vulnerable confusion that finally became our new battle order. In *Laura*, we ended up leading the second flight in the high-right squadron. The group flew on and, as each safe minute passed, we blessed our luck, hoping it would hold. But we knew it couldn't last, this soothing peace; it couldn't last.

"Flak! Flak at ten o'clock."

We were passing Klagenfurt. The bursts were high and to our left, edging toward us as the batteries corrected their fire. It was closing on us. Crystal fragments of steel burned the air around us while we blundered through the greasy traces of brown and black smoke. Our squadron lead plane suddenly showed a stream of flaming oil from his number-two engine. I watched curiously to see how quickly the pilots could shut down the engine and feather the prop. It was secured within minutes. The flames subsided, but a mist of smoking oil trailed the plane, leaving a widened, curling ribbon of black behind us. The damaged plane didn't waver but held the lead steady, not yielding our course. It was a violent passage of about ten minutes before we were out of the range of the guns. It was an eternity, a second-by-second deliverance from each exploding shell. And there was no end, only another beginning.

"Top turret to pilot. They're back. Three o'clock level." Pete hesitated, as though he were puzzled. "Queer—For Christ's sake! They're JU-88s, a string of them! I make out six. Off about a thousand yards, on our course. The rest of you guys? Do you see anything else?" Each gunner reported in negative; no other enemy planes in sight. It didn't seem possible that they were throwing these old bombers at us. They were slow and not heavily armed, easy targets for our packed firepower.

"They're turning— Rockets! Jesus, they're shootin' fuckin' rockets at us!"

A cluster of white tracks moved gracefully toward us, arcing away from the bombers like the start of a fireworks display. Each rocket was followed by a core of pulsing orange light that refracted through the exhaust vapors, making shimmering circles of yellow and red. They passed about fifty yards in front of the lead squadron, and their auras faded as their vapor tracks blended together to form a thin cloud through which we passed, spilling the curves of whiteness over our wings and engines.

"Bandits. Twelve o'clock." It was Andy's voice, our navigator. The words were spoken quietly. I could barely hear him on the intercom. He knew there was no need to shout, no need to summon us with a brave rallying cry; it was only a matter of making it known—they had returned.

Two waves were coming straight in, ten in each line. They were ME-210s, two-engine fighters with plenty of firepower. One line was attacking level, heading for the lead squadron; the other line of ten was slightly higher, and were sliding over the top of their comrades, positioning for an attack on our squadron.

"Ten coming in. Eleven o'clock high."

The top turret and the nose open fired. I could see the blinking wing guns of the incoming fighters, and I watched the white lines of tracers merge before me. Black bursts of twenty-millimeter shells stitched a line over our left wing. Our squadron leader began to go to pieces: large chunks of metal blew away from the lower part of the nose; the chin turret was hanging at a strange angle; the end of his right wing blew away, and the plane flipped over. It continued to turn, performing a looping barrel roll of flame before it fell from us in an almost vertical dive. The fighters broke to our right except for one flaming coffin that continued through our formation, miraculously missing the left wing of the lead flight by inches.

As the frenzy of the battle raged, my terror faded and I waited for my death. I no longer saw them: the 109s, the 410s, the 210s, and the 190s, coming at us from all directions. I no longer saw the horror of my comrades burning and dying. I shut my soul to everything but the plane ahead of me. I held *Laura* steady under the tail guns as though she were nailed there.

Sweat covered me: it ran down my back and between my buttocks; it streamed down my chest; my eyes burned with it. My crotch and thighs were soaked with urine. I crouched in my small seat, strapped to it so I could barely move. Life-giving air came into my lungs from a slender rubber tube that could be severed with a boy's jackknife. Goggles shielded my eyes from the blasts of ice-cold air pouring through the ragged holes in the windshield. A band of rubber plastic around my throat with two small diaphragms pressed against my vocal cords allowed me to speak; but there were no words: the maelstrom roared around me, and only my gasping breath pulsed through the unmindful slender strands of wire.

After a long, long time, some words were spoken to me, words I could barely comprehend.

"Bombardier to pilot. We're coming up on the IP. Bomb-bay doors are coming open."

We had made it! We had made it to Regensburg!

The group wheeled in a shallow turn, settling in on the angle of attack. We were on the bomb run. The fighters were gone, but ahead of us loomed a wall of flak. It was more than enough for our ragged band of fourteen bombers. We had lost seven, and were now down to five in the lead, five in the left, and four in my right squadron. We plunged into the darkness.

Laura was rocked by near explosions. She was vibrating, trying to fall off on her right wing. Paul's voice came on the intercom. "Number three—number three. Manifold pressure's gone. Oil pressure's dropping."

"Shutting down number three." I hit the feathering button.

Paul's hands moved fast: throttle, off; fuel, off; oil pump, off; switches, off. "Number three, secure."

The vibration lessened. Paul and I watched the blades slow down, and we waited for them to rotate with their edges facing into the wind. If the blades failed to feather, we would have an almost impossible drag on our plane: the broad area of the three blades, flat in the wind, would be a barrier, slowing *Laura* down. We would be forced to fall behind the formation, and the German fighters would make short work of us.

Paul's hand pounded my knee. "It's okay. She's feathered. Okay to trim."

I advanced power slightly on the other inboard, then adjusted the rudder and aileron trim to compensate for the dead engine. Paul came back to me. "I'll give you a damage report when we're out of this stuff."

The flak engulfed us. It was so intense we could only feel the turbulence from the near bursts; we were in a swirling torrent that obscured the individual explosions except when they came close and fire blazed out of the shadows. Something slammed into the armor plate on the back of my seat; a gaping hole appeared in the Plexiglas over my head.

A plane was falling out of the lead squadron. I watched for chutes. Suddenly she blew; a tremendous explosion of flame and debris leaped outward. The shock wave rocked the squadron, and we struggled to recover. We had to keep the formation tight; we couldn't fail now. As we fought to control our planes, the group leader's voice came in on a command frequency. "Steady. Steady. Hold it steady."

Laura lurched upward.

"Bombs away! Bombs away!"

Three tons of bombs had dropped out of the racks. The group started a wide turn to the left, nosing down in a shallow dive to clear the inferno. We leveled off at twenty-two thousand feet and began our long journey home.

We were mauled on our return. The battle was a series of violent sporadic attacks by German fighters now disorganized and without the concentrated fury they had been able to throw at us on our way in. They were rising in smaller numbers. Some of them couldn't get back to us: the time it took them to land, refuel, climb to twenty-two thousand feet, and search for us as we pushed hard for the coast made interception more a matter of luck than anything else. But those who found us fought with a ferocity that our reduced numbers and battle-damaged planes could barely endure. They slashed at our formation with an abandoned savagery to make us pay for the rubble and corpses of Regensburg, for their comrades blasted out of the air; they slashed at us in their rage against an onslaught they knew would never end. We lost two more bombers to these furious attacks, and by the time we reached the Adriatic the original group strength was reduced to ten aircraft.

Ten B-17s crossed the coastline, ten torn machines carrying exhausted men, wounded and dead men. And those who lived watched the calm sea pass beneath them; they watched the towering cumulus along the coast swell upward in a billowing stream, forming great castles of purple-and-white fleece. They watched and saw nothing. Their vision still held the battle, and they stared with unseeing eyes at the splendor of the sky and sea.

We peeled off over the field. *Laura* was laboring now. The feathered engine was vibrating badly, probably from structural damage in the mount. Number one was running rough. I made the downwing leg short, turning for my landing as soon as the end of the runway passed under the left wingtip. When I cut back the throttles, Paul quickly followed my lead, setting up for full power if we had to pull up and go around again.

"Booster pumps, on; manifold pressure and RPM, okay; fuel mixture, okay. Twenty degrees of flaps, coming down."

Laura sighed, banking high in the tight turn into the field. She lurched irritably when Paul hit the toggle switch and the wheels dropped into the down position.

"Wheels, down and locked."

The falling turn was almost complete, and I tried to gauge my roll-out so I would be lined up with the runway.

"Give me full flaps."

"Full flaps, coming down."

The wings were level. We were at three hundred feet and lined up right on the money. I had seconds to adjust the trim, to correct the dragging pull away from the dead engine. We crossed the end of the strip, and I pulled the throttles all the way back against the stops and set the friction brake. *Laura* yielded to the loss of power, to the drag of flaps and wheels, sinking, sinking toward the steel mat. I gentled her fall, slowing her descent with back pressure on the wheel, holding her off, holding her off. I felt the tail wheel touch and then heard the screech of rubber as the main gear hit. The steel mat rattled under us as we rolled toward the end of the runway. We were down.

Ahead of us, off to the side of the taxi strip near the end of the runway, I could see the crash truck and two ambulances waiting. We were rolling too fast. I still hadn't touched the brakes, not wanting to challenge the hydraulic system, even though the hydraulic pressure indicator showed that the pressure was normal. We were nearing the end of the runway and I couldn't delay any longer. The brakes grabbed; little jerks of restraint now curbed *Laura*, slowing her to a sedate speed. I turned off the runway onto the taxi strip, moving slowly toward the nearest ambulance.

I pulled off the strip and, as soon as I stopped rolling, the medics were on board. One of them came forward through the bomb bay and onto the flight deck. He stared at us for a moment.

"You guys okay?"

I heard myself answer, "Yeah, we're okay."

The medic was holding on to the back of my seat. He could barely keep his balance as he tried to stand on the hundreds of shell cases on the deck. His eyes took in the shattered windshield, the holes in the overhead Plexiglas, Paul's window covered with oil, the three ghostly faces staring back at him.

"You sure you guys are all right?"

Pete put his hand on the medic's shoulder. "We're okay, Sergeant. Just take care of the gunner."

"Yeah, okay. Okay. We'll have the man off in a couple of minutes." He hesitated as though he wanted to say something else, but then he turned and headed back through the bomb bay.

While we waited with the engine idling, Paul brought up the wing flaps, opened the cowl flaps, shut the booster pumps off, locked the gyros, and shut down number-two engine so I could taxi with the two outboards. He looked over his shoulder for Pete. "Any more coffee back there, Pete?"

"There's half a Thermos left, still hot." Pete poured a cup and handed it to Paul.

I watched him sip it. His face was pale and streaked with grease and smoke. A faint pink line marked where his oxygen mask had pressed against his skin. His hands were steady.

"Do you want a cigarette?" I offered my pack to Paul.

"No, no thanks. You know I don't smoke."

"Well, I just thought you might want to start some bad habits. It's going to be a long war."

He didn't smile but looked down at his coffee, swishing it around in his cup before he gulped it down. "I never did give you that damage report on number three, did I?" Then he looked at me. "Did I do all right, Jack?"

"You were fine, Paul. You were abso-fuckin'-lutely fine."

I turned back to my window. The medics were taking Marty out. His body was covered with a blanket and strapped to the stretcher. I motioned to Paul to unlock the tail wheel.

"Tail wheel, unlocked."

I advanced the outboard throttles and moved *Laura* back out on the taxi strip.

"Lock the wheel."

"Tail wheel locked."

As we approached our stand, I could see the ground crew waiting for us. Their faces were grim; there were no smiles. There would be none of the obscene banter that always greeted us after an easy mission. I turned *Laura* in and shut her down.

I stood beside *Laura*, looking up at her for a moment. She was still smiling over her wineglass, but she showed wear from her encounters. There was a shell hole in her right knee and new oil stains soiled the rosy curve of her breast. Were her eyes still the same? I didn't think so; she looked tired, worn by what we had done to her.

The trucks hadn't come to take us to debriefing. I walked to the edge of the steel mat and off into the dry winter grass. Looking to the west, my eyes followed the slope of the land toward the far mountains. They were too far away to see, but they were there, because I could see the clouds rising up from them as they always did in the late afternoon.

It was then that I felt the wind. It brushed against me gently, rustling through my flight suit, touching my face, my throat. It nestled against the palms of my hands. It was cool and sweet, silent except for a murmuring, a whisper of moving air bending the grass around me. It moved through my hair, it moved under my jacket, softly flapping it aside to stream upward over my back and chest, coiling about me, now strong, now exquisitely tender. It was like a divine pity, caressing me, soothing me. The wind, the holy wind. I stood fixed to the earth, rooted in a perfect timeless ecstasy.

It was long ago, and he has not returned. The young man still stands in the wind. He will always be there, holding my youth forever to him, secret and quiet, never moving, never yielding to time nor the endless seasons of snow and sun. He is gone from me, and I shall never come upon him again.

Chapter VI

A COSTLY ERROR

Poor naked wretches, wheresoe'r you are,
That bide the pelting of this pitiless storm,
How shall your houseless heads and unfed sides
Your loop'd and window'd raggedness, defend you
From seasons such as these?

—WILLIAM SHAKESPEARE
King Lear,
Act III, Scene 4

The group began the task of rebuilding. Major Billings pulled me off the battle orders again and assigned me temporarily to the role of squadron check pilot. There were five new crews coming in to replace our losses, and Billings was adamant that their proficiency must be assured before they joined the squadron on any operational flights. Billings also wanted me to help Captain Salinas by flying check flights on planes that Mike felt could be repaired and brought back on the line. The work suited me. It left me little time to dwell on the hard missions ahead.

Mike's situation was extreme. There were only two undamaged planes in the squadron. With a certain reluctance, I volunteered the information that I had some technical background and perhaps could help by doing a bit more than simply flying the check flights and the slow-times. Mike promptly introduced me to the Boeing technical manuals and to T/Sgt. Sam White, who was the boss of the engineering hangar. Sam dragged me into the chaos of his world without any delay, assuming that I understood everything he said to me. His was a recital of disaster: there were a thousand problems and the solutions could have been categorized as nearly impossible, impossible, and totally impossible.

During the days that followed, I don't know how much help I was to Mike and Sam. Probably the most important thing I did was to aid

Mike in persuading Billings and Devereaux that they had to bring in some more planes from Foggia Main. They had brought in one and, from their cursory reviews of Mike's daily reports, they had concluded that Mike could work miracles and bring the squadron up to operational strength in a couple of days. It couldn't be done.

Major Devereaux and Major Billings were intelligent men, and I could not understand why Mike's precise assessment of the damage situation did not convince them to act immediately. It was not until I put in my two cents' worth that Devereaux and Billings agreed to pull in two more planes from Foggia. Why they listened to me and not to Mike, I cannot say. The fact that Mike was a graduate engineer and a man of exceptional judgment did not seem to impress them as much as the mystique of pilots, whose innate knowledge about everything relating to airplanes was to be relied on, and not the opinion of anyone who was outside the pale of their brotherhood.

But this kind of arrogance, this mystical faith in the omnipotent wisdom of pilots, was pretty much confined to ambitious men in command positions. A few of them actually scorned the mundane work of the engineers and the ground crews, and half believed the foolish boast "I can fly the boxes they came in." The line pilots, however, were less sanguine, and sought Mike's counsel as often as they could. In spite of the courageous élan of Devereaux and Billings, and sometimes the mad determination of Colonel Belcher, our group commander, the line pilots subscribed more sensibly to the conservative philosophy "There are old pilots and there are bold pilots, but there are no old, bold pilots."

As much as Belcher, Devereaux, and Billings would have liked us to be flaming heroes, we could not manage to play the role. We were drab workingmen who did what we were told to do as best we could. Our best was our commitment to the hard task of war, which we met as common men enduring the trouble of each day as it came. We were rarely brave, and some of us were cowards. We trembled, cursed, and grumbled. When it was beyond bearing, we were silent. There were a few, like Paul, who were indifferent to death, who praised God and flew their missions sure of glory one way or the other. But they were, we thought, a little mad.

Through the month of March, I saw little of Mac and Paul. When I wasn't flying transition with the new crews or flying check flights for Mike, I was working with Sam in the repair hangar. The work I did for Sam was not as difficult as I thought it would be. The Boeing technical manuals were excellent documents with complete information, in minute detail, on everything one needed to know about the anatomy of a B-17. My work was only a matter of extracting the data I needed and preparing it for Sam and his men in the form of a rough sketch with a material list and occasionally a few calculations. The calcs were only required when I had to depart from the requirements in the technical manuals because the material available in our inventory was not precisely what the manual specified.

I rarely got back to my tent. Many nights I slept on a cot in the Engineering Office and sometimes in Mike's tent, where he lived in lone squalor amid empty cans and bottles, books, grease-stained clothes, and posters of pouting half-naked girls whose sullen faces promised a tedious hour or two of whining complaints after the pleasure of their company. The debris and the display of modest pornography contrasted strangely with the B-17 engineering drawings that were strewn on his bunk, on the floor, on a wretched desk, and spilling out of two ancient filing cabinets.

Mike's tent made me yearn for the comfort of my own, where Paul kept everything neat as a pin. He even had Mac tidying up once in a while. Oddly enough, they were becoming good friends, and I rarely saw one without the other. They were special: the brute of a man, Mac, blundering through the area with Paul alongside of him, elegant and slim. Mac was now belligerently protective of Paul, like a bear with a cub. Paul in turn treated Mac with an affectionate patience and endured Mac's rough ways, as part of his devotion to the reality of the world and the goodness he perceived in it.

Although I was away from Mac and Paul most of the time, I managed to keep track of their progress. During the first two weeks of March, Mac had got in three missions and Paul had flown two. Paul's last mission was with a Lieutenant Clark, who was one of the more experienced pilots in the squadron, with twenty-six missions to his credit. I had a chance one night to talk with Bernie Clark at mess, and I asked him about Paul's performance.

Bernie had just finished eating and was drinking his coffee when I approached him. Without answering me, he motioned me to sit down beside him. Bernie was a big, rawboned man with a relaxed, gentle manner which is often common among physically powerful men. He seemed to be pleased to have me join him.

"Oh, you mean Paul Leigh?"

"Yes," I said.

"What about him? Is he a pal of yours?"

I told Bernie that Paul was a tentmate and I had checked him out. I added, "He flew Regensburg with me."

"Oh, Jesus," Bernie groaned. "Wasn't that a ball buster? I was so scared I didn't know whether to shit in my pants or wind the fuckin' clock. How did Paul do?"

I said, "He did fine. Real fine."

Bernie lit a cigarette. The white cylinder looked tiny in his hand. "Yeah, he's a good kid. Good pilot. It was a milk run so I let him fly the bomb run. Steady as a rock. Flies good across the cockpit. I put a word in for him with Billings. Tell me somethin', is he always quiet and polite like that?"

I tried to think about how to answer the question, and then Bernie came up with another one.

"How about the kid and McCarthy? That's a damn funny pair. Now that Mac, he's a mean bastard. How is it he and young Paul get along?"

I gave Bernie a lame answer. "I don't know. They're so damn different in their ways, but maybe their differences are a kind of reassurance for each of them."

"What the hell are you talkin' about? Don't be so goddamn obscure."

"Well, Paul wants to believe in the goodness of everyone, and maybe he perceives Mac's anger as Mac's way of seeking the same thing. You know, the purifying flame stripping away all the horseshit."

Bernie laughed. "Speaking of horseshit, Jack, you're shoveling your share. And Mac?"

"Sort of the same thing. To Mac, Paul is the virtuous, brave, and honest man he knew he would find if he knocked enough phonies on their ass. Paul is his prize, the proof of his tough faith."

Bernie laughed again. "Jack, you are absolutely full of crap. Come on, let's go up to the club and have a few beers. I've got to hear more of this."

As he rose from his seat, Bernie struck me on the shoulder in a friendly way. My arm went numb and I felt an exploding pain in my elbow. I knew it was going to be a rough night, and it was. Bernie plied me with beer, switching to gin and grapefruit juice as time happily passed. I never did recall much of the conversation except I think we generally covered everything from the Boston Red Sox to T. S. Eliot, with some brilliant excursions into politics and history, or so it seemed at the time.

Three days later, Mac was killed.

I didn't know the full story until hours after the accident. My first awareness of something wrong came as I was standing by at the end of the runway waiting to take off on a check flight. The tower had told me to hold until the planes returning from Zagreb had landed. When the planes came over the field and peeled off, there were five planes not seven. I switched my radio to the squadron frequency and listened. There were two planes down about thirty miles northeast of the field. Mac! Mac was on that mission!

After the squadron had landed, I called the tower and told them to scratch my flight plan. I was returning to the hardstand.

"Roger," the tower said. "Anything wrong?"

"No," I said. "Please advise engineering."

"Wilco. Out."

I had a terrible feeling, a dread of confirming Mac's death. I positively knew it had happened. I could smell the stinking presence of it; it was near me. "Oh, Mac! You crazy bastard! What have you done?"

My copilot, who was one of the new pilots going through his brief transition training, was puzzled by my behavior. "Anything wrong, Jack?"

I said, "Yes. I think my tentmate bought it. Look, as soon as we get back to the stand, I want you to secure the plane and then go over to engineering and tell them I've scratched this flight. Okay? I'm going back to Operations and find out what the hell happened."

It took forever, or so it seemed, before we got back to the stand. As soon as we stopped, I set the brakes and scrambled out of my seat, telling Charlie as I left, "We won't make our flight today. I'll see you tonight. Tell Mike. I'll explain it to him later. Thanks, Charlie."

I tried not to drive the jeep too fast. The sloping dirt road that ran from the field to the main highway was rough, deeply rutted from the winter rains. As I neared the highway, I began to feel Mac's presence. I could hear his gruff voice on the night we stopped at the farmhouse on our way to Bari. "See, Jack, I told you we'd find a place to stay. Hey, that kid sure can sing!" I could see him staring into Maria's eyes, his bulky form leaning toward her, caught in a tenderness that I had scorned. I could smell the pipe he used to smoke when he settled in the tent at night.

"Oh, Mac. For Christ's sake, I'm sorry. I'm so damn sorry."

The sentry gave me an indifferent salute, and I passed through to the Operations shack. Captain Ewell was the only one there. When he looked and saw me coming into the office, he didn't hesitate. He knew I wanted to hear it, fast and straight.

"Yeah, McCarthy's dead, along with nineteen others—for no fuckin' reason at all."

"What happened, Jim? What the hell happened?"

"I only know what Billings called in. They were letting down through a thin cloud cover. Either they hit some rough air or somebody screwed up. I don't know. Devereaux's gone to the crash site with a couple of ambulances. Want some coffee?"

I shook my head. "No. No thanks, Jim. I'd better get up to the tent and go through Mac's stuff."

"Yeah, you'd better. The ghouls will be with you as soon as they confirm the casualties."

By "ghouls" Jim meant the people who were required to collect and seal all the effects of anyone killed or missing in action. These men had to be indiscriminate in their work, and everything, no matter what it was, went into the cardboard cartons. A man's personal effects had to be culled by his friends; they could include things that would be painful for his family to see, pitifully trite things that might soil the memory of the man—pornographic books or pictures, indiscreet letters, things of that sort. Then there were the spoils: whiskey, a few cans of beer, cigarettes, a good razor, candy, and tidbits from home, which were all liberated from the man's hoard for the common larder of the tent. Each death yielded these inheritances which we wore, used, drank, smoked, or ate. And for a brief time, until we forgot, these gifts made it seem as though the man were still there.

I asked Jim. "Is Paul around?"

"No. He and Bernie Clark grabbed a jeep and have gone chasing after the C.O. and his meat wagons. They left about thirty minutes ago."

As I left operations, Ewell called after me, "When you're finished, come back and pick me up. We'll go down to chow together."

I made my way through the olive grove to the tent. When I went in, Paul's fastidious housekeeping was evident. Everything was in its place. My gear was neatly arranged in my footlocker, my bunk was made, and I wouldn't have been surprised if even the mice who lived under the floorboards and who often scrambled over us at night hadn't been charged by Paul to shape up and tidy their quarters for his inspection. It was as if in greeting that three of the tiny creatures came out from the boards around the stove and scurried toward me. I was sitting on Mac's bunk. He used to feed them crumbs every time he came in the tent. I found his biscuit tin and sprinkled some crumbled pieces on the floor. A fourth mouse joined his friends and, while they

nibbled happily, I began the sad chore of going through Mac's belongings.

I found nothing. I had half expected to find something from Maria, some remembrance, a letter or a photograph, but there was nothing. He had kept two recent letters from his mother and father. There were three letters from his brother, who was a pilot instructor at Maxwell Field. There were two battered copies of *Field and Stream*, three cans of beer, two cartons of Chesterfields, a catechism, two pipes and a tin of tobacco, a half-eaten box of chocolates, rosary beads, two textbooks on navigation, a piece of D ration tropical chocolate, and a tin of shortbread biscuits. As I sat there touching Mac's little possessions, I was awed by them, by their simple meanings, by their wise modesty, as though I were a devout pilgrim who had come upon the relics of a great and noble king.

Tomorrow won't be so bad, I thought. Maybe tomorrow will be better. I watched the mice leave their feast, one by one, and return to their nests under the floorboards. I put Mac's beer, the candy, the cigarettes, and the tin of shortbread in my footlocker. I smoothed Mac's bunk and stretched out on my own to wait for Paul. It was quiet, everything was so quiet. I didn't sleep right away but fell into a restless desire for sleep. My memory searched for peace, for a way out of the sadness, wandering and uncertain until it came to a quarry wall where white stone circled a pool of clear blue water. It found the warm shelf of rock above the pool where I used to lie naked in the sun. It found the sweaty arrow of a boy diving through shafts of light into the joy of spray and foam. I slept.

When I opened my eyes, the afternoon light had faded into a gray early twilight. Paul was lying on his bunk, his hands clasped behind his head. He knew I was awake, and without moving, he said, "Do you want to hear about it?"

"Yes."

"Mac's plane was on Billings's left wing. Going through the clouds, the flight leader of the second flight failed to control his plane when they hit some turbulence and he collided with Mac's. Do you remember when you cussed me out for letting the wing drop and I almost went into Ewell?"

"Yes. I remember."

"You were right. You said something else later, after you calmed down."

"Never mind that now, Paul. What happened to Mac?"

"Well, when the planes hit they flamed right away. The guys didn't have a chance. But it was funny about Mac."

"What do you mean—funny? For Christ's sake, get on with it."

"Well, Mac must have been blown clear, but he didn't have his chute pack on. He fell through the roof of a little farmhouse. There was an old man and his wife outside clearing their garden—getting it ready for planting. Mac went right through the roof. He landed on their kitchen table—flattened it."

"Did you see him?"

"Yes, I saw him." Paul was silent for a moment. "There was no blood; only a little from his mouth. He was flat on his back; he was staring at the hole in the roof. Doc examined him. He said every bone in his body was smashed. They couldn't pick him up. Jack, they couldn't pick him up! He was pulp!"

Paul got up from his cot and went to the door of the tent. He stood with his back to me; and after a time, he said, "I think I'll go down to Operations. The battle orders should be posted by now."

I asked as gently as I could, "Is there anything else, Paul?"

"They used stretcher poles. They made a rig out of stretcher poles. They lashed him to it and put him in the ambulance."

"I'll walk down to the shack with you. I promised Jim Ewell I'd pick him up for chow. Do you want to go with us?"

"No, thanks. I'm not hungry yet."

As we walked toward Operations, I saw Rich Egan coming through the trees. I hadn't seen Rich for some time, and it was reassuring to observe that he hadn't changed: his white face was shadowed by a two-day growth of beard; his thick black hair was uncombed and sticking out in all directions; he was wearing the filthiest striped T-shirt I had ever seen, and he reeked of stale beer.

"Hey, you guys. I'm sorry about Mac. I'm damned sorry."

"Thanks, Rich," Paul answered him, looking him over with a trace of a smile.

"I was just checking the battle orders. I'll be Ewell's navigator to-morrow—lucky bastard. Did you know that Mac's pilot was named McCarthy too? That would have been his fiftieth mission—he almost made it."

"Rotten luck," I said. I remembered the man, a tall fellow, quiet, with a good reputation. I had no idea he had that many missions. "What do you think happened, Rich?"

"There's nothing to think about, I *know* what happened." Egan's pale eyes stared at us; he challenged us. "Bob McCarthy was as good a pilot that ever put on a pair of pants, but he was half dead, his nerves were shot. He didn't have another mission in him. When they went into that cloud bank, he fucked up, he did something stupid." Egan shifted his glance back and forth, now at Paul, now at me. "You don't believe me, huh? Huh? Bob McCarthy was the best, the fuckin' best; but I don't give a shit who you are, there's a fuckin' limit!" Rich kicked the dirt in his rage; stones and dust flew at us. "Ah, what the hell do you jerks know, you and young Jesus there—what the fuck do you know." He walked away still cursing, shaking his head. He waved his arms in the air, railing at heaven, at every saint he could flay with the whip of his tongue.

Paul watched him. "He's just as mad from the back as he is from the front. He's totally wrong you know—about the crash."

"He isn't mad. Egan's a man of great passion. All the best Irishmen are men who roar against the world. And what do you mean, he's wrong? How can you be sure?"

"Billings's tail gunner saw the whole thing. Bob McCarthy had his plane in perfect position on Billings's wing when they were in the muck. The second flight leader was the one who lost control—for whatever reason. He yawed toward his own wingman and pulled up to avoid hitting him. When he pulled up, he went right into Bob. That's the way it happened."

"Does it really matter? Does it really matter? The poor bastards are all dead now—Bob McCarthy, our Mac, all of them."

"Perhaps it doesn't matter, but there's something I wanted to say to you a while back when you shut me up."

"Oh, about the time I cussed you out for sliding toward Ewell?"

"Yes."

"Hell, you weren't that close. I was just looking for an excuse to take some skin off you."

"It was after you calmed down, and we were on the ground. You said, 'Never, never let the plane fly you. You must never lose your concentration, especially when you're flying formation. When you're in that seat, you're not a man; you're not a personality; you're not allowed moods or distractions. You're a component, the most critical component of your machine. You are allowed no margin. There are no excuses.' "

"Yeah, I remember the lecture."

"Well, I'm grateful. I was really angry because of the way you swore at me. But you were right, and I want to thank you. I'll never be the cause of an accident like today's. Never."

"I hope not." His earnestness was getting on my nerves. I wondered if he felt any sorrow at all. He was as much a fool as Egan. Did he have any grasp of the horror of that long, long flaming fall to earth? Did he really think God had killed twenty men to teach him a lesson?

When we reached the Operations shack, Paul stayed outside to check the bulletin board and the battle-order listings for tomorrow's mission. Jim Ewell was just hanging up the telephone as I entered the office.

"That was Mike Salinas," Jim said. "He's looking for you. I told him we'd meet him at chow. Okay?"

"Yeah, that's fine. Poor Mike, we were just about getting out of the woods, and now two more planes are gone."

"And two crews," Jim added.

"Hell, the crews are nothing. We can always get men." I knew I was being ridiculous. There was absolutely no reason for burdening Jim Ewell with my bitterness. I couldn't help it. An anger raged inside me.

Jim didn't say anything for a moment. He looked at me in a concerned way. "How about a belt before we eat? I got Billings's good stuff right here in the desk." He didn't wait for my answer but got up and pulled two glasses off the shelf. He poured each of us a generous shot.

At that moment Paul appeared in the door. "Hey, is it okay if I change my mind and eat with you fellows? I guess I am kind of hungry."

"Of course," I said. I regretted the harsh thoughts I had about him. He looked lost. I made up my mind I would try to get back to the tent more often.

Jim asked him, "Are you flying tomorrow? Would you like a drink?"

I was surprised when Paul said, "Yes—to both. I'm flying with Bernie. Just two fingers, please."

"I didn't know you drank, Paul," I said.

"Well, I don't very often. I used to have a little bourbon with my father and my grandfather—you know, on special occasions."

When Jim handed him his drink, Paul held it to the light like a connoisseur. "Good color," he said. And then he added, "If you'll permit me? To the men who died today." We drank, and then Paul raised his glass again. "I hope God doesn't mind the way Mac talks. He really blistered your ears sometimes." Paul downed the rest of his bourbon. His eyes filled and he reached for his handkerchief. "That whiskey isn't as smooth as my grandfather's. It takes a little getting used to, I guess." He wiped his eyes and held his empty glass toward Jim. "Another two fingers, if you please, sir."

Chapter VII

TARANTO: AN INTERLUDE

I fled Him, down the nights and down the days;
    I fled Him down the arches of the years;
I fled Him down the labyrinthine ways
    Of my own mind; and in the mist of tears
I hid from Him . . .

—FRANCIS THOMPSON
"The Hound of Heaven"

By the end of March, Mike Salinas and his engineering people had our maintenance problems well in hand. The intensity of German fighter resistance had lessened, with a consequent reduction in our losses. Supplies and parts were coming in better, too, and increasing numbers of new crews and new planes had built the Fifteenth Air Force bomber strength up to over seven hundred planes. There was talk around the squadron of the start of the bombing campaign against the oil fields in Rumania. The main target would be Ploesti, a vast complex which had only been attacked once by the ill-fated low-level mission from North Africa on August 1 of 1943. The losses on that mission had been staggering: fifty-three Liberator bombers had been shot down; four hundred and forty-six men were killed or missing; seventy-nine were interned in Turkey; forty-four were wounded. The men who had made this raid had come a long, long way, over two thousand miles from their bases in North Africa to Ploesti and back; and they did it without fighter cover and against fierce fighter resistance provided by German, Rumanian, and Bulgarian planes. When they finally fought their way through to the target area, they had to make their bomb runs through barrage balloons, cutting the cables with their wings, through a flaming holocaust of exploding oil and into the horror of the great guns of Festung Ploesti firing at point-blank range. The way back was a journey of sorrow, of endless fighter attacks against the crippled bombers that fell flaming into mountainsides and fields.

Some staggered to the coast of Greece for a long reach across the
Mediterranean, mortally wounded and falling with guns and engines
silent, at last touching the tops of waves and entering the green depths
of an ancient sea far from home.

This gallant attack was followed in late 1943 by the hard bloody
work of the infantry, the British Eighth Army and the American Fifth
Army, who invaded Italy from Sicily across the straits of Messina, and,
in late November and December, cleared the Foggia plains, making
it possible for the Fifteenth Air Force to establish a position within
range of Ploesti. Soon it would begin, completing the work of the
brave airmen who flew the epic raid from North Africa.

My role hadn't changed. I was still doing chores for Mike, but my
work load was light, and there was not enough to keep me busy through
the day. I idled hours away reading and playing bridge. I didn't play
bridge well; but I was better at it than at poker or at dice and I lost
less money. I finished reading Hudson's *Green Mansions,* and I was
wandering in the convoluted prose of Carlyle in *Sartor Resartus,* understanding very little of what I read. I received a late valentine from
Jean. Only Jean with this missile of extravagant sentiment could so
blithely elude the maudlin clichés of war. It had a sweet verse, asking
me to be her valentine, and unfolded to display a large velvet heart
saturated with perfume. I tacked it to the tent doorframe and its fragrance lasted for days. And while it lasted, it cast a spell over Paul and
me; the traces of scent led us to reveries of silk and loved voices, and
we fell into long silences as we stared at our books, sometimes glancing
up at the bright red heart on the door.

It was nearly the end of March. It didn't seem they were ever going
to put me back on operational duty. I was perfectly content to have it
that way, although I knew Major Billings was aware of my cushy
situation, and he would soon be pressuring Mike to release me back
to the squadron. My return to combat, however, was to be delayed
for at least a few more days. Jim Ewell and I were to fly down to an
abandoned Italian airfield just outside of Taranto. We had been assigned the task of checking the place out to see if it could be used as
a rest camp.

Billings's instructions were, as always, to the point. "Get one of
Mike's old kites and get your asses down to Taranto. We've got a
couple of surveyors down there checking over the field. There's shell
craters all over the place, but they've marked a landing path with panel
markers. You shouldn't have any problems. Oh yeah, the grass is pretty
long so you'd better drag the field a couple of times before you go in.

And don't bust up Mike's airplane; I don't want to hear him pissin' and moanin'."

I asked, "What are we supposed to do when we get there?"

Billings looked me over. "Jesus, Jack, the longer you're in the Army the more you look like a civilian." I was wearing a red T-shirt and suntan pants that were less than clean. No hat. No insignia of rank. "Where's your insignia? Where's your goddamn flight cap?"

"My insignia's on my shirt back in my tent—so's my hat."

"What the hell are those things on your feet?"

"Those are moccasins, Major. They're really comfortable."

"The next time I see you," Billings snapped, "I want to see you in uniform, with a goddamn tie, with your goddamn hat and with goddamn shoes on—shined. Do you read me?"

"Yes, sir."

"And when you go down to Taranto, I want you to look like an officer and not like a goddamn bum."

"Yes, sir."

"Okay. Where were we? Oh yeah, when you get down there you'll contact an Italian civil engineer. His name is Darcy, Signor Vincente Darcy. He'll give you a preliminary outline on what has to be done. Also, contact Maj. Earl Haff. He's the Army engineer who is heading up the surveying party; he'll also be the cognizant engineer if we decide to take the place over. Now, what I want from you two is an opinion from our point of view. I'm interested in what Darcy and Haff can tell you about electrical power, plumbing, mess facilities, the condition of the field, and all that, but I want mostly a reaction from you guys. Is it suitable for our people? Or isn't it?"

"Does Darcy speak English?" Jim asked.

"Yes, so I understand. Anything else? No? Okay. Get down there as soon as you can."

Jim and I flew to Taranto the following day. The weather was poor with a low overcast at about four thousand feet. There were patches of fog at ground level. We flew at twenty-five hundred feet where visibility was as good as it was going to get. We had a flight engineer with us, an Italian-American sergeant who could interpret for us if Billings was wrong about Signor Darcy's linguistic skills. The sergeant's name was Joe Aducci.

The overcast was lowering. We were in and out of gray scud until I throttled back and dropped to fifteen hundred feet. Jim was dozing in the copilot's seat. He had refused my offer to fly the trip, preferring to loaf in the right seat. When we had made our preflight he had said to me, "No, you know these crates of Mike's better than I do. I don't like flying these old shit boxes. You take it."

Throttling back again, I set the RPM to seventeen hundred and let the old girl ease down a gentle glide slope. Jim was sound asleep. Sergeant Aducci was sitting in the top turret watching wisps of clouds spray over us. I could hear the squealing resentment of the turret's train gears as he turned and turned, trying to find a view that wasn't obscured by ground fog. He finally gave up; the turret was quiet. I brought her down to seventy-five feet, proceeding toward Taranto at this low altitude as a way of amusing myself. The mists were clearing at ground level, changing to thin curls of fading vapor in the warming air. The land rolled beneath us, a pale green panorama streaked for a moment with yellow and then returning to green; so arid for spring, so unlike the lush green hues of New England. Occasional stands of trees bounding the windward sides of fields flew by us. Stone walls, clutches of poor houses, empty roads, three children who waved, boulders leaning out of the earth, a small black dog, a wretched cow drinking from a pond, plowed fields: all were consumed in our thundering passage.

"Hey, Lieutenant! Sheep at twelve o'clock level. You'll huddle the shit out of them if you go over them."

Pressure on the right rudder, aileron, back pressure on the wheel, and the great slab of wing slanted perpendicular to the earth. I pulled her hard in a ninety-degree turn. Jim was startled awake by the abrupt change in direction. From his window he saw the ground, much too close, spinning by him. "What the hell is going on?"

"Sheep!" I yelled. "Sheep attacking, twelve o'clock! There's hundreds of 'em, Jim! Big woolly bastards." I rolled the wing level and pushed her down to the deck.

Faintly from the turret I heard Joe's voice cry above the roar of the engines, "Yippee! Wahoo!" We ran from our gentle enemy, the sheep, shattering the quiet of the land with the great noise of our thirty-ton machine hurtling toward Taranto as though she were being chased by the hounds of hell.

"You crazy bastard!" Jim was laughing now. "They ain't kraut sheep; they're Italian sheep."

I didn't answer. The buzz job was getting me, holding me in a fascinated concentration as I drove her even closer to the ground. I was running away. The bastards would never catch me. Never catch me. I fled across the plains; the old engines hammered, growing hotter every minute. I fled toward the sea where foam crests surging up the shore would hold my shadow for a moment, and then I would be gone.

"Back off, for Christ's sake, Jack! Back off! You're too fuckin' low! Pull her up!"

I let Jim's words touch me. I eased her away from the earth. When she was high enough, I dropped the left wing, brought the controls to neutral, and then pulled hard back on the wheel. She soared toward heaven like a bird on a summer day.

"Oh, for God's sake," Jim moaned. "You can't chandelle this old lady. Please. Please get this goddamn kite to Taranto and stop screwin' around."

I put her back on course and slowly climbed to two thousand feet. "When are we supposed to get to Taranto, Jim?"

"How the hell do I know? You've loused up my ETA for fuckin' fair. You ought to write a goddamn book—tactics for evading sheep. Christ." Jim was disgusted with me.

We arrived over the airfield at three o'clock. I began a slow spiral descent. The panel markers were clearly visible. "Wheels down, and give me flaps—twenty degrees." I turned to Jim. "I'll drag her slow over the field a couple of times. Okay?" Jim nodded.

We made two passes, but it was impossible to determine the terrain, whether it was rough, sloping, or as smooth as it appeared. Long straw-colored grass covered the ground; it looked like a small field of wheat. Traces of mist trailing from low cumulus clouds wandered with us as we slowly dragged our plane upwind over the panel markers. Pale yellow waves passed beneath us, shimmering now into gold and orange by a touch from a lone shaft of sunlight filtering down from an open patch of sky. The edges of the field were darker. Along the downwind boundary, I saw a fence and the ruins of an old wall. This hazard to our landing approach showed bright spots of blue, brilliant red, and purple along its length; early spring wild flowers, I supposed. It was a lovely field for any purpose, except for landing a B-17. It was very small.

After the second pass, I asked Jim, "What do you think?"

"It'll be tight, but I think we can get in."

"Yeah, maybe we get in, but how about getting out? We'll need a hundred-mile-an-hour headwind."

"You're the hotshot pilot. You worry about it. C'mon, let's get this bucket on the ground." Jim was still angry.

I turned from downwind into my base leg and then made the final turn into my approach. I had decided to make a long approach, dragging her in just above stalling speed. Jim held off full flaps until we passed over the wall. She touched down easy, swishing through the grass before she hit. The ground surface was smooth and firm.

"Nice landing. Ver nice." Jim was apparently feeling better about me. "She isn't rolling too fast. The grass must be helping to slow her down."

I let her roll for a few moments, then gently began to apply the brakes. We were about seventy yards from the end of the field when I brought her to a full stop. Jim shut down the inboards and I left the outboards idling.

A jeep was coming toward us. The driver, young Pfc., came alongside my window and motioned me to follow him. We rumbled along in his wake toward a stand of poplars at the side of the field. As we approached the trees, I could see three trucks, one of them a tanker, and two small liaison planes. The jeep driver led us into a position parallel with the small planes. He then made the motion of dragging his fingers across his throat, the signal for us to shut down our engines. I pushed the throttles forward, cut the fuel, and Jim and I began quickly to go through our checklist for securing the aircraft.

There were two small hangars; both were deserted. The sergeant's voice echoed in the empty space as he walked with us, briefing us in a casual way while we waited for Major Haff and Signor Darcy.

"The facility used to be an Italian auxiliary field. They had a few fighters here and some infantry liaison and spotter aircraft. It's been abandoned for about a year. It's in good shape. The barracks, the mess hall, and . . ."

"What about power?" I asked.

"Well, we're running one diesel generator now, which is enough for our needs. Major Haff and Darcy are planning to hook up with a main power source in Taranto if you people move in. Would you gentlemen like some coffee?"

The sergeant led us into a group of offices that were partitioned off in an area adjacent to the large hangar door. The offices were all empty except one, larger than the others; it was furnished with two desks, a conference table with eight chairs, and four filing cabinets. On the conference table there was a goose-neck lamp that the sergeant snapped on, and the depressing shadows of the place were relieved by a cheerful glow of light. On top of one of the filing cabinets was an old three-burner grill, a ubiquitous presence in military life. The sergeant opened the cabinet top drawer, pulled out a can of coffee, sugar, and a can of evaporated milk.

"It won't take a minute," he said. He filled the pot with water from a large Thermos container. "We haven't got the water hooked up yet. I bring some over every day from the barracks. By the way, my name is Borg, Sgt. Peter Borg."

I introduced myself, Captain Ewell, and Sergeant Aducci. We shook hands, and I found I was very curious about Sergeant Borg. There was something different about him, an exquisite gentleness that could not be entirely masked by his G.I. clothing nor by his agreeable forthright manner. He was, by any standard, a handsome man. When he looked at me, his expression was one of concerned deference. I did not think this effect was his intent but perhaps was my reaction to his pale complexion and the intensity of his features, which were finely drawn and perfectly proportioned. He was slender, of medium height, and he seemed incapable of an awkward movement. There was no overt sensuality in his manner, yet I was sure that Peter marched to a different drummer. I smiled at him as he handed me my coffee. "Thank you," I said.

"You're welcome, Lieutenant. It's hot, but I wouldn't vouch for anything beyond that."

Jim Ewell seemed disturbed. "I can't say I feel very positive about this place. It's flat, drab—depressing. It would drive the men bonkers."

Borg smiled. "I agree, Captain Ewell. It is drab, and I can't give you any reason why it should be used as a rest camp. If it were closer to the sea perhaps, but it isn't. The Gulf of Taranto is about twelve miles away."

"What about Haff and Darcy? How do they see it?"

"Well, they're more inclined to recommend it as a staging area for supplies and equipment coming in from the port."

"Yeah, that probably would be better," Jim said.

There was the unmistakable sound of a jeep approaching the hangar. Sergeant Aducci shook his head. "Lord, that thing needs a muffler." It came rattling through the open hangar door, bringing with its shattering presence a swirl of dust and the stench of burning oil. It screeched to a halt just outside the office door. Two men clambered out: an older man wearing light pants and a leather jacket and a younger, heavyset man in uniform. Sergeant Borg led us out of the office and introduced us to Major Haff and Signor Darcy.

Major Haff said, "I'm sorry we're late. Couldn't be helped. I'm glad you fellows squeezed in the field without bustin' anything." He rubbed his hands together and chuckled, as though he had made a very amusing joke. We all smiled weakly back at him. "I hope Sergeant Borg has been able to give you a preliminary briefing on our situation here."

Major Haff was obviously a very self-conscious man. His pleasant, rugged features were flushed by his effort to assume the role of the assured senior officer. His forced affability had the style of a shy schoolboy remembering his teacher's prompting, "Don't forget to speak clearly and directly when you're in company, and don't mumble." He shifted awkwardly from one foot to the other, not seeming to know what to say next. There was a brief silence, and I noticed Sergeant Borg looked particularly distressed as Haff stumbled on.

"Er, you fellows must be hungry. Right, Vince? Have to get you some chow. Right? Well, we'll move right along. We'll move right along. Vince, do you think Carla would mind fixing dinner for us? She is such a charming girl. Peter, why don't you tidy up and follow along. I'm sure these fellows will have some questions you'll have to answer. Details, you know. Details. Yes, we'd better get along. Better get along." This little monologue caused the major even greater discomfort. His face was quite red; there were beads of perspiration forming on his upper lip.

Sergeant Aducci was totally insensitive to the major's problem and, without realizing how welcome his outburst was, he blurted out, "Christ, Major, you ought to get that jeep fixed. I never heard a machine sound like that in my life. You'll get yourself killed driving around in a piece of shit like that."

Sergeant Borg kindly continued the diversion. "Yes, you're right, Sergeant. I'll get the command car, Major. It will be more comfortable—and safer." He smiled at Major Haff, reassuring him it seemed that he had done well and that the worst part of the encounter was over. "I'll come along a little later in the jeep."

"Now, Peter, you must be careful. You drive much too fast, you know. Much too fast." Haff turned to Signor Darcy. "He does, you know, Vince. He drives much too fast."

Darcy was an intimidating man, at least to me: the quintessential European indulging the brash American. He was years older than we were, probably in his fifties. He wore an old felt hat that he pushed back on his head as he spoke to Haff, and even the common gesture seemed particularly graceful to me. I smiled in admiration, as though I had never seen a man push his hat back from over his eyes before.

"Peter will be fine, Earl. He's a very good driver. And I have already made arrangements with Carla. She said she'd be delighted to have us." Darcy's voice was cultured, urbane. His slight accent enhanced the sound of each word. He proceeded to ease the initiative away from Major Haff. "Why don't we go back to the office for a moment while Peter gets the car. Earl and I have copies of our report for you to pass on to your commanding officer. We think it's quite clear, but I would like to touch on some of the points."

When we were seated at the conference table and had refilled our coffee cups, Darcy began his presentation, which covered everything from sewage disposal to the average yearly temperatures and the incidence of venereal disease among the ladies from Taranto. In spite of his articulate discourse, I found the subjects dull; and he was becoming increasingly pedantic, talking down to us in a patronizing way. The ordinary things he said were implied to be the result of wise reflection; he seemed to perceive in them subtle, hidden meanings he didn't think we could quite understand. I was becoming restless. I wasn't the only one. Jim was yawning and Sergeant Aducci was having trouble with his eyes, constantly blinking them and then opening them in a desperate effort to stay awake.

I listened to Darcy's words finally winding down. "I know I've covered these subjects only in a superficial way, but everything is in the report. I trust by the time you leave tomorrow you will give us your feelings on the matter. Thank you, gentlemen."

It was dusk when we left the field. Captain Ewell, Sergeant Aducci, and I sat in the back seat. Major Haff drove with Darcy sitting beside him in the front. Neither Jim nor I felt like talking; we were both too tired and hungry. Sergeant Aducci slept. Haff was silent, concentrating his attention on the road. Darcy, on the other hand, was full of talk. He had turned in his seat to face us and he was once again the schoolmaster lecturing the dullards.

"Some of the history of Taranto might interest you gentlemen; in fact, I've been considering organizing tours for your fellows if you establish a rest camp here. What do you think? Little culture—that sort of thing?"

"Sounds interesting," Jim said. I detected a flat hardness in Jim's voice, a little more of Kansas than usual, and a sure sign he was pissed. He murmured under his breath so only I could hear, "Who gives a shit."

Darcy carried on. "The original city of Taranto was named Tarentum. It was founded by Spartan emigrants somewhere around 700 B.C. It later became the sovereign city of Magna Graecia and vied in power with Rome itself. There's a splendid cathedral and a very impressive castle built by Charles the Fifth. Really, I think your fellows would find it all very interesting, particularly some of the modern stuff—you know, when the Normans captured it in 1063 A.D. Robert Guiscard was really a rascal, don't you think?" Darcy laughed at his little scholarly joke.

Ewell answered him. "I suppose a tour like that wouldn't hurt them, but I don't know, Vince, I can't cotton to this land. It's dead, worn out. What the hell has all your history left the Italian people? Nothing but poverty and dust to scratch in. Ever been to Kansas, Vince?"

"I don't entirely agree, Captain," Vince said. "And no, I've never been to Kansas, but I know it's in the central part of the country— one of the Plains States I think you call them."

"You're sharp, Vince. Really sharp. Maybe I'm wrong about the value of your history, but, oh Lord, wouldn't I love to be back in Kansas right now. Over eighty thousand square miles of rolling prairie. It's beautiful, Vince; you should see it."

"I'd like to, Captain Ewell. I'd like to very much."

"Now that's where I want you to set up a tour, Vince. That would suit me fine. Just fine."

Darcy was silent for a moment, and then he said quietly, "I wish I could, Captain Ewell. With all my heart, I wish I could." He turned to face the front of the car, but then turned back to us again. "You must forgive me, Captain, if I talk to you and your friends as though you were all little boys, for that is how you seem to me. It's my age, I guess." He laughed. "Too much war, too much. I have been fighting for a long time, before you were even born. For me, it has been long, very long. Now I can only do little things like find a place where your men can rest; where they can eat, drink, see a few sights, forget about the war for a while, and maybe find a nice girl—if they have luck. So you see, you have to bear with me, to indulge me if you will, while I talk about the troubles of Taranto: the Spartans, the Romans, the Lombards, all the old men, the old wars."

The car rolled on toward the bay. We felt the wind rushing against our faces as we peered into the darkness. Out there were ghosts. I could hear the soft thunder of hoofs of great horses. There was a sound of armor, of steel touching steel, ringing in the night. I could almost see the plumed helmets, the gleaming tips of lances, and the fluttering pennants of the host. The monotone of priests intoned the breviary; I could hear them faintly as they reminded God of their presence, seeking His blessing for the slaughter they would bring to the land.

I was startled by a flash of brief light. It was Jim, lighting a cigarette. He spoke to Darcy in a friendly way. "Signor Darcy, don't worry about us. We're just the new kids on the block. Hey, when this is all over, you come to Kansas. I'll buy you the biggest, sweetest steak you ever put your teeth into."

"I may do that, Captain Ewell. I just may do that."

"Call me Jim, Vince. All my friends call me Jim. C'mon, tell us some more stories about Italy."

Major Haff was waving something in his right hand, "Here now, I want everyone to brighten up. No more talk about wars." His voice was cheerful, entirely unlike his painful effort back at the field. "It's open, Vince. It's good stuff, real calvados."

Darcy pulled the cork free and raised the bottle to his lips. "Marvelous idea, Earl." He took a long swallow, then passed the bottle back to us. We drank. There was a hint of cider without the sweetness. I had taken a full mouthful, swallowing it little by little. It was too much, much too much. This brandy was made for men's souls and shouldn't be guzzled.

The last half-hour of the drive, which brought us to a stone house on the Bay of Taranto, seemed but a moment. In spite of Haff's admonition not to talk about war, we plied Darcy with questions about the history of Italy. He told us old stories while we passed the bottle of calvados, without pause, from front to back.

Darcy's voice was as intense as the brandy; between the two we were drawn, unresisting, into a world of kings, knaves, fools, nobles, traitors, and common men struggling to survive. He told us of centuries of war, of famine and plague, of unrelenting butchery. Our minds were driven to an inevitable wonder how any people could have lived through such a past. When we spoke of this, Darcy answered, "Any study of history will provoke the question: How does the common man endure? And perhaps the sadder, wiser question should also be asked: Why does he bother? After fifty-six years, I cannot answer either of them."

He was telling us about Sir John Hawkwood when Major Haff brought the car to a stop. We didn't get out but sat listening to Darcy. "He came from nothing, the second son of a minor English landowner. He and his infamous White Company, a force of over six thousand men, fought for thirty-five years in Italy during the fourteenth century, selling their services to the highest bidder. He was a vicious and evil man. When he died, he was rich in land and admired throughout Europe and in England. The bastard was buried with honors in the cathedral of Florence. They even put a commemorative fresco for him over the door."

"For God's sake. Never mind about Sir John Hawkwood. Let's get something to eat. I'm starved." Major Haff was unbelievably asserting himself.

"You're right. I have been jabbering on, haven't I? Am I seeing things, or is that our jeep over there? Peter must have taken a shorter route."

"Yeah, that's it," Sergeant Aducci grumbled. "There's not another one like it, believe me."

We entered the house into what appeared to be a reception room or a small study. We couldn't see very well. Shadows darkened the sides of the room. The only light came from a small lamp that was seated on an ornate desk near the entrance door. The glow from the lamp revealed the elaborate scrollwork along the edge of the desk; it made no intrusion into the shadows. There was an agreeable soft sound of music and a woman's voice singing sweetly above it; it was *La Traviata*, "Addio del Passato," one of the few arias I knew well.

> Addio del passato bei sogni ridenti,
> Le rose del volto gia sono pallenti.

I heard the click of a latch. A door opened in the rear part of the room and a woman stood outlined by the light beyond her.

"Ah, Vincente," she said. "How good to see you. Please come in. Peter and I have been waiting for you and your friends."

Darcy embraced her. It could have been the final scene of a play, the way they were framed in the door. When he released her, his hands rested on her shoulders. "My dear Carla, how wonderful you look. Yes, there is no doubt about it; you are more beautiful than last week. Absolutely no doubt about it."

"Now, Vincente, stop your foolishness. You only love me when I cook for you. Isn't that true?" Without waiting for his answer, she turned to us. "Please, gentlemen, come in." Her English was as perfect as Darcy's but her accent was different. As Major Haff approached her, she smiled and presented her cheek to him, murmuring, "Dear Earl. Dear Earl." He kissed her in a shy, awkward way, obviously delighted by this tendered intimacy which perhaps he thought she might withhold because we were there.

Carla led us to a table placed against long windows facing the sea. The sky had cleared. Through the windows we could see a highway of glistening light on the water reaching toward the horizon where the moon was beginning to rise for its familiar journey across the sky. There was no one in the room except Sergeant Borg, who was seated in a high-backed chair twirling a glass of red wine in his hands. He smiled and nodded but didn't speak.

"Now, please, gentlemen. Help yourself to drinks. There is scotch and brandy. There is also wine; the red is a Barolo, and not bad; the white is an especially nice Orvieto. Now I must see to your dinner." Before she left, she spoke to Darcy. "Vincente? A moment, please." She took his arm and drew him aside to a corner of the room. They spoke quietly in Italian. I poured myself a scotch. They spoke only for a few moments; then I watched Carla walk across the room with the grace of a ballerina leaving the stage.

She was unlike anyone I had ever seen, and I was not prepared for the effect she had on me. Her hauteur impressed me, as had Signor Darcy's, and her kind manner, like his, did little to diminish the distance of worlds between us. Her face was classic; the severity of flat planes of bone and white skin contrasted with her mouth, which was full and expressive, sometimes musing with a provocative sensuality, and sometimes very still, as pensive as a troubled child's. She was wise not to admit any distraction to the purity of her features nor to the compelling gaze of her dark eyes; her hair was drawn back away from them to the nape of her neck where it was fastened with a small gold clasp. When she walked or made any movement, her body, even covered as it was by a drab, shapeless dress, declared her elegance. "See how beautifully I did that. Watch my back now, how straight it is. If I turn and move my arms from my sides, is it not a breathless moment? If I smile at you and walk toward you in this wonderful way, will you not die of pleasure?"

She served our dinner effortlessly: steamed mussels, sautéed sole accompanied by a thin pasta with white sauce, and finally warm cream-filled pastries with our coffee. As she served, Carla listened attentively to the conversation, nodding her head when she approved of what was being said and frowning severely when she disagreed. I found myself trying to be amusing when I spoke, trying to impress her like some young schoolboy exploring for the first time the labyrinth of passion for an older woman. After she served our coffee and left the room, I relaxed from the tension of my foolish performance and began to listen to what the others were saying.

Major Haff was talking about the air base, giving us a cogent analysis of its potential as a supply depot rather than as a rest camp. He was very much at ease. Smoke from his cigar curled about his face; his wineglass was in constant motion as he waved it at us when he was intent on making a point. When it was still for a moment, Peter filled it, smiling at Haff.

Signor Darcy remarked about the good shellfishing in the area, particularly in the Bay of Piccolo for oysters and mussels. In answer to our questions about Carla, he slowly sipped his brandy as if to overcome a reluctance to speak of her at all. I didn't think his reluctance was real but more of an actor's device to hold our attention. He told us finally, with many pauses, she had married young, to a scholar who had been a professor of history at Padua University. The marriage was brief. Her husband died in a Fascist prison during one of Mussolini's more brutal purges. In her youth, Carla had been a dancer and had toured in Europe and in America. Darcy and his wife had befriended her after her husband's death. Darcy's voice trembled with emotion when he said, "She is a daughter to us, not so young nor so vulnerable anymore, but still and always a dear child to us." He again turned his attention to his brandy, staring at the amber liquor in his glass. His voice was calm as he continued. "She works occasionally as a translator; and recently she has been much in demand as hostess for the American and British brass in Taranto, arranging dinners and entertainments, that sort of thing." There was one more thing he had to say. He didn't say it to us; it was more like an afterthought, an incomprehensible thing he said to himself, trying to understand it. "They put her in prison, too, you know." The room was very quiet. "I do not know what they did to her. I dare not ask. I never want to know."

A string ensemble was playing softly on the recording machine. I guessed it was either Vivaldi or Bach. From the back of the house I could hear women's voices, laughter, and then there was the sound of a door opening, some words in Italian as the door was closed. Carla entered the room.

"How quiet you are! Ah, you're listening to my Vivaldi. I came to join you for a drink before I send you home, but I have a better idea. Why don't we take our brandy and coffee and go out in the fresh air for a little while. It would be so good for you. We can sit on the sea wall in the moonlight. You go ahead. I have to get my shawl. I'll be with you in a moment."

Major Haff scooped up a bottle and said, "I'm ready." He was a bit on the drunk side. I poured hot coffee into my cup, adding a generous splash of scotch. Jim did the same. Aducci filled his wineglass. Sergeant Borg took coffee.

Vincente was composed now. He sounded almost cheerful. "I'll wait for Carla. You fellows go ahead."

We sat on the concrete cap of the sea wall, which extended about two feet above the promenade. The promenade followed the curve of the harbor. We could easily see down it a long way, for it was bathed in a silver light except where it met the wall, and there a sharply defined shadow made a parallel border to it. Below us a few fishing boats were secured to a dock. We could hear the water lapping against the hulls.

I watched the two of them approach us. She was holding his arm with both of hers; her head was against his shoulder. Behind them, the stone front of the house shone brilliant white in the moonlight. From the dining room, where we had sat moments ago, the window made a small warm pattern of yellow against the ghostly coldness of the façade.

When they joined us, they were both laughing. Carla, between gasps for breath, explained. "Vincente had been telling me about your vulgar airplane. How absolutely awful!" What Carla was referring to was a painting on the side of the plane, directly over the bomb bay, of a comic-strip character of Al Capp's. The painting was of a crude, hairy fellow named Typhoon McGoon crouched with his pants down in an appropriate position to simulate defecation as the bombs dropped. "Really," Carla said, "you Americans are terrible. You make a joke of everything. You would go to your death with that stupid thing on your machine?"

"I'll tear it off with my bare hands, Carla, if it displeases you," I said.

"Ah, now you're teasing me. Can't you ever be serious?"

Vincente kept the light touch, determined not to allow the conversation to become depressing. He gave us a hilarious account of his first trip to the States when he had been assigned the task of negotiating a contract with General Electric for power-plant machinery. It had been many years ago, and the encounter of this sophisticated young Italian with the ladies of Boston must have been as he said, "Unbelievable. My God, if she invited me to her apartment for a superb evening of dining and seduction, how could she possibly have fed me a pulpy tomato stuffed with an abominable mess of oily tuna fish and a bottle of warm Coca-Cola?"

The moon was rising higher in a star-filled sky. All of the surfaces of the sea were shimmering silver. From somewhere far out in the bay, the deep sound of a bell tolled, sorrowful and somber. For the world's sake, we shared the beauty of the night and touched each other for the first time. We drank our coffee, our wine, our brandy. We told each other stories. We were the Magi, not three but seven, led by God to this place. We waited for a sign.

Chapter VIII

BACK TO LONGSKIRT

If there were dreams to sell,
Merry and sad to tell,
And the crier rang the bell,
What would you buy?

—THOMAS LOVELL BEDDOES
Dream Pedlery

It was nearly eleven in the morning when Sergeant Borg drove us from the barracks to the field. We had slept late at his urging to do so the night before. He had said there was no hurry and we might as well sack in, for he needed time for his work party to cut a swath through the grass diagonally across the field. He thought it would take about three hours for the surveyors to set up a line for the Italian workmen to follow; he also told us Major Haff had worked out our minimum roll requirements based on our estimated weight. By preparing a diagonal run, Haff had determined he could give us almost four thousand feet, which would be more then enough; that is, if the long grass were cut to provide something like a runway. Our weight was critical, but Mike Salinas, with his usual foresight, had rigged our plane as light as possible. There were no guns or armor on board. The wingtip tanks were empty; the main fuel tanks were only half full, and we had used a part of that weight during our flight down from Longskirt.

We had lingered over breakfast, enjoying extra cups of coffee with our cigarettes while we chatted with Sergeant Borg. My mind hadn't been entirely on the conversation; thoughts about the squadron had distracted me. I was still thinking about the squadron now as we bounced along in Borg's dilapidated jeep. When he finally pulled off the highway and onto a narrow dirt track leading to the west side of the field where our plane was parked, I began to feel an increased sense of urgency. What was I doing here? I had to get back. As soon as the jeep stopped, I quickly clambered out and stood in bright sunlight near the poplars.

It was too far south to hear them or to see them; even so, I stared into the incredible emptiness above me wondering where they were. The answering silence and the vast savannah of blue which held my gaze seemed ominous to me, as though something were terribly wrong. I should have heard the thunder of engines; I should have seen hundreds of dark images of bombers and vapor trails of fighters streaming north above them. The peaceful quiet of the morning, the fragrance of the dew-drenched earth, and the azure sky, which was marred only by a small mare's tail of cirrus very high in the west—it was all wrong, there was some strange deception. I looked away from the sky toward the horizon, still searching for my comrades, but the illusion was secure: the undulating land stretched before me, crowded with golden grass gently moving in the wind. There was nothing else.

I pulled myself up through the nose hatch and went aft to the flight deck. Jim Ewell was already in the copilot's seat, glowering and impatient. "C'mon, let's go. Let's go."

Aducci was standing outside in front of number-one engine with a fire extinguisher cradled in his arms. Like Ewell, he glared up at me, apparently irritated by the delay I had caused staring up at the sky, wondering about the squadron.

"We got plenty of time," I said.

"Billings will be pissed if we're late," Ewell grumbled. "C'mon. Hurry it up."

I gave Jim a grimacing smile. "Fuck Billings. Fuck 'em all."

We quickly went through our checklist, and I signaled to Aducci we were ready for engine start.

"Energize one." I waited. "Start one." She coughed, gasped, and sparks flew out of the open cowl flaps, but she started. The engine ran very rough.

"Try leaning her out and running her up to two thousand," Jim suggested. He shook his head. "Christ, what a bucket."

I moved the mixture control to lean and then advanced the throttle slowly until the engine reached two thousand RPM. The port wing vibrated in resonance with the rough-running engine; the flight deck was shaking as well. Two loud explosions announced the engine had cleared some condensation or some carbon and the vibration subsided. Dark, insolent smoke drifted in through my window. Sergeant Aducci was laughing, but he gave me an okay sign and moved toward number two.

"This fuckin' thing will blow up before we get off the ground." Jim was feeling better. We were rolling.

"Ah, she's all right. Christ, for a minute there I thought it was the ignition harness, especially when all the bloody sparks were coming out."

We taxied, following the panel markers downwind over a surprisingly smooth surface. Sergeant Borg's work party had done an excellent job. When we reached the last of the markers, I stopped her and we ran up each engine through our takeoff power settings. Number one was still rough. I gunned the port engines and brought her into the wind. When she was on the precise compass heading Borg's surveyors had given us, I set the directional gyro at zero.

Jim called out, "Flaps. Twenty degrees, coming down. Cowl flaps trailed."

I left the brakes on, and both Jim and I kept pressure on the pedals. Sergeant Aducci, who was between us in the jump seat, called out the manifold pressure as I advanced the throttles. The plane trembled, trying to surge forward away from the restraint that held her. When Aducci's call reached thirty-three inches, I gave Jim a nod and we released the brakes. She lunged at the runway. Her lunge was brave, but she was less than a greyhound breaking from the gate; she was more like an old lady trying to get out of a chair. She waddled toward midfield, accelerating at a maddeningly slow rate. I advanced the manifold pressure to forty inches and waited for something to happen. Number-one engine responded with an explosive backfire, and then settled down to a smooth roar of power. We passed midfield. Aducci was driving me crazy. He kept repeating the same speeds. "Sixty. Sixty. Sixty-five. Sixty-five." We were running out of runway. A looming hedgerow was rushing toward us. "Seventy. Seventy-five. Eighty. Eighty-five. Ninety." From my side window, I watched the oleo strut begin to extend; the plane's weight was lifting off the landing gear.

I yelled to Jim, "Wheels up." He hit the toggle switch. I eased back on the yoke and she came off the ground, laboring but steady. For a brief part of a second, the hedgerow was incredibly detailed through the windshield and then, as if by some astonishing magic, it disappeared. We were airborne.

While Jim was milking up the flaps, I reduced the manifold pressure to thirty-five inches and set the engine speeds at twenty-three hundred.

No one spoke. Jim closed the cowl flaps and shut down the booster pumps. He then stretched his arms wide above his head like a tired man. Looking up through the Plexiglas, he casually observed, "Hairy. Very hairy."

I eased the plane into a climb, heading for five thousand feet. I was concerned about two fighter fields just south of Longskirt. It was one o'clock; in an hour or less, the fighters would be returning from their morning sorties and escort assignments, coming in low and fast to their bases. I didn't want to be in the way; I wanted to we well above them.

"Sergeant Aducci, I want you in the turret. Keep your eyes open for returning fighters. I want them below me. If you see anything near our altitude, let me know immediately."

When I reached five thousand, I leveled off and reduced to cruising power. Number one was running smooth. The sergeant's turret was constantly turning as he watched for the returning fighters. From the flight deck, I could see only clear sky; there was nothing in sight.

Jim was slouched in his seat, sound asleep. His angular frame was awkward in repose. The copilot's straight-backed bucket seat was not made for comfort, but Jim had made the best of it. He had eased his back down against it as he had surrendered to sleep; his bottom had moved forward to the very edge: he was an inch away from sliding off of it entirely. This forward motion was restrained by his feet, which were held firmly in place by the rudder pedals; as a result, his knees were forced upward to form two extreme angles. In this fetal posture, Jim's knees were even with his face. He looked ridiculous and very uncomfortable. His strong features were softened by sleep. His eyes, which were worn to pale blue by long gazes in the sun of his beloved Kansas, were not mocking me now but were peering inward, resting on some image in a pleasing dream. The dream must have been pleasant for his mouth was curved in an unrepentant grin, and he was enjoying whatever it was that was passing through his mind. It couldn't have been about his farm, although I knew he loved it; his grin was too salacious. There must have been things about Kansas that Jim had never told me.

"Turret to pilot. There's some fighters coming in low from one o'clock—P-38s. I see ten."

"Anything else, Sergeant?"

"No, that's all."

A few moments later, Aducci called out a squadron of P-47s heading north, probably tactical fighters on their way to an infantry support task. Marvelous low-level stuff, busting the hell out of tanks, trucks, artillery, and German infantry. I wondered why I ever decided on heavy bombers. Like every other thing I have ever done and regretted, it seemed like a good idea at the time.

We proceeded on to Longskirt. I began to let down and entered the traffic pattern at two o'clock. Jim, who had at last left the coils of his lustful sleep, was looking out of his side window as we flew our downwind leg. He spoke to me quietly over the intercom. "Where the hell is everybody? Christ, the whole bloody squadron's gone to glory. Holy shit, there's not a plane left on the stands. We're all that's left. We'll have to fight the fuckin' war by ourselves. Just you and me, kid."

"Wheels down."

"Coming down."

I turned on my base leg, steepening my turn with the nose down and onto my final approach. It did seem strange to see the field so empty. As Jim had said, all the stands were empty except in Mike's area where I could see three planes shrouded by staging.

"Flaps."

"Full flaps, coming down."

We touched down and rolled toward the end of the runway. I wondered if the mission today had been Ploesti.

When we taxied in, Captain Salinas was at the stand chatting with the crew chief. His jeep was parked nearby on the grass; it looked like a new one. I wasn't surprised. If anyone could wangle a new jeep for himself, it would have to be Mike. He wasn't only a good engineer, he was an incisive opportunist, a master of quid pro quo dealings with his counterparts in other squadrons.

Jim and I secured the aircraft, and I spent some time writing up the erratic performance of number-one engine. After completing my engineering notes in the Form 1, I made one last check to be sure the master switch was off and then followed Jim forward and out through the nose hatch.

As I dropped from the hatch to the ground, I heard Mike's remarks to the crew chief. He was giving the chief instructions about tomorrow's bomb load. "Tell the armorers it'll be straight demolition stuff. No frags. No incendiaries. We haven't got confirmation from wing yet, so I'll leave it up to you guys whether you want to load early or not."

The chief asked, "Will it be a mix, or what?"

"Right now, they're saying it'll be probably all five-hundred-pounders."

The chief looked uncertain. "What do you think?"

Mike hesitated, and then said, "I'd wait. Those guys up in wing shit their pants before they can decide to head for the latrine. They'll change their minds a hundred times before six o'clock."

"Yeah, you're probably right, Captain. We'll wait."

Mike turned to us. "How did it go?"

Jim ignored Mike's question. "Where's the squadron? Where did they go today?"

"Wiener Neustadt. Synthetic refineries. Maximum effort and all that crap. We got up two squadrons."

"Any strike call yet?"

"Yeah, we got a strike call at twelve thirty-five." Mike looked at his watch. "They're due back in about forty minutes. Want some coffee?"

Jim said, "That sounds good to me." He turned to me, smiling. "How about you?"

"Sounds good to me, too—and James, old fart, someday you'll be proud to tell your children you rode the sky with me, the Scourge of the Hun. And thanks for your stinking navigating."

"Bullshit."

Mike Salinas was indifferent to our exchange. Such bickering as Jim and I engaged in was a common patois used by friends in the squadron; it passed for conversation and allowed one to maintain a silence about the unrelenting inevitability of one's fate. It was a language of special constraint. There were no words for the men who were killed. There were no words for survival, except sometimes a whore's promise in one's soul of maybe, maybe. There were no words for the horror of our bombs, or for the thousands who perished in their flames, beyond the comfortable abstractions one used after a mission, "Yes, we covered the target well today." And by such fragile devices, we did our obscene work and endured, becoming strangers to our past, becoming uncaring men without pity.

We waited in Mike's office for the return of the group. The coffee was not like Carla's; it was very strong and bitter.

"Mike, when the hell did you make this pot? It's bloody awful."

Mike peered at me over his cup. "You're going back on operationals, you bastard. Billings gave me the word. You're also going to labor in my vineyards in your spare time, so don't get me pissed. By the way, you've been promoted—why, I'll never understand. There's a copy of the orders up in your tent. Paul's got them."

"A first lieutenant now, my, ain't that grand." Jim sighed in despair. "God help us all, he's going up the ladder."

Mike held up his hand. "Wait a minute. I think I hear them."

It was not a sound; it was in the beginning a fearful trembling, as if the earth itself were shuddering under the weight of a mighty Juggernaut stirring and moving toward me. In a moment I began to hear them, faint at first, but swelling in strength as each second passed. It was not like a storm of cracking explosions across the sky that faded into rumbles of thunder and then began again; it was resolute, an intolerable crescendo of engines shattering the air. I leaped to my feet

and ran to the door, eager to see them. When I came outside, they were there, where I knew they would be, coming in low from the northeast. The roar of strident power overwhelmed my senses; it entered into me, slamming into bone and muscle, bursting in my head. My heart soared up to them. Ah, my comrades, my comrades, the joy of your return, the glorious tumult of your return.

I was not aware of Jim and Mike standing beside me until Mike touched my arm and motioned to the jeep. Jim and I followed him; Jim climbed into the front with Mike and I vaulted into the back. As we hurtled down the dirt road heading for the flight line, I watched the group make its first pass over the field. A squadron of six planes peeled off as the group continued on, making a three-hundred-sixty-degree turn to begin another pass and release another squadron. By the time we reached the flight line, the first squadron was followed by a second squadron peeling off, and then a third. The traffic pattern became a column of B-17s strung out on the downwind leg, the base leg, and the final approach. They were touching down at about thirty-second intervals. The steady cadence of screeching tires hitting the steel mat was accompanied by the intermittent squeal of brakes. These sounds were a petulant counterpoint to the sullen roar of the planes still aloft waiting to enter traffic.

A flight of P-38 fighters flashed over the field followed by a lone P-51. The 51 saluted us by pulling up and executing a perfect climbing roll. Jim looked up; his eyes followed the fighter's maneuver with scornful contempt. Jim could not abide flamboyance of any kind. He meted out his courage as it was needed, no more, no less. If his life was the stake and he found it an appropriate measure to give, he would give it with a steadfast calm or perhaps with no more than one softly spoken "Ah, shit."

We waited until all the bombers were down; all were in their stands except five that were still lumbering down the periphery strip wearily seeking rest. Mike was staring at the sky. He said, "There's seven missing." Neither Jim nor I spoke. Mike muttered, "Jesus, seven." He started up the jeep. "Let's get up to the debriefing and find out what the hell happened."

The large room in Operations was nearly full. Each crew was isolated, or as isolated as the space allowed. They were seated at long tables and in turn were being questioned by four officers from Intelligence. Smoke from cigarettes, cigars, and a few pipes drifted up shafts of sunlight pouring in from two large windows on either side of the room. The clatter of coffee cups was distinct, but the voices of the men were blurred in an incessant, loud, discordant noise reverberating throughout the room. There were so many men talking at the same time it was impossible to hear what was being said unless you stood near one table and concentrated on a particular man as he responded to a question. I heard fragmentary parts of conversations while I moved around the room looking for Paul. The crewmen were dull with fatigue, but their voices were edged with impatient anger at the importunate insistence of their interrogators.

"How many MEs?"

"Oh, I don't know—a lot."

"How many?"

"Oh, maybe twenty, maybe thirty—when we rallied off the target."

"Any more? FWs? Two-tens?"

"Yeah, there were some more."

"Where?"

"Six o'clock. They were workin' over the second wave. I couldn't see. Ask Sal over there, he's the tail gunner."

"Did you see Lieutenant Turner's plane go down?"

"Yeah."

"Any chutes?"

"Naw. No chutes."

"Are you sure there were no chutes?"

"Of course I'm sure. Nobody got out, Captain. I told ya, nobody got out. The fuckin' thing blew apart!"

"Now, Sergeant, take it easy. Just take it easy. We'll be through this in a minute. Flak. How was the flak? Moderate? Heavy?"

I walked away.

Paul found me. I was leaning against the wall, trying to stay out of the way until the debriefing was over, when he appeared in front of me. My God, he was smoking—one of those foul cigars that Billings favored.

"You're smoking that stinking thing! My boy, what are you coming to?"

Paul smiled, shifting the cigar expertly to the corner of his mouth before he spoke. "I flew copilot with Major Billings today—squadron lead. He said I did okay. I fly in the left seat from now on. First pilot at last. Isn't that great? The least I could do was accept his offer of a smoke. Oh yes, before I forget, the major wants to see you and Captain Ewell tonight, after chow. By the way, congratulations on your promotion."

"Thanks."

He was not the same. He had changed. Maybe he had never been the shy, tentative fellow I thought I knew. Maybe I had never really looked at him. The man who stood with me now was as modest in his manner and as courtly as before, but these semblances of gentleness were not enough to mask the unyielding assurance he revealed to me as I watched him coolly survey the chaos in the room. There was no perceptible difference in his demeanor, and he appeared wholly detached from what was going on around him; yet I sensed his will, striving to withhold any expression of displeasure or contempt. Because

I knew him well and in the past was used to searching for his moods, I looked around the room, trying to see what he was seeing, to hear what he was hearing.

The words were loud and many of them were coarse. Men filled their mouths with doughnuts and gulped coffee as they described the deaths of enemies and friends. They looked at photographs of the target and their fingers touched the shining surfaces, "Yeah, right there somethin' big went up. I could see it real good when we rallied—smoke up to twenty thousand feet." "Over there, see, right there, nothin' but flame." "The group bombardier hit the aiming point right on the fuckin' money. Beautiful pattern. Beautiful." They called across the room to comrades they thought they would never see again, greeting them with affectionate curses, "You rotten bastard, you made it! How to go, baby! How to go!" "Hey, Frankie, you wop asshole, come over here. I've been lookin' all over the goddamn place for you. Christ, I thought you went down with Turner." The men's words were old words, banal and vulgar, and had been said before, ten thousand times after ten thousand battles. The joy in their voices would not be stilled. Their Te Deum rose to heaven, "We praise Thee, O God . . ."

To Paul, of course, it was unbearable, an unseemly display by his standard of exquisite restraint. When at last he felt he had done his penance and had given his presence for a sufficient amount of time to the ritual of camaraderie, he turned to me and said, "Okay, we can go now."

As soon as we were outside, Paul stretched his arms wide and arched his back. "I'm awful stiff," he said. He looked around, puzzled. "Where's the trucks?"

"Never mind the bloody trucks. Come on, we'll walk back."

He walked beside me, his hands clasped behind his back. The dirt road was covered by a light brown silt and our footsteps left small puffs of dust trailing behind us. For ten minutes Paul didn't say a word. He stared at the ground, occasionally kicking at a stone with dull ineptness. I tired of the silence and prodded him in my usual tactful way. "What the hell's the matter with you?"

Paul took off his flight cap and slapped it lightly against his leg as he walked. He ignored my question. The afternoon was waning; frail white patterns in the sky were not quite clouds but were tenuous threads holding the little moisture they had been able to suck from the dry earth.

"Come on, Paul, what is it?" I tried to be less abrasive.

"It's Bernie—Bernie Clark. He went down today. I was supposed to fly with him today until the last minute when Major Billings shifted my assignment."

"Who else did we lose?"

"Well, the group lost seven: our squadron lost two—Sam Turner and Bernie. No one got out of Sam's plane—it blew almost as soon as it got hit. I saw four chutes out of Bernie's, then he slid underneath us and I couldn't see if there were any more. I asked Sergeant Pena, our ball turret, but he said he didn't see any more chutes."

"I'm sorry. Bernie was a great guy." Then I added lamely, "He'll be okay. He'll probably sit the war out in some German camp. His chances are good, they're really pretty good."

Paul looked at me coldly. "You don't give a damn, do you? You don't give a damn about anything. And if you want to know what's troubling me—it's you. I'm getting to be just like you, I don't feel anything. Bernie was a good friend, and I feel nothing. Nothing—God help me."

He shocked me. His voice was hard, desperate with shame that he could not grieve for Bernie. There was no point in being maudlin; it was the last thing he needed. "What you need is a good belt of bourbon—and a boot in the ass. Everybody dies, don't worry about it. It goes with the territory."

Paul shook his head. "You're hopeless, absolutely hopeless. How can you talk like that?"

"It's easy, my boy. Just cultivated ignorance—you have to work at it."

"No, really, Jack. Don't you feel anything about all this? Anything?"

"Yes, I do. When I fly a mission, I'm scared; when I'm not flying, I'm bored. When they get killed, I'm glad it's not me."

"Is that all?"

"That's it."

"I don't believe you. I don't believe you at all. What would you do if I were killed?"

"I'd think for a few minutes of what a pain in the ass you were, and then I'd go through your stuff to see if I could find some dirty pictures or some booze."

Paul finally laughed. "Well, you wouldn't be entirely disappointed."

"What, you devil! Have you got some dirty pictures?"

"No, no." He was still laughing. "No, but I got some whiskey for you. Sergeant Petrosky got it for me. He went visiting a Polish regiment that's at an Eighth Army rest camp just up beyond Lucera. He swapped cigarettes and green American dollars for it. We got a quart of Jameson's

Irish. It's not bourbon, but it's very good—at least Pete said it was."

"Paul, you're a splendid fellow, a jewel, the best friend I ever had."

Paul looked at me with tired disapproval as he might have at an unrepentant sinner. "You're a liar. You're such a liar."

We stretched on our cots while we read our letters, only leaving them for brief seconds when we reached for the whiskey. Paul seemed content. He had a long letter from his girl, and he read it again and again. After making me promise not to read any of the contents, he showed me the salutation which, as he pointed out, was "My dearest Paul" instead of the usual modest "Dear Paul." His eyes were bright with pleasure at this gentle boldness. For Paul, it was positively erotic. He kept reading the letter until he fell asleep, still clutching it in his hand. A cool wind rustled through the tent. I got up from my cot and went over to look at him. He was out like a light, totally and completely out. I pulled his blanket up and over his legs. He didn't stir.

I took my three letters and headed for the club, leaving Paul to sleep for as long as he could before evening mess. His outburst had surprised me. Two months ago, if he had been angry with me, he would have sulked, responding when I badgered him into a conversation with polite but sullen brevity. Today he came right at me, making it clear that he did not approve of what seemed to him to be my callous indifference to the losses in the squadron. He blamed me for his own lack of feeling which, in time, he would come to understand was not an insensitivity that he and I alone were privy to; all men in combat must come to it. To feel sorrow, to grieve for the dead, to weep in despair, was not what we were asked to do. To kill, to maim, to destroy, to die, these were our tasks, and we were to do them without too much fuss. Sometime later there would be ceremony.

The club was quiet. There was one bridge game going on which I kibitzed until I became disgusted with the poor play and wandered over to the bar. Sergeant Paoli, a fat, ugly gunner, was bartending. He looked like a ward boss from the North End of Boston, and he had the savvy of one.

"I hear you're going back on operationals, Lieutenant."

"Yep, that's right."

He precisely assessed my feelings. "Well, you can't expect a good thing to last forever."

"What have you got?"

"Gin—and some lousy rum."

"Gin, I guess—with juice."

As he prepared my drink he said, "Things are a little better now. We're not seeing as many fighters. The flak's a little worse, though. Too bad about Clark and Turner's boys."

"Yes," I said. "Too bad."

"You know, it's funny. I remember the night you and Lieutenant Clark tied one on up here. Geez, he was a great guy. I never laughed so hard in my fuckin' life. Remember that story he told about the guy who pissed over the wall?"

"I remember the story, Sarge. But you know what I remember most about that night? It was the way he hit me every time he laughed. Christ, my arms were black and blue for weeks."

Sergeant Paoli laughed. "It's a good thing he liked you. He sure was a big, strong guy. How's the drink?"

"Fine."

"You're shittin' me, Lieutenant; it's a little better than cat piss. Right?"

"Right."

Somewhere, not far off, I heard a B-25 flying very low. I could always tell the sound of a B-25. It had an odd configuration for its exhaust collector ring. The engine always clattered.

I took my drink to a table to read my letters again. I had one from my mother, one from Sandy, my oldest brother, and one from Jean. My mother's letter was in her usual scrawl; it was a challenge, like a puzzle. It was full of family gossip. The only concern she expressed was for my father who was working long hours at the shipyard and getting very little rest. She gave me a delightful account of the escapades of my big cat, Bruno, and the wear and tear he was enduring in pursuit of sex. "I really think we should get him altered. What do you think? Oh, well, we can decide that later." Her restraint made me smile. She said nothing of her fears, but I knew her prayers were battering heaven day and night.

Sandy's letter, in his neat backhanded script, was written on engineering graph paper. His short, cynical observations about the state of the world assured me he was in fine fettle. At the end he told me he had bought a new record album I must hear, the Brahms C Minor Symphony conducted by Toscanini. He also was sending me a copy of T. S. Eliot's *Four Quartets*; that is, "If Millie will ever get off her butt and mail the goddamn thing. I'm never home these days. Thank God the package stores are open until eleven!"

Jean's letter I had saved for last; I had not opened it. I stared at it for a long time, admiring the elegance of her hand. I took a sip of my drink, then I lit a cigarette. I looked around the room. Sergeant Paoli was drinking coffee while he idly turned the pages of a magazine. The bridge players were crouched over their cards. There was no one at the craps table. I would not open it right at this moment. I would wait. The envelope was light blue; the right-hand corner was slightly crimped. It was too close to my drink and there was a wet spot. I moved it. My hands were damp. I wiped them on the sides of my pants. I opened the envelope.

Ah, the words, the dear words. Little things lifted me from the pages, touched me, and were driven away by a sound in the room: by a man's voice, a glass banging down on a table. I bent over the letter, shielding it with my arms. Billy, her father, was fine. She and her mother had gone shopping in Boston; they had lunch at Filene's. As she sat at her father's desk writing the letter, she was watching the rain through the window. The maples in the yard were laden with large drops of water. Two bluejays were quarreling on the lawn. On Sunday, my mother and her mother had dinner together at Johnson's. I could hear Jean's laughter as she described my mother's hat. "You know Ma and her hats. This one was a blue straw with little red flowers stitched along the sides. I told her it looked great, and she beamed. I would love to know what those two talked about. Wouldn't you?" I followed her down a path she had made sweet and fair for me. She did not speak of the war but led me away from it, quieting my fear as she would have a child's by showing me all her bright beads of memory and of promise. When I came to the last words, the last three words which were placed, as they always were, just above her name, I stared at them, at their unbelievable revelation of love. I stared at them.

"Hey, Lieutenant, you'll wear that letter out. Here you are, it's getting kind of dark in here." Sergeant Paoli placed a dish holding a small burning candle on the table. "Letter from your girl?"

I looked up at him, over his great belly, and grinned into his homely face. "Yeah—three full pages."

"Any pictures?"

"No, no pictures."

Chapter IX
JIM EWELL TAKES OVER

Yes; quaint and curious war is!
　You shoot a fellow down
You'd treat, if met where any bar is,
　Or help to half-a-crown.

—THOMAS HARDY

I had finished my dinner; Paul was still working on his. It was seven o'clock. The mess was half empty and very quiet. Paul was diminishing a mountain of hash, boiled potatoes, and peas with unhurried dispatch. Occasionally he stopped, carefully placing his knife and fork down on his plate before he reached in his back pocket for his handkerchief, which he used to touch his lips as he contemplated the food remaining before him. There was no question that everything would be consumed; it was just a matter of how much time it would take.

As a point of habit, I nagged him. "You eat too much. Do you realize you eat too much?"

Paul did not totally ignore me: he nodded, acknowledging that I had spoken to him. He accepted my irritating commentary as an expression of concerned friendship on my part, something he appreciated but not anything he felt obliged to respond to any more than a monk need respond to the itch of his robe or the buzz of a fly. He continued to eat, wiping up the last crumb of his food with a piece of bread, which he put in his mouth and chewed with ruminant pleasure.

"You look like a goddamn cow."

He continued chewing.

"Do you know you look like a goddamn cow?"

Paul washed his bread down with a gulp of coffee. "You better go see Major Billings," he said. "I told you he wants to see you and Captain Ewell. Remember?"

"Yeah, I remember. I'll go in a minute."

"You'd better go now. You shouldn't keep the major waiting." He looked at me in a concerned way. "And don't get drunk. You're flying tomorrow."

"Are you?"

"No, I've got a couple of days off."

"Good. The sky will be safe. All I have to worry about is the krauts."

Paul grinned. "Beat it, will you?"

I got up from the table and left him.

Jim Ewell was with Billings when I arrived at the Operations shack. Billings looked very tired. His face was gaunt with fatigue; his eyes were dull and lifeless. Too many missions, I thought. Too many cares, but mostly, too many missions. His voice was not hard as it was before. It was listless. Each word was formed with an effort and there were uncertain pauses as though it were difficult for him to speak at all.

"Ah—congratulations on your promotion, Lieutenant."

"Thank you, sir."

"The report—the report on Taranto. Have you read it?"

"No, sir, but Signor Darcy went through it with us."

"Oh, I see— Well, fine—fine. I wanted to discuss it with you tonight. No, not tonight. Later—we'll discuss it later—yes, later."

There was a long silence; Jim lit a cigarette. Billings's sunken eyes stared at me.

"You're back—ah, back on operationals. Right?"

"Yes, sir."

"Good—good."

I could hear voices outside. Someone was singing. After a time, the major spoke again.

"You will still help out Captain Salinas?"

"Yes, sir. I've spoken with the captain."

"Good—good."

Jim said, "May I fix you some coffee, Major?"

"No, no. Thanks, Jim. I think I'll just hit the sack. Thank you, gentlemen."

When we were outside, Jim asked me, "What do you think?"

"He needs at least a week of doing nothing."

"Yes, I agree." Jim flipped his cigarette at a butt can. It came close. "I've talked with Major Devereaux. He's aware of Billings's condition, and he has already relieved him of all duty for at least a week."

"Then what?"

"And then Devereaux is putting him on a ground assignment for another week or two. After that, I don't know."

"He'll be back in less than two weeks," I said. "Count on it."

"You know," Jim said, "you may be right. One of the few fuckin' times in your life, you may be right."

"Well," I said, "I'll see you later."

"No, no. For Christ's sake, wait a minute. We've got to talk."

"About what?"

"About a lot of things. Come on, we'll go up to your tent. Paul's got a bottle of Irish. Right?"

"How the hell did you know?"

Jim laughed and grabbed my arm. "Come on, come on," he said.

When we were in the tent, Ewell sat on Mac's bunk, taking a large sip of the whiskey I had poured before he spoke. Paul started to leave but Ewell called him back. "Stick around." And then he asked, "How was Billings today? How did he seem to you?"

"It's funny," Paul said, "I was going to speak to Jack about it. He was quiet, very quiet. A couple of times he fell asleep. Is the major all right?"

"No, he's not all right," Ewell said, and he briefly described Billings's condition. He ended by saying, "Both Jack and I feel he's exhausted, just plain fuckin' exhausted. He'll be grounded for at least a couple of weeks." Ewell sat quietly for a moment; he took another swallow of his whiskey, then he said, "Whether you like it or not, I'm the new operations officer. Devereaux wants me to take over until Billings is back on the line."

"Congratulations, Captain Ewell." Paul was as always properly predictable.

"I'm sorry, Jim," I said. "You have my condolences."

"I don't want your condolences, I want your help. I'm going to need all I can get—even if it's only for three weeks. Now, here's the situation.

"We've lost almost all of our best pilots—Turner, Coursey, Clark, Bob McCarthy, and a couple of others I can't think of right now. They were all capable of flying squadron lead—and they did. They took a big part of the flying load away from Major Billings. When they bought it, Billings tried to take up the slack by flying lead on almost every mission. He's paying for it now, right at this moment. Tomorrow, I'm flying lead. The next one, you fly." Jim pointed to me. "After that, I don't know. I'll have to play it by ear. Devereaux has orders not to fly more than two missions a month, so I can't count on him."

"How about Lieutenant Myerson?"

"Yeah, I hear he's pretty good. What do you know about him?"

I told Jim what I knew, which wasn't much. "I've talked with him a few times—you know, at mess, up at the club. Intelligent guy, low key, the crews all want to fly with him—a good sign, I think. The major spoke about him once, mentioned something about his 'exceptional qualifications.' "

"Hey, he's good," Paul said. "I flew with him once. He's really good."

"Well, fine," Jim said. "I'll look over his record. But we're going to need a couple more. When Billings comes back I want him to be able to sit on his ass for a while and run the squadron." He gave Paul a searching look. "In a couple of weeks, I'm going to be looking at you."

Paul was shaken. "Not me. Not me. I've just been checked out for the left seat. You've got more experienced men than me."

Jim was different. He had changed in the past hour. His mocking humor was gone; he was all business. "Lieutenant Leigh," he said, "you'll do what I tell you to do. Do you read me?"

"Yes, sir."

"Good. You'll fly with Jack when he leads, and with four or five more missions, you'll be on the roster. You got that straight?"

"Yes, sir."

"And you, Jack, I want those reports from engineering more concise. You have a tendency to rattle on. Any questions?"

"No, not right now."

"Fine. Paul, pour me another small one, will you?"

Yes, Jim was different. He seemed suddenly to have aged. He was slumped forward, his elbows resting on his knees. He stared at the tent floor while Paul poured his whiskey and placed it on the cot. Without looking up he said, "What a lousy fuckin' business." He raised his head and looked at me with a trace of a smile. "A lousy business, right Jack?"

"A lousy business, Jim."

The group flew north over the Adriatic Sea. It was a short haul today to the submarine pens at Pola, a small city on the western point of the peninsula that protruded into the sea between Fiume and Trieste. There would be heavy flak but we did not anticipate any fighter resistance. The Udine patrols rarely stretched that far to the southeast. It was nine o'clock. We were to hit the Initial Point at ten-thirty. At twenty thousand feet the air was smooth; and our squadron, holding the low-left position, had little difficulty in maintaining a tight formation. Ewell's lead was steady; his slight course corrections were accomplished with skillful gentleness so those of us who were folllowing his lead did not have to violently jockey our throttles to hold our spots. Overhead, an escort of P-38s snaked across the blue sky. They lazily crisscrossed our formation in loose elements of three. I listened to their chatter.

"This is Blue Squadron leader. Are you my fuckin' wingman or ain't you? Get in here. Get in here."

"Temper. Temper."

"Never mind the shit, get in here."

A singing voice broke in. "Oh, give me a home—"

"Knock it off. Knock it off."

There was quiet for a moment, then the voice came back, very softly, but determined to finish the refrain, "—where the buffalo roam."

"Bandits! Bandits! Twelve o'clock level!" The new voice was tense with alarm.

Six ME-210s were attacking the lead squadron. I could see the tracers streaming out from the bomber's turrets; black explosions appeared above the group leader's plane. The German fighters didn't press their attack but broke for the deck with eight P-38s screaming down after them. I still had my radio selector on the fighters' channel, and I could hear the flight leaders yelling. "Break right! Break right! Charley, break right!"

Ten P-38s held their altitude to provide top cover for their comrades, who were swarming below them in pursuit of the MEs. The ten now swept forward over us like wolves stretched flat with hunger for their prey. "Blue leader, do you have contact?"

"Negative. Negative."

The bomber formation pressed on, indifferent to the melee: the slow, sullen progress never faltered, never changed; it moved with a purpose beyond understanding. A wide vapor trail lay behind us, a defiant pennant without valor proclaiming stubborn, plodding persistence, nothing else. The strike would be made. No matter what it cost, the strike would be made.

We had long ago forgotten why we served with such obsessive devotion. We had long ago forgotten how we came to be here. We knew only the compelling imperative of the mission; it had become our life, the reason for our existence. We had nothing to do with victory or defeat, nor were we a part of any global strategy. This was our work, ours alone. We did it because it was given to us to do, or perhaps we did it because we could not bear the shame of being less than the man beside us. We fought because he fought; we died because he died. I cannot remember or think of any other reasons.

The fighters were gone, both ours and the Germans'. The ten P-38s who were covering their friends were now far ahead of us, following the chase back toward Udine. I switched back to the command channel. A red flare rose from the group leader's plane in a gentle, climbing arc and then fell slowly, sputtering on its way beneath us; this was a signal to change the formation from a box of four squadrons to a column.

The column of squadrons was a new technique that sought to provide greater bombing accuracy on a target of limited size where broad saturation would be ineffective. In our normal box formation of one or two waves, only the group leader's bombardier was responsible for bombing accuracy. When he dropped his bombs, we all dropped. His

aiming point was determined on the basis of optimizing the pattern on the target, a diamond-shaped coverage that would destroy a number of facilities within a fairly large area. Bombing in a column, with each squadron bombing independently, offered a better opportunity to damage the submarine pens, which were narrow concrete revetments able to easily withstand a casual hit or two. If only one squadron could succeed in laying down a concentrated strike of thirty tons, the destruction would be significant. If two or more squadrons could place their bombs on precisely the same spot, it would be hell below and the submarines operating out of Pola would not be doing business for some time to come, although the resilience of the Germans often stunned us. They came back again and again, perhaps a bit weaker each time than the last, but we could rarely shut them down for long.

Men who have never fought, chauvinists who pipe the tune of moral invincibility and the courage of their "brave boys," would be shocked to find the enemy is neither craven nor irresolute; neither is he stupid. He fights as well as you do, and often better. He bleeds and dies in lonely agony, as you do. He, like you, is given to jokes, small wonders, dreams, love, and the pleasing taste of cold beer. He, like you, knows the bile of fear, the unbearable terror of battle and the shaking exhaustion of those who survive it. He knows all this, as you do. And he goes on and you go on until it is over for him and over for you, or until they tell you to stop.

When we finished our maneuver, which was quickly done, our squadron was third in the column of four squadrons. Ewell had us slightly below the second squadron so our seven planes were clear of the prop wash, a turbulent, churning wake made by the two squadrons ahead of us. I didn't like this formation, nor did any of the air crew; if there were tactical advantages, there were also hazards. Going over the sub pens we would be presenting four separate targets to the flak gunners. They could practice on the first, leisurely adjust on the second, and clobber the third and the fourth. There was an added peril after we dropped our bombs. Coming off the target we would be vulnerable to fighters: instead of having the packed firepower of twenty-eight planes, our squadrons would be isolated in seven-plane elements and would be easier bites for the German fighters.

"Bombardier to pilot. Over."

"Pilot. Over."

"We're coming up on the IP. Okay?"

"Roger."

I couldn't remember the bombardier. Was he the dark kid? I could never remember any of them. When I briefed the crew, I tried to fix each face in my mind, but it never worked. Today the only one I knew was Lieutenant Egan, the navigator. Hell, everyone knew Rich . . .

I kept my eyes on Ewell's plane, waiting for his bomb bay doors to open. The first shell blossomed over the lead squadron, four more incredibly leaped out of the clear sky. They were high. Now the explosions were lowering and getting very thick ahead of us. The first squadron entered the storm. The second squadron followed with deliberate élan; unperturbed, it beckoned us. "You see, it's easy. Nothing to it. Come on with us. Come on with us."

I watched Ewell's bomb bay door swing open. At the same time I heard our bombardier's voice. "Bomb bay doors, coming open."

I heard the slow whine of the door mechanism.

"Bomb bay, open."

The copilot and I put on our flak helmets. I pulled my flak vest down, trying to be sure my genitals were covered.

"Pilot to radio. Over."

"Radio. Over."

"Is the gunner out of the ball turret?"

"Affirmative. He's out."

We began our bomb run.

The shooting was accurate. Five successive explosions were close, much too close. The German gunners had honed their fire on the first two squadrons, who were now past the target and were rallying back toward the sea. Shell after shell burst between my left wingman and me; the tip of his right wing blew away. Fuel from his wingtip tank sprayed between us in a fine mist that widened as it streamed behind us forming an unwelcome cloud of one-hundred-octane fuel in the path of the trailing squadron. Thumping blows hammered underneath us; some black puffs were far enough away to be benign companions to our passage and the ragged fragments never reached us. An orange flame covered the windshield in front of me; there was not time enough for terror. The violence I stiffened for ended when the plane shuddered in the concussive blast and staggered out of it. I couldn't comprehend how we had survived one that close. Smoke streaked past my window. I fought my panic. I fought my passion for a steep dive away from this barrage of flying iron. Just a little longer. Hold her steady, just a little longer. Again, the black bursts were leading my right wing.

The bombardier was merciful. I heard the click of the intercom and then his calm voice. "Bombs away. Bombs away."

Ewell broke our straight course by leading us down and to the left in a rally away from the target back to the sea. Flak followed us but it soon trailed off with a few random bursts that exploded to our right and well above us, staining the sky for a while until the day was perfect again, as perfect as any man could have wanted it.

"Check in. Check in." The copilot was confirming the status of the crew and checking for battle damage. I listened as I trimmed for a slow descent back to Longskirt.

"Tail okay."

"Left waist okay."

"Right waist okay."

"Radio okay."

"Ball turret okay."

"Top turret okay."

"Bombardier okay."

The last check was with the navigator, our one and only, Lt. Rich Egan. He was not all right. "Those bastards blew away my chart table. My Mercator charts too—they're all burned to shit. Who's goin' to pay for all that? I want to know, who's goin' to pay for all that? I'm goin' to send a fuckin' bill to Hitler. I'm goin' to—"

"Okay, Rich, okay," the copilot said, soothing him, trying to get him to shut up. "We'll take up a collection."

The other crew members couldn't let it go. "Hey, Rich, you don't need that stuff. You never know where the fuck you are anyway."

"When we get back I'm goin' to kick your silly ass all over the fuckin' field. You got that, you dumb fuckin' Swede?"

The banter went on as we flew over the tranquil sea toward home. When we were low enough to come off oxygen, I had two cups of cold tomato juice and a half of a Spam sandwich. The copilot and I spelled each other while we ate. I lit a cigarette and continued to listen to the crew rag Egan.

"Hey, Rich, they say you're such a lousy navigator you need a Seeing Eye dog to take you to the latrine."

"Well, if I need a dog, I know where to find one, you stupid bastard."

"Hey, Rich."

"Yeah, fuck you too, Tommy."

"No, no kiddin', Rich, listen. Is it true you were the group lead navigator on the Steyr mission?"

"Yeah, that's right."

Another voice broke in. "Oh yeah, I remember that. The group ended up in fuckin' Oklahoma."

"How to go, Rich baby. How to go."

I should have shut them up. There was a chance of fighters following us off the peninsula, but a very remote one. My left wingman was feathering his number-four engine, the one nearest to his mangled wingtip. There was no sign of fire. There was evidence of leaking oil; the lower side of his engine housing was black with it. The wingtip fascinated me: shreds of metal were flapping wildly in the windstream; I could see the outboard frame, which appeared to be intact. Another problem for Captain Salinas. I wondered how Mike would repair it: probably a whole new outboard section—maybe a new engine mount. The engine was feathered now. I wondered who the pilot was. He was good; with all his troubles he hadn't wavered an inch from his position in the formation. The copilot waved from the damaged plane, giving me an okay sign with his thumb and forefinger formed in a loop and his other three fingers straight up.

I called the tail gunner. "How does the fourth squadron look? Can you see them?"

"They lost one, sir. He got it just after they dropped. He went into the sea. I saw four chutes."

"How do they look now?"

"They look okay, sir."

"Thanks, tail. Out."

We flew on toward home. The sun was high over us; the sea was beautiful beneath us. The radio operator had picked up a German station; it was a man's voice, a powerful baritone singing the ballad "Lili Marlene." I sang along with him, trying to remember the words, "Underneath the lamppost by the garden gate . . ."

After securing the plane at the hardstand, I talked with the crew chief for a moment about the damage up forward in Egan's area. He scribbled a note on his clipboard and then asked, "Anything else?"

"No, she was fine—no problems."

"How was the flak?"

"Lovely, just fuckin' lovely."

The chief laughed. "Okay, Lieutenant, I'll look her over."

My left wingman had just pulled into his stand, which was next to mine. I watched him maneuver the plane around in a three-sixty turn so she would be facing the taxi strip. This was something we were all supposed to do, but few of us did. Captain Salinas bitched about it constantly. "Turn her facing the strip when you come in and you're light. Think of my tires for Christ's sake. It'll take you three crummy seconds." I took a rueful look at my plane, which was parked facing the wrong way with one wheel nearly off the stand. Sloppy, I thought. Very sloppy.

I was curious. I wanted to know who my wingman was. It was not my habit during briefing to particularly note any pilot's name. I usually just jotted down each plane's number and where it was placed in the formation. When I did write down a name, it was to identify a man for whom I felt a certain wariness, a man who could kill you by making a stupid mistake. Such a man had killed Mac and nineteen others. But today was a different circumstance. I wanted to know the wingman not because I considered him a hazard in the air but because he had demonstrated the kind of reliability and composure Captain Ewell was looking for; besides, as I said, I was curious.

Perhaps ten or fifteen yards separated the two stands. The ground between, which was pleasantly yielding to walk on, was made up of tough weeds growing close to the soil. As I walked I noticed the thick layer of weeds would hold the impression of my boots for only a moment; then, with deliberate resolve, the stubborn greenery would return to its original state and the shallow print of my foot would disappear before my eyes. This phenomenon amused me, so I stood in the middle of the swirling pattern stomping my feet up and down, watching the wretched sward's refusal to retain any evidence of my having passed this way. In time my amusement changed to melancholy, and I felt as though I had come upon a confirmation that I was truly lost. Soon I would fail even to throw a shadow in the sun. No one would ever speak my name.

The wind blew the cold metallic smell of airplane against my face; my mouth tasted of oil and cordite; stale sweat reeked in my nostrils. I saw the bursting orange flames again in front of my windshield. A nauseous spasm rose in my stomach. I wanted to vomit.

"Jack, what the hell are you doing?"

I looked up and saw Phil Myerson standing a short distance from me. So he was the wingman. I should have known. I managed to stammer, "I think I'm going to puke."

"No, no," he called. "Hold your hands over your head and take deep breaths." Staring at him stupidly, I did as he suggested. I must have looked idiotic because Phil was smiling, and Phil didn't smile often. His advice didn't help. I puked anyway.

He walked toward me. "Are you all right?"

"Yeah, I'm okay. Something I ate no doubt."

"Yes," Phil said, "I know." He was standing in front of me now, staring at me in a detached way. "Are you sure you're all right?"

"Yes, really, I'm fine."

"What the hell was that war dance you were doing? I thought you had gone bonkers."

"No," I said, and pointed down to the green ground cover. "I just thought this was funny stuff to walk on. I was—well, sort of checking it out." My actions must have seemed insane to him; and then to puke—good God!

Phil appeared to consider me at this point as reasonably normal. He looked me over carefully. "Yes, you seem to be good now. Your color's better." He tapped his finger against his mouth. "Well, if you're rational and your stomach's settled, I want to show you something. I understand you work with engineering."

I mumbled a few vague words about assisting Mike Salinas as I walked with Phil toward his plane, and he gave me little cause to speak again for some time.

"I want you to take a good look at the wing. I had the devil of a time getting her back. The wingtip wasn't the problem, but you know, on a short haul like that, the wingtip tank should have been empty. You see, the explosion must have twisted the whole bloody thing. The wing is completely out of rig. I had full left aileron trim on all the way back, and Joe and I had the wheel cranked over as hard as we could trying to hold that damn wing up. Landing was bloody awful. I didn't dare slow her down—scared to death the damn wing would stall out. The tower was screaming bloody murder at me. Well, what could I do? I had to bring her in hot. I think I burned out the damn brakes." He paused to light a cigarette. His Zippo lighter refused to ignite, and in angry frustration, he threw it down on the mat. "Goddamn it! Doesn't anything work around here!"

"Take it easy. Here you are." I lit a match, cupping it from the wind as I held it. He placed his hands over mine while he took his light; they were trembling. He took a long drag, holding it for a moment before he lifted his head and blew the smoke upward with a hissing sigh. His agitation seemed to lessen.

He shook his head, as if puzzled, and then spoke in a quieter way. "What the hell am I raving about? Can you tell me? It's all routine, isn't it? One gets his ass shot off, another doesn't. The sun comes up, the bloody world turns— Where's my pipe? I can't find my pipe." His hand flapped wildly against his pockets; then he walked away from me toward his B-5 bag which had been thrown on the mat below the forward hatch. His arm dove into it, rummaging through his gear until he came upon his beloved pipe. "Ah, here it is," he said. The briar was then chastised by several hard taps against his hand. It was filled, tamped very carefully, and tamped again. I watched him, wondering when it would occur to him that he didn't have any matches and that he had just thrown his lighter away.

"I don't have any damn matches."

I handed him mine. He took them without a word; he struck five of them before he got the pipe going. He had forgotten his cigarette, which was still smoldering on the bomb cart where he had placed it. Some of the smoke from the pipe drifted my way. It was a rich fragrance untainted by any scent other than that of fine tobacco.

I said, "That's good stuff you're smoking."

"Yes, my father sends it to me. Comes from a shop in New York. He's smoked it all his life—all his life." Myerson's voice trailed off. The sun was lower now. From where we stood, Phil's plane was shining in a bright, golden light. On the far side of it, a long shadow stretched away from us. The ragged wingtip defined the extreme end of the shadow, and on the ground the tattered edges of the metal made trembling images like the fluttering wings of small black birds.

Phil was quiet now, withdrawn, and sucking on his pipe in his usual reflective way. His brief outburst had disconcerted me, and I had trouble reconciling his anger and his excitement with the bland detachment with which he ordinarily viewed even the most violent incidents in the squadron, although I should have immediately understood that he had to react in some way to his experience. Fighting the instability of a badly damaged plane for over two hours, a plane that was determined to flip over on him, was enough to make a pilgrim out of any man; to hold it in formation as well was a superb excess of will, an act of purpose beyond reason except for a special few. He was, without doubt, the kind of pilot, the kind of man, that Ewell needed.

Like many extraordinary men, Phil didn't look the part; he was somewhat frail, nondescript, one whom you would not remember or make it a point to speak to: his face was pale and always reflected what seemed to be a petulant disapproval of everything before him. In the end, my assessment of him came to nothing. Four days after the Pola mission, Lt. Philip Myerson was killed on a routine sortie up to Avisio where we bombed a bridge. A piece of flak blew his arm off and he bled to death on the way back.

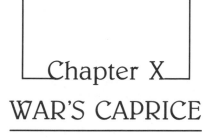

Chapter X

WAR'S CAPRICE

Move him into the sun—
Gently its touch awoke him once,
At home, whispering of fields unsown.
Always it woke him . . .

—WILFRED OWEN

To remember war is not so much to try to reveal its brutal matrix as it is to try to understand it, if that is possible. Not to understand it, you see, as a political or historical event but as an event apart from what is proposed to have caused it, as something alone, by itself, like the flight of a bird or the sound of a wave surging against the shore. For war is in our nature as it is in the nature of the wind to drive the wave or to enter the spirit of the bird. When you come to war, you are certain you have come upon it before. Somewhere, from your ancient memory, you know it; you know you must submit to it, that you must be borne by its awesome power and embark upon a perilous journey. I remember the darkness of my journey, but, as I have said, it was a darkness I knew would come. I traveled through it with dreadful apprehension and without understanding. Even now, looking down the worn corridor of time, I cannot see clearly.

It was April, a time of beginning stirring out of the late warming days of March into the sun of spring. A few bright flowers were showing in the fields around the airstrip. While I was waiting to check-ride a new pilot, I saw small bits of yellow, incredibly delicate blossoms, peering out of my friends, the weeds, at the edge of the hardstand. Squadron life had taken on an air of routine. We were settled in, and it seemed as though we had never lived in any other place. Our casualties were down; we were relaxed, beginning to believe the old lie again. Like the foolish children who chased the sly ratcatcher down the cobbled streets of Hamelin, we followed dreams.

Egan hadn't started a fire in weeks; in fact, he was showing ominous signs of sanity. He was shaving every other day. Art Dillman had cleared a space behind his tent and had put up a small fence for his dachshund pups. Art, too, was yielding to the gentle season; his clarinet wandered softly through songs of Schubert and Satie while the pups frolicked about him ecstatic in their new freedom.

Paul was trying to learn Italian, with little success. He could not seem to manage the clean consonants or the open vowels required to effect the pleasing rhythm of the language. Everything he said came out slurred in a strange South Carolinian version of Italian that appalled Tony, an Italian boy who worked in the squadron area and who tried to help Paul in his stubborn effort to become a sophisticated man. Paul, in turn, tried to help Tony with his English. Both Tony and Paul were unrelenting martinets: Paul on English grammar and Tony on Italian pronunciation. They bickered endlessly in a patois that was barely comprehensible, although each one seemed to know what the other was driving at. I couldn't decide who fared the worse in those exchanges. Tony yelled the louder so he appeared to prevail, which must have been the case, for he was learning English much faster than Paul was learning Italian.

Replacement crews were arriving with bewildering regularity. We were pressed to find quarters for them. There were new faces everywhere, and I found them all to be a cause for sullen anger. These brazen innocents who presumed to take the places of my dead friends seemed like children on their first day at school, so confused, so insufferably agreeable. Their vulnerability did not appease me or soften my attitude toward them. I was perversely determined to ignore their presence. When I did have to deal with them, I was impatient and needlessly curt. I remember one boy in particular who infuriated me because he giggled when I told him he had to use his flak helmet for a wash basin so he should never piss in it. He angered me even more by seeming indifferent to my warning that he must never speak to Captain Ewell in the morning before Ewell had a cup of coffee and at least two cigarettes. In time, however, I came to accept them as they had generously accepted me from the very beginning, and I came to regret my harshness when they, too, left me to join the better company of my lost friends.

With new crews came new planes. Mike Salinas had them on the line in less than six hours. If we had to, we could have put up a squadron of twelve or more. Every day, Captain Ewell's schedule called for some kind of training flight. I was processing new pilots and copilots through orientation and transition flights at a rate of six a day. Ewell had also added another chore to my already swelling list, that of setting up the automatic pilot on planes to be used as squadron lead planes on the following day's mission. This was a time-consuming task requiring a delicate series of adjustments to sort out the variables of this sophisticated device.

The autopilot was electronically connected to the plane's control surfaces through a number of balancing potentiometers. It controlled the movement of the rudder, ailerons, and elevators through varying degrees of responses of rate, ratio, and sensitivity, depending on the pilot's preference and the amount of turbulence the plane might be encountering. It had two primary functions: during a long flight, it could relieve the pilot of the tedium of manually controlling the plane in the three dimensions of flight, and it could hold a heading with amazing precision; it could also be used on the bomb run as an alternate to the pilot's directional indicator, a rather primitive instrument the pilot used to respond to the bombardier's final heading adjustments made in the course of the run from the IP to the target. But using the PDI always provoked the bombardier's frustration: either the pilot's reaction lagged or he failed to keep the directional indicator centered. When flying lead, the better option was to use the automatic pilot and link it directly to the bombsight. In this mode, the plane's controls would respond immediately, accurately, and only to heading corrections made by the bombardier.

My own preference on a bomb run was to use the PDI to pick up the first major drift corrections made by the bombardier. These large corrections, I felt, could be made smoother in the manual mode and would be less challenging to my wingmen and the second flight's efforts to hold their position in the formation. After the first corrections were accommodated and the bombardier began to fine-tune his drift, I linked the autopilot to the sight, finishing the run to bombs away with the sight in total control of our heading. On the run, I also optioned not to use the autopilot's elevator control; it had a tendency to lag, which was not significant in normal flight but was unacceptable when level flight was an imperative. By simply holding my airspeed steady and watching the altimeter, I could better satisfy the assumptions of our predicted airspeed and altitude, which were already loaded in the sight.

But on occasions, when the weather was less than good and the target was covered, our precious techniques meant little to us. A mission to Padua, where we bombed the railroad marshaling yards, or what we guessed were the railroad yards, was a case in point. The weather was poor that day, with broken clouds at various levels below us; at our altitude of twenty-two thousand feet, icy flat patterns of cirrus were beginning to form. We were supposed to have gone to Vienna but were blocked by heavy cloud banks over the mountains. Padua was a secondary target we were determined to hit, for if we came back to Longskirt with bombs still in our racks, there would not be credit for a mission. It was an uneventful sortie: we got only a brief glimpse of the target as we started our bomb run. I followed the first squadron in, with my squadron huddled around me like sheep in a strange pasture. I never saw the IP, and could only vaguely surmise where the target was from one glance I had of curving railroad tracks and a cluster of shrouded brown sheds before the ground was obscured by sweeping streams of dark mist. There was no movement of the PDI so I presumed the bombardier wasn't seeing anything either. I flicked the automatic pilot on and linked it to the bombsight. A few random bursts of flak now joined us; at the same time a rain squall engulfed the squadron. The bombardier was not making any drift corrections. The squadron proceeded on through the weak challenge of scattered shell bursts until the bombardier's voice came on the intercom, "Bombs away."

I wondered what we had hit. It would have been a miracle if we had nailed the target. As we rallied toward the sea, I looked to the south where the sky was lighter and promised better weather for the journey home. We continued to let down, heading for the coast below Venice. We were encountering moderate turbulence, and streams of freezing rain were tumbling over the wings. It was later, when the weather had eased, and the engineer was handing me my coffee, that I considered the obscene thought—maybe the bombs went into the city. Christ, maybe they went into the city. I called the bombardier.

"Pilot to bombardier. Over."

"Bombardier. Go ahead."

"Did we hit the target?"

"Cripes—I don't know. I think I had the sweep angle okay. I could only see for a couple of seconds before it closed in. I couldn't do anything about the drift. There was nothin' in the sight but a lot of gray crap. I just don't know. We could have been way off, to the right or to the left. I just don't know."

"Yeah, I see. Okay, Hank. Thanks."

I didn't think about it anymore. Instead, I watched the sky, enjoying the patch of blue I saw opening up before us between about ten and fifteen thousand feet. It had been an easy mission, a milk run. A few more like this and I'd have a ticket home. I'd be sitting at the bar at the Red Coach Grill in Hingham with my arm around Jean, feeling wonderful—absolutely wonderful.

At the debriefing, my mood returned to its normal state. I snapped at the officer who was questioning me, "No, I don't know what the fuck we hit. Call photo recon and have them take a look—that's what they get paid for. Isn't there any bloody coffee around here?"

"Look, Lieutenant, I'm just trying to do my job. I ask the dumb questions; you answer them. Okay?" He was smiling at me in a patient, appealing way. "Here," he said, "I've got a spot of something better than coffee." He fumbled with the lower drawer of his desk and came up with a paper cup that he handed to me. "Take a couple of sips of this; you'll feel much better. Real mother's milk—delights the tummy, warms the heart, 'ravels up the sleeve of care,' as the bard says, or said somewhere or other. Brandy, my boy. Drink up."

"Thanks, Captain," I said. He was older than I, probably in his thirties. My guess would have been a banker, an accountant, maybe a lawyer; whatever he was, he was unlike any intelligence officer I had encountered before. He was balding; his side remnants of dark hair, which were kept short and neatly trimmed, defined a precise boundary to the translucent fuzz on top of his head. His pink-and-white complexion was as rosy as a girl's; his features were regular and without distinction except for his eyes, which were blue and brightly curious. He wore dark-rimmed glasses that provided a frail credibility to his maturity; without them, I would have taken him for a precocious boy having a wonderful time imitating his father. He read the questions he was required to ask of me, and I was required to answer, as if they were delightful little jokes he had especially prepared for our entertainment on a drab, rainy afternoon.

"Now, let's see. You don't know whether you hit the target or not. Correct?"

"Correct."

"You don't give a shit?"

"Correct."

"The flak—light, heavy, or moderate? You must say heavy, otherwise my report will be extremely dull."

"Light, very light—and inaccurate."

"Ah, well. Fighters? Now don't tell me there were no fighters."

"No fighters."

"Really, this won't do at all. By the way, my name is Stoner, Capt. Jacob Stoner." He reached across the desk and shook my hand firmly. His face was familiar to me; I was sure I had seen him before—not during my Army life, somewhere else, a film, or maybe a photograph in a magazine or a newspaper. He was staring at me with an expression of severe disapproval. "Come, come, Lieutenant, I want the truth about what happened today. The truth, do you understand?" In mock rage, he shook his fist; his chin was thrust forward, challenging me to tell him a story that would satisfy his absurd demands. "By God, sir, if you don't tell me, it's Siberia for you."

The word Siberia did it. Yes, yes—it was Lenin. He looked like a young Lenin, the Russian leader of the Bolsheviks. "Please, comrade," I said, "I'll tell you what you want to know. Not Siberia. Please, not Siberia."

"Comrade?" Stoner leaned forward, squinting at me in bewilderment.

"Yes," I said. "Hasn't anyone noticed before? You look like Lenin."

Stoner blithely adjusted his style, and began to play the new game. He looked around the room in furtive despair; Hollywood's best tradition of craven evil was being well served by his performance. He cringed behind his desk; his eyes were wide in desperate alarm as he dissolved before the contemptuous gaze of Lt. Basil Quentin Flasher, ace pilot and America's most feared secret agent. "You capitalist swine!

You've found me out at last! No, maybe you're one of Trotsky's gang. Reactionary pig! . . . Do you really think I look like Lenin?"

"Yes, very much so."

"Hmm—strange." He tapped his pencil against his cheek. "My wife, when she is in one of her affectionate moods—you know what I mean—has said I have an extraordinary virile, intellectual presence; but I always thought that was just something she said to persuade herself I was worthy to serve her nerves of delight. Who was the poet who talked about 'nerves of delight'?"

"I don't know. Byron maybe?"

"No, I don't think so. Do you suppose she suspected something? Could she have possibly realized I was not simply the most pedestrian lawyer in New Jersey? How could she have possibly known?"

"Women are usually very perceptive about such things," I said.

"Good heavens."

"It's all right, Ilyich. Your secret's safe with me."

He grasped my arm with his hand. "Thank you, my dear fellow. Now, let us get on with this damn junk." He asked me a few more routine questions about the weather, the morale of the crew, any troop movements I had seen, about any submarine activity coming out of Pola, until finally he pushed his chair back and said, "I've kept you long enough. I can finish up without holding you. Thanks very much." He grinned at me. "Lenin, huh? I really look like Lenin. Isn't that something." This was the beginning of my friendship with Jake Stoner, whom I called Ilyich Ulyanov from that day on.

Three days after the Padua mission, we went back to Wiener Neustadt, this time in splendid weather with only a few pale streaks of cirrus stretched across the blue sky. We crossed the coast west of Pola, having climbed to twenty-one thousand feet, and proceeded north, staying well to the east of Trieste. As we pressed on, we came too close to Graz; scattered bursts of ground fire reached for us but it was high and to our left.

Our luck didn't hold. We were jumped by fighters as we approached the target and would have been hit hard again after we came out of the flak if it hadn't been for the joyful interdiction of the two squadrons of P-51s who took the bastards off our backs. None of us had spotted our fighters sitting about two thousand feet above us; neither had the German MEs who had approached us low from the southwest. Fighter cover over a target this far from our base was a new experience; the rumors about the new P-51s must have been true. We had heard that their range had been greatly improved, and they would be able to cover any target in Europe. What this meant for us cannot be described, no more than one can describe the flowering grief of tears or the exultant joy of a child running across a field. Wired and strapped to our biers, we yelled into our oxygen masks as we watched the sweeping curve of the attack. White traces of vapor streaming from their wingtips spilled through our formation like the breath of angels. We were saved.

I led my flight into the flak, indomitable and serene until my terror returned with the violent explosion of the first close burst, which staggered the plane and almost tore the wheel out of my hands. For a brief moment, I had forgotten what I have not forgotten since: one is never saved for long.

The group lost two planes; but our squadron came through un-scathed except for the usual evidence of that insolent, wayward bitch, luck, who ruled our lives with her gambols and all the bloody things that amused her. She moved from plane to plane, and those she chose not to destroy, she visited in her way, leaving vile reminders of her malice. Sometimes she would barely touch you, which was her way of saying she would be back; sometimes she played games smashing things around you: pipe, cable, instrument panels, turrets, and a Ther-mos of tomato juice splattered around the flight deck like a joke for blood. She tore a gunner's parachute harness away from his body, and scratched his belly with her nails.

Oh, she was quite a girl! My ball turret gunner could attest to that: she sent one of the MEs' shells up between his legs while he lay fetuslike in the womb of his turret, and she touched him only lightly with shards of steel and Plexiglas, leaving him stunned, staring at his twisted guns and bubbles of blood seeping out of the burned holes in his pants. A ten-degree-below-zero gale was blowing around him when the waist gunner pulled him out of the wrecked turret. He was nearly frozen. The waist gunner got an emergency oxygen bottle on him and then cut away the lower part of the wounded man's flight suit. Both legs, between the knees and the groin, were badly torn and encased in crusting wet ice. The radio operator came aft to help out, and the two men worked together cleaning away the mottled scabbards of blood, urine, and hydraulic oil. They gave him a shot of morphine before they bandaged him, which was crudely done, but was done well enough to reduce the bleeding. The radio operator then dragged the gunner forward into the radio compartment where it was clear of the freezing wind now blowing up through the ruined turret. When we landed and I was able to look in on him, he was lying on the deck wrapped in a blanket, barely conscious, with an unlighted cigarette dangling from his lips. When he saw me, he tried to grin. The cigarette fell out of his mouth. I picked it up and lit it before I held it for him so he could take a drag. He was pulling on the butt pretty well when the medics came on board and took over. This was nothing serious for our lady, mind you, just a little fun with one of the boys.

We did everything we could to please her: we showed her trinkets, crucifixes, St. Christopher medals, the foot of a rabbit, vials of holy water, small pieces of paper with prayers written on them, lucky coins, sacred photographs in gold lockets, a pair of loaded dice, a pressed flower from a girl, a picture of a child in an embossed leather case, and many other beloved charms. But we never really knew what she thought of such things. When she kissed one of us in a rare act of sweetness, the rest watched in wonder. Why him, we thought? Of all of us, why him?

When we landed at Longskirt after flying for over seven hours, we thought we were done with her for the day; but she was no different than any other god who has to be constantly adored. We must have been remiss in our devotions, for she had one last trick, one last punishment to remind us she was not pleased with the poor things we placed upon her altar.

I was talking with the crew chief about the ruined ball turret; not exactly talking with him as much as I was belaboring him with my usual fatuous observations that I can never restrain when I'm confronted by something incomprehensible. "Why wasn't he killed? Look at the goddamn thing! Just look at it! Look at the size of that hole, right by the gun handles! Christ!"

The chief shook his head. "Yeah, he was lucky—very lucky. Was he badly wounded?"

"No," I said. "When the medics took him off at the end of the runway, he looked okay—a little gray, but he looked okay. He was dragging on a butt, and he told the medic he had a whiskey ration due—and it should be a double."

"Hey, what's goin' on over there?" The chief was looking toward the stand next to ours. "They're taking a guy out of the forward hatch. Christ, that's funny. They didn't call in any casualties."

We walked across the space between the two planes, breaking into a run as we neared the stand. I recognized the copilot, Rob Andrews.

"Rob, what's wrong? Who got hit?"

"It's the bombardier, Sully. We don't know what happened. He's dead. There's not a mark on him. No wounds—nothin' but he's dead."

They had laid him on a steel mat. His head rested on a folded brown blanket. Someone had closed his eyes, and he looked peaceful, as though he were in a deep sleep. His face was composed and natural, entirely free of any expression of pain or fear. The sun was shining down on our little group; the steel mat under our feet was shimmering like a hundred mirrors, dazzling our eyes. As I looked at this insane caprice of battle, at this death of a young man who now was so quiet in the sun, I heard myself make my usual banal remark, "Ah, the sun is good; he'll be warm." The words were so stupid; I was grateful that only Robby heard them.

"Did you know him?" Rob asked.

"No. No, I didn't."

"His name was Sullivan, Lt. Barney Sullivan—Sully. A helluva guy."

This pilot was kneeling beside him while the crew watched, silent, not moving from where they stood, not willing to yield their bondage to the dead man. He still held them in his thrall. The pilot's hands gently explored Sully's body, his legs, his torso, and ever so gently, under his back. He unbuttoned Sully's shirt and ran his hand inside along the chest and stomach. He withdrew his hand and stared at it— nothing, no blood. He put his face close, peering at the back of the neck, the face, and then he moved his hand over Sully's head and through his hair. Suddenly his hand stopped. Now he saw it, a thin red crescent perhaps an inch and a half long on the right ride of Sully's temple, just under the hairline. For the first time, I heard the pilot's voice. It was soft; I could barely hear him curse. "Ah, shit—the bastards. The dirty bastards." After a moment, he looked up at the crew. "Would one of you boys get another blanket out of the plane? We'd better cover him now. The medics will be here in a minute." His hand never left Sully's face. He kept stroking it as he might have caressed a child of his own.

Rob was still beside me. He looked at the body of his dead friend, puzzled and disbelieving. "We thought he was asleep," he said. "All the way back, he was sitting in his seat hunched over his sight. That's what the navigator told us; he thought he was asleep. When we got out of the plane, he didn't move—just stayed there. Cripes, he must have bought it after the bombs went. We had a couple of close ones about then. A little piece like that—Christ."

An ambulance pulled into the stand and came to a screaming halt beside the plane. Doc Javit was with two medics. He appeared to be sober as he moved quickly toward Sully's body, at the same time

speaking to the medics, "Get the stretcher." The noise of the rear door
of the ambulance being opened, the clatter of the stretcher being
dragged from its rack, were offensive and callous reminders that even
death was no more than a routine, something to be handled coldly
with indifference and dispatch. Doc's examination was cursory; he
crouched down for only a few moments, turning Sully's head roughly
so he could see the wound in the best light. He said nothing, but rose
to his feet motioning to the medics to put the body on the stretcher.
As the ambulance moved away, I watched it for a while, racing down
the taxi strip.

"Fuck you, Doc," I said. "Fuck you."

I didn't say a word after I cursed Doc, not to anyone. I wasn't sure
why I had cursed him. I walked down the taxi strip to the dirt road
leading to the highway. I didn't go to debriefing. Captain Ewell would
not be pleased. What could he do? At worst, rant at me for an hour
or so. It didn't matter. I felt tired; I felt overwhelmed, like a man
trapped in a circumstance from which there was no escape, where
every way was blocked except the one hopeless way before him.

My anger would not leave me. I trudged along the edge of the road
staring at the ground. I kept seeing the face of the dead bombardier,
so composed, so quiet; I kept seeing the wind ruffling his hair as we
stared at him awed by his stillness. I kept seeing the gray face of my
ball gunner trying to grin, half dead from shock and the loss of blood.
What absurd devotion! And they were only a pittance against the
ghastly final payment that would be made to kill a madman whose
vile spoor now fouled all of Europe, a madman who should have been
culled by God the moment he drew breath.

Nothing gave me peace; nothing gave me any understanding. I
stopped walking for a moment to light a cigarette. There was no sound
except the murmur of the wind. A jeep that had passed me minutes
ago was now far ahead of me, just a wisp of swirling dust moving
toward the highway. I stood perfectly still and listened to the songs of
two birds pierce through the fabric of silence, stitching it with a pattern
of shrill, golden sound. A movement in the road caught my eye; it
was a very small lizard stirring the dust as he made his way to the grass
near where I was standing. He paused, raising his tiny dragon head
to peer about for the shadow of hawks or for any other lurking creature
for whom he was prey. Before he moved into the grass, he paused
again for a last look and then dashed into the greenery no more than
an inch away from my foot. On the sky's edge, near the horizon,
stately cumulus clouds were forming against the now darkening blue

of heaven. Of two of them, I made out Spanish galleons under full sail with high aft peaks; of one, I made out the face of a woman with long hair; of one, I made out a man's face with pouting lips like Neptune blowing the wind; and one was too challenging for me. I could not decide whether it was a dog or maybe a small deer. Suddenly, I realized I was terribly thirsty. I really could use a couple of beers. A good cold Pickwick ale! God, wouldn't that be marvelous.

When I went to the movies with Sandy or went for a walk with him and one or two of his friends, we usually ended up in the Brick Grill in Weymouth Landing. It was always Pickwick ale we drank, a sturdy ale sometimes referred to as poor man's whiskey. It had a wonderful flavor, full-bodied with a good tang to it. When Bill Walsh, the stolid, solemn bartender, who ran a quiet place or God help you, served Pickwick from the tap, we knew it would be just the way we wanted it: cool and with a creamy head of foam about a half an inch thick.

As I walked up the road toward the squadron area, I thought of Sandy, of the good times that were not so long ago, of long talks, of days on the river in our old canoe, of Sunday morning treks through the Blue Hills with Peg, our little terrier, trotting along with us; and I thought of cold New England winters after a fresh snow when Sandy would drag me with him and his friends to trudge around the streets of Weymouth and Braintree, listening to the crunch of dry snow under our feet while we talked about everything and laughed about everything, as young men will always do at such times. I couldn't remember what we said, but I remembered the nights; I remembered how bright the stars were shining brilliantly above us in the cold, black sky.

Sandy was almost five years older than I; he was slight with dark hair that he parted on the side. He wore glasses, had a game leg—the result of a boyhood accident and two months of hell in the hospital with blood poisoning—and he sported a small mustache that drove everyone in my house to near madness because of the time he took in the bathroom grooming the infamous thing. His complexion was pale, and he was particularly vulnerable to bronchial infections, but this chronic weakness never kept him down for long; he always managed to subdue his illnesses with curses and complaints, grumbling even at my poor mother when she rubbed his thin chest with sticky mentholated unguents, or at night, after he went to bed, tucked a blistering hot water bottle against his back. He gulped aspirin, sipped hot lemonade, submitted to Musterole plasters and, when he was older, switched to hot buttered rums with sticks of cinnamon, a potion he also used to wash down countless small pink quinine pills he claimed did him more good than anything else.

Sandy read incessantly; his mind was incredibly efficient and agile; it catalogued, organized, and stored what he wanted, carefully discarding the dunnage from the great cargoes of information he brought to it. Politics, art, history, music, economics, and literature were the mainstream of his interests, but there were delightful tributaries where he poked and picked, finding thousands of treasures that amused him: the care and feeding of Lippizan horses, the spheres of influence of the five nations of the Iroquois, the character of cats, the metabolism

of birds, how to tie a hangman's knot (he used to hang our young sister's dolls as she directed him to when they were naughty), Dorothy Sayers detective stories, and he particularly loved villains; Iago, Torquemada, and Caligula were three of his favorites. He was amoral; he never considered good or evil as anything more than words that covered mere expedience. He loathed the arrogance of power; he feared the abyss of poverty and ignorance. He pretended to be self-centered and affected a gruff manner when he abused any one of us, although each vied for his attention and was always pleased to be singled out. I never knew anyone quite like Sandy. I loved him, and I loved the frail body he held in such contempt. I loved the blazing, stubborn strength of his spirit which had guided me once and could guide me again if we could sit together for a few moments at Bill Walsh's bar drinking cold Pickwick ale as we talked.

But what could he say to me? Even Sandy would have to be circumspect. He would sip his ale, squinting at me in an intense, puzzled way, listening while I talked about my bewilderment, listening to my stories about one bitter day following another. He would let me talk until I had nothing more to say. Then we both would be quiet, and Bill would wipe the bar and take our two glasses away to draw two more from the tap. Sandy would squirm on his stool trying to get his stiff leg in a comfortable position before he spoke. There would be a hesitancy in his voice at first, an implied warning that he was not going to offer me a bone for comfort; instead he would recite a dull account of situations in the shipyard, of the difficulty he was having with the design of a high-speed turbine, of problems with a reduction gear, of flawed castings; and perhaps he would say one trite thing about the war: that it would be over soon. This would be all. He would not tell me the lie he knew I would not believe. He would not give me a single word to change the reality I knew or to lead me to an illusion that there was any other way without dishonor.

After a time, we would go outside and stand together for a moment before we parted, watching a few cars pass in front of the green neon lights blinking from across the square where the large, bright window of Arthur's Delicatessen challenged the darkness and welcomed the weary traveler. Sandy would embrace me before he turned away; his thin shoulders would be hunched against the chill of the night, and I would watch him until he disappeared around the corner heading for the bridge that crossed the Fore River and on to the hill beyond it where our house would be waiting for him.

Chapter XL

PLOESTI

Throw away Thy rod,
Throw away Thy wrath;
O my God,
Take the gentle path!

—GEORGE HERBERT

Nights in the squadron area were quiet; it was a time dedicated to chores, which were listlessly performed, and to the languid camaraderie of cards and dice. Books were only half read as we wandered in and out of the stupor of sleep. Old letters were held again; the crinkled paper and the dear, familiar scrawls, like the holy Talmud, told us what we had been and what we might be again. We stared at them for long moments, trying to remember, trying to remember. We sipped drinks at the club and watched cards drop on the crude, bare tables to become the stuff of legends, lies, and boasts. The muffled sound of dice tumbling in a felt-lined box was prelude to fortune's whim, and the players, intense and passionate, threw the white cubes as though their souls were the stake.

I couldn't always join my comrades after evening mess; I was often summoned by Captain Ewell to help him process the paper interminably fluttering down from group and wing headquarters. Critiques of missions, statistics on dropped tonnage, citations, promotions, confirmations of orders, tracts on sexual hygiene, engineering bulletins, long-range weather forecasts, and various impedimenta that covered every subject and defined an appropriate military response for every calamity from a dripping penis to Armaggedon, all were making an old man out of Captain Ewell. His squadron clerk, Staff Sgt. Billy Chambers, tried to persuade Jim not to concern himself, that he would take care of these routine matters as he had for the major; but Jim was overwhelmed by his new responsibilities, and he couldn't let anything go across his desk without agonizing over every possible ramification. As Sergeant Chambers told me, "He'll stare at a piece of paper for hours, trying to make up his mind whether he should route it to somebody, or file it, or post it on the bulletin board, or send it to Major Devereaux, or wipe his ass with it. With all due respect, sir, I think I'm goin' to have to shoot him. He's driving me crazy."

"When is Billings coming back?" I asked.

"The major said in about a week."

"Well, hang in there, Billy. You can make it."

"I don't know, sir. He's holdin' up the fuckin' war. I have to sneak stuff out to the officers who need it when the captain isn't around. Even the major is bitchin' because he isn't getting his stats and all that other junk he gets every two or three days. And he's wreckin' my files. He puts everything in the wrong bloody place."

I sympathized with the sergeant. Captain Ewell was a fine pilot, a natural combat leader, but he also was a lousy administrator. I didn't say so to Billy, but I was certain Jim Ewell belonged only in one or two places: either in the left seat of a B-17, leading the squadron, or on his farm in Kansas staring at a mule's ass for ten hours a day. "Look," I said. "The weather's going to be good for the next few days; Captain Ewell will be flying his butt off. You'll have plenty of time to get things in order before Billings comes back. And maybe you'll get lucky."

"What do you mean, sir—lucky?"

"Well, the krauts might take the captain out of your hair."

"Naw. Don't get me wrong, sir. The captain is a great guy. This just isn't his cup of tea. Naw—I don't want that kind of luck. No way." Billy laughed. "Besides, he makes a helluva good cup of coffee. Major Billings never does that."

Since I contributed nothing to the resolution of Jim's problems, and since, on too many occasions, I was used by him to support his equivocal responses to Billy's pleas to move the paper, I decided to do the sensible thing and stay out of sight. I was always in the middle of the confrontation: either being bullied by Sergeant Chambers to agree with him that such-and-such an order should be posted for two days and then filed, or being wheedled by Jim to be on his side. "Well, I don't know. I think these orders should go to Devereaux for his review before we post them. I think there's some clarification needed, and I'm not going to call wing unless Devereaux agrees. What do you think, Jack? Don't you think that's the right way to handle it?"

I sought refuge with Mike Salinas, even though he had little need of me now. His situation had tremendously improved. He had a new engineer assisting him; he had a stockpile of tires and critical parts, and he had made an arrangement with Foggia Main to have his engine changes done there, which meant that slow-times were a thing of the past. Foggia had test stands, two of them.

When I described my predicament to Mike and pleaded for sanctuary, he seemed puzzled. "You know, I thought Jim was a real take-over guy. I remember that first night, after he was assigned the job when Billings had to bail out for a spell, he seemed to know just where he was going; he seemed to have a handle on the whole damn operation—funny."

"As far as the missions go," I said, "he's first rate. He's doing a great job with the crews. The armorers think he's the greatest guy that ever came down the pike. They love the way he stands up to the boys in wing and the group to get the bomb loads firmed up early. His leadership in the air is superb. It's just the routine office junk; it's driving him bonkers." I paused for a moment, and then I added, "Billy Chambers said he's going to have to shoot him."

Mike laughed. "Oh, poor Jimmy. I know what he's going through." He pointed to a pile of paper on his desk. "Look at that shit. Most of it's new inserts for the technical manuals, some of it's crap, and maybe one or two might be worth reading." He picked one off the top. "Listen to this. 'AAF regulation 62-15 requires that all AAF engineering officers certify that they have read and understand all instructions contained in EIF revision sheets listed and numbered below. When you receive the EIF material listed below, sign the bottom portion of the form, detach at the dotted line, and return the receipt (properly executed) to your Operations Officer.' Shall I read on?" Mike asked.

"No. No, please; I know what you mean."

Mike threw the paper in a basket marked ACTION, which contained as many documents as there were in his basket marked INCOMING, but not half the staggering number there were in his basket marked FILE. He stared at the piles of paper. Without taking his eyes off them, he asked, "Do you think the krauts have all this horseshit?"

"Absolutely. They're sticklers for documentation. A wonderful people. They even piss by the numbers."

"Ah, well." Mike sighed. "I've got to find a job for you. Let's see. How about looking at bomb racks?"

"Huh?"

"Yeah, we're having some problems with malfunctions. Look into it for me. See what you can find out. When can you start?"

"Not tomorrow. I'm on the battle orders."

"Okay then; the day after." Mike looked at me with a wry smile. "You know, you're a bastard for leaving poor Jim in the lurch. You're really a no-good bastard."

"Yes," I said, "I know."

It was going to be a clear morning. In the semidarkness in the back of the truck rumbling down the highway to briefing, I could see the stars near the eastern horizon turning pale in the glowing rim of yellow light that led the sun upon us. There were no clouds. There was nothing to mar the serene beauty of day breaking, a day that would be again indifferent to our wretchedness. I folded my arms close around my chest and trembled. I always trembled now before a mission. My mouth was very dry. I had traveled this road too many times. I had become too used to it for it to matter. Like Bill Sykes's dog sniffing the sweet promises of dawn, I waited for the first kick, the first blow. I waited, like that poor beast, to endure the day.

There was something different at briefing. I couldn't sort it out. From what I could see and hear, it was like any other day: there was the same hum of voices, smoke swirled up toward the roof beams, an occasional tense laugh broke the somber monotone of sound like the hysterical screech of chalk on a blackboard. But there was something threatening . . . something.

"Attention!" The orderly's voice was loud, silencing the room. This brief silence was immediately followed by the clattering din of one hundred and thirty officers quickly standing to come to attention. The group commander walked briskly down the aisle toward the stage; he looked straight ahead; his face was grim. When he took his place on the stage behind the small podium, he turned and said a few words to one of the briefing officers, and then he turned and faced us.

"As you were, gentlemen." He paused, waiting for us to become seated. "I want to speak to you this morning before we proceed with our regular briefing." He paused again. The mission map was sitting on its tripod stand about three feet away from the colonel's right hand. He held the felt-tipped pointer, the doom stick, in his left hand. The map was still covered. "Gentlemen, today marks the beginning of our campaign against the oil fields in Rumania. Today, gentlemen, our target is Ploesti."

The silence in the room was broken by half-stifled groans, by men shifting in their seats as if to try to move out of harm's way. I felt the edge of panic, the saving, urging impulse to run, to get away from it, the word, the terrifying word—Ploesti. The man beside me leaned forward and muttered, "Oh, Christ. Here we go."

I stared at the stage, watching the colonel play his role. He peered around the room, waiting for the men to quiet down. His eyes were searching, eagerly, cruelly searching through us to find the one poor pilgrim who might say no. The bastard, I thought, the dirty bastard. The colonel nodded to his aide, who was bursting with desire for his little moment of drama and who could not control his excitement as he flipped the black cloth away from the map. He was barely able to restrain a proud smile at the stunned reaction to the long, eastward journey of the tape that stretched deep into Rumania to a point just north of Bucharest. The colonel tapped his pointer on the map. "There, gentlemen; there it is—Ploesti, a complex of eleven refineries with all the support installations: rail yards, tank farms, pumping stations, cracking plants—plenty for everybody. Every plane that can fly will be in the air today, our Fifth Wing and all the B-24 boys. This is the beginning, gentlemen. This is the beginning."

The colonel was smiling. Christ, he was smiling. Oh, it's going to be a bloody party; we'll all have a wonderful time. The damn fool, the goddamn fool. And then he spoke again, a few quiet words that wiped away my anger and my contempt.

"I'll be leading the group today. There's no way you're going to leave the old man home on this one." The men responded with cheers and laughter. The tension was broken. My heart lifted to their raucous declaration. I joined them, clapping my hands in joyful affirmation of our comradeship. Yes, we'll do it. Yes, by God! Yes! Yes! We were all mad, as mad as men must be to cheer the words that would send them against a terrible fortress halfway round the world from home, to cheer as though it were a splendid game that only they could play.

A voice called out from the center of the room. "Colonel?"

The colonel looked down toward the speaker with a grin, enjoying this brief camaraderie before the mission. "Yes, Lieutenant. What's on your mind?"

"Well, sir, what I want to know is, is this trip really necessary?" The men in the room roared with laughter at this reference to the gas-rationing slogan used back in the States.

The colonel's grin broadened into a smile. "Son, you can bet your ass it is." And then he raised his hands over his head, waving them to stop the manic celebration that followed his answer. "We've got to get on, gentlemen." He waved his arms again and called out in a louder voice, "We've got to get on, boys. I'm taking up too much time." He waited for a few moments for the room to become quiet, and then he turned to the briefing officer standing behind him. "Major Roberts, please carry on."

The briefing was the usual settling-down kind of comfort of any familiar routine. The wheels of the machine began to turn, and we inched toward the inevitable events before us. The past was gone, all the days and all the years were gone. Tomorrow could not be seen; it was too far away, beyond the eternity of nine hours through which we must pass to come to it. We were bound and locked to the day. There was nothing else; nothing before and nothing after. If wife, mother, child, or a beloved friend called to us, we would not hear; if they stood beside us, we would not see them.

We formed the group over the field without incident. The colonel's lead was steady; his climbing turn, gathering the flock, was gentle and perfectly controlled: not so fast that the outside planes had to pound their throttles to keep up, and not so slow that the inside planes had to endure the terror of trying to hold their positions with their airspeeds dropping dangerously close to a stall.

An overloaded B-17 stalling out under a thousand feet met its spectacular end in seconds. It happened when the lead was bad or when a bad lead combined with turbulent weather. It happened when a pilot, fearing the embarrassment of dropping from his position in the formation, hesitated a fraction of a second too long before dumping the nose of his plane to regain a safe airspeed. When his inside wing lost its lift, he never had to worry about being embarrassed again. Three tons of bombs, twenty-seven hundred gallons of high-octane fuel, about six thousand rounds of fifty-caliber ammunition along with oxygen tanks, hydraulic and lubricating oil, all hitting the ground at over two hundred miles an hour, left nothing but a steaming black smear. It happened like other incidents referred to as "unfortunate accidents" in the form letters sent home to the families. It happened, but it was nothing to worry about; in a little while grass grew over the dark stains, and there was nothing to see, nothing to remember.

We made our rendezvous with the wing precisely on time. Our group's position was on the extreme left of the echelon; the Ninety-ninth was on our right. It was splendid; there were airplanes everywhere, all heading east. The air was smooth, and it must have been dry for there was not a trace of vapor trail behind us. P-38s slid over the formation, drifting toward the southeast. Every time I saw them, I felt the same yearning to be as free as they were, to move as they did in soft, curling patterns above the bombers, or to roll away in a flash of motion as though abandoned to some impulse of delight. The sky was more a playground for them than a battlefield, or so it seemed to me. I knew they fell and died as we did, but theirs must have been a brighter heaven.

To our left, P-51s sped past us in loose elements of three, heading for the target, where their task would be to clear out any enemy fighters who might rise to intercept us. They would hold the air over Ploesti and cover us for those vital moments when we were most vulnerable, after we had dropped our bombs and were rallying off the target. It was then, when we came out of the barrage of flak, when damaged planes staggered and began to lag, when the empty spaces left by our fallen had to be filled, it was always then that the German fighters hit us hard. We had seen it before: fighters swarming around the laggards, killing them like wounded beasts whose death was certain because they couldn't keep up. We always had to leave them; the formation had to survive. It was the law for us, and it had to be obeyed. Maybe it wouldn't happen today; maybe the 51s would be there.

Our squadron was flying the low-left position, and I was tail-end Charlie, the seventh plane filling the box of the second flight. Captain Ewell's instructions had been clear. "I want you to cover our ass—and make sure your gunners keep their eyes open. Keep me out of trouble back there."

It was difficult to see. The sun was blazing in my eyes. I tried to hold the flight leader's plane in the upper right quadrant of my half of the windshield, but I kept losing him in the blinding sunlight. I could only recover his image by lifting my plane so he would be between me and the sun, and I couldn't hold this position for long because I was then battered by the prop wash from his left wingman. I was drowned in sweat and desperately fighting disorientation. In another thirty minutes, the sun would rise above my line of vision, and I would be free of it. At the moment, it was torture. I struggled in my chamber of dancing light between the two wingmen and the flight leader, guessing where they were half the time. Clues were given to me and were then quickly taken away, obliterated by golden lights shimmering with such intensity I could not look into them. For a moment I could see a wing, and then a glimpse of a tail assembly, two tail guns gleamed ahead of me. My left wing was buffeted by prop wash, and I eased back my outboard throttles to drop below the stream of turbulent air; at the same time, I tried to keep my plane steady with aileron and rudder. The sun rose higher as each minute passed until it shone above all of us. It shone above our planes; it shone above the land and the snow-streaked peaks of mountains. We were no longer caught by its fierce glare; it looked beyond us to the west and to the great sea behind us. And far beyond the sea, its first rays were lifting the darkness that brooded over a troubled land.

We were ninety minutes from the IP. I motioned to the copilot to take over. I called our flight engineer who was in the top turret. "Pilot to engineer."

"Engineer over."

"Sam, check the wingtip tanks, will you?"

"Yeah, okay. Hold a second."

I wanted to confirm the amount of fuel remaining in my outboard tanks. If possible, I wanted them empty and vented when we reached the IP. On the bomb run, my ideal situation would be to have the outboards empty and the main cells full. It would be the least explosive situation with the minimum amount of vapor in any of the tanks.

"Engineer to pilot."

"Go ahead."

"You got about seventy minutes."

"Okay, I'm going to lean her out a little. Check them in an hour, and let me know."

"Wilco. Out."

After I adjusted my fuel mixture, I began to fiddle with the engine speed of number four. It sounded slightly out of sync. The copilot didn't appreciate my interference. He came on the intercom to let me know it. "It's all right. Leave it alone."

"The hell it is," I said. I kept fiddling.

"You're making it worse."

"Bogeys! Bogeys! Ten o'clock."

I looked out over the left wing and I could see them: ten dark specks, far out of range, paralleling our course. My binoculars were not under my seat; I had forgotten. I called the crew. "Pilot to crew. Look around. See if you can spot any others. Pilot to tail."

"Tail to pilot. Over."

"Anything behind us?"

"Nope. Clear as a bell."

"Top turret to pilot. Over."

"Go ahead."

"I think they're 190s."

"Okay. Keep your eyes open."

"Sir? Where the hell are our P-38s?"

"They're chasing trains or blowin' up fuckin' schools. How the hell do I know?" And then I eased my tone. "The group leader's probably already called them, Sam. Don't worry; they'll be here by noon to-morrow."

Sam came back on the intercom. "Jeez, thanks, sir. I feel a helluva lot better now. . . . Yeah, they're 190s. I can see them pretty good. They seem to be just lookin' us over."

"Ball turret to pilot. Over."

"Yep. Go ahead."

"There's six MEs below us."

"How far below us?"

"Oh, about two thousand feet."

"Okay. Out."

The German fighters were obviously tracking us. Their radios would be buzzing with information: our numbers, our airspeed and altitude, course headings, the distance between the groups in echelon, the distance between the wings . . . and their command headquarters would be making excellent use of it. There would be no surprises. How could there be on such a splendid day?

Paul was flying the right wing position on the squadron leader. I could see his plane clearly now. He looked good; he was holding his spot, and he wasn't wobbling all over the sky. He was close in, but not too close. He was just high enough for his port guns to clear Ewell if he had to fire over him. I wondered what Paul was thinking about, probably some romantic nonsense comparing our attack on Ploesti with his doomed heroes at Gettysburg who had followed Pickett out of the woods and across the Emmitsburg Road on that bloody July day. Was he thinking before this day was done he might lie, white and still, on the slope of these eastern mountains as they had on the hill that climbed to the cemetery on the ridge? I looked toward his plane again; it hadn't changed. No, Paul wasn't dreaming about old ghosts. He was in the same dumb stupor of obedience that I was, aware of nothing beyond the instant he was in.

My thoughts were fixed on the two barrels of tail guns in front of me. My eyes never left them. The barrels moved to the right. I touched the right rudder and they were framed again where I wanted them. The barrels raised an inch and began to slide to the left. Back pressure on the wheel; light left rudder. The barrels slowly returned to their original position, pointing at me from the center of my windshield.

They were coming toward me; I eased back on the outboard throttles, just a touch. The barrels were still, and then they began to move again. The game went on. My responses with aileron, rudder, and elevator were gentle and would have been imperceptible to anyone beside me who was unfamiliar with the exquisite control and concentration needed to fly a steady position in a bomber formation. The flight leader's tail guns were my point of reference. I could not allow my plane to waver from them. I was tied to them by a fragile string; it must never break.

"Engineer to pilot."

"Yeah. Go ahead."

"We'd better switch, sir. The wing tanks are almost empty."

"Okay. We'll switch to the main cells. Are the 190s still out there?"

"Naw. They're gone. Somethin' must have spooked them."

"Okay, Sam. Out."

The ball turret came on the intercom. "Ball to pilot. Over."

"Go ahead, ball."

"The MEs are still under us. They've moved up a little. They're out of range, but I'd like to give them a squirt. Okay?"

"Yeah, let 'em know we see them. Just a couple of short bursts. We don't want to waste any ammo."

"Roger."

I heard the chug of his twin fifties. A pause. Another burst, a bit longer than the first. The ball turret came back on the intercom. He was laughing. "They didn't like that. They screwed off. Aw, they were probably low on fuel anyway."

"Bandits! Bandits! Eleven o'clock level!"

Two flights of MEs were crossing in front of us, heading south. I counted twenty. I could hear the whine of the top turret following them. The bombardier, who acted as gunnery officer, came on the intercom. "Hold it. They're too far out. Hold it."

I waited, not wanting to interrupt the bombardier if he had anything more to say to the gunners. He anticipated me. "Bombardier to pilot. Over."

"Pilot. Go ahead."

"They're heading for the center of the wing, or maybe for one of the B-24 groups up ahead of us. I switched to command a few minutes ago, and one of the group leaders was calling for fighter help. Where the hell are the 38s?"

"I don't know, Nick. Keep your eyes peeled."

"Wilco. Out."

"Pilot to navigator. Over."

"Yeah, Jack?"

"How much longer to the IP?"

"Twenty minutes." The navigator paused, and then he spoke again. "We're going to have a headwind on the bomb run."

"How bad?"

"I don't know—maybe ten knots."

Jesus, a long run, and of all the places to have one. "Okay. Out."

The fact that winds aloft were difficult to predict didn't keep me from cursing the group meteorologist. There were over eight hundred guns down there. Our angle of attack couldn't have been worse. It was wrong, dead wrong.

"Bandits! Bandits! Six o'clock high!"

White traces streamed by my window about twenty yards off the left wing. The turret behind me fired two long bursts.

"They're breaking low to nine o'clock!"

"Bombardier to tail. Any more back there?"

"No. There was three of them. They're headin' for the deck. Can't see nothin' else."

We were very near the IP. Far ahead of us, the sky looked different. There was a band of brown haze from eighteen thousand feet up to about twenty-three thousand. It was not easy to see; you had to know what you were looking for. I knew what it was; I had seen it before. Flak. The dirty strings from a flak barrage drifted in the cold wind. Less than five minutes ago a group had gone through it, and now the shreds of smoke were fading and were barely visible. A black column was rising from the ground in the southeast. Someone had hit something big, something that had violently blown. The swirling, greasy smoke was leaping upward, widening as it climbed. The group began to make a gentle turn to the left. As my left wing dipped, I could see a cluster of white buildings below us shining bright and clear in the sunlight. I wondered how one would say God have mercy in Rumanian. We were at the IP. We were beginning our run.

There was not a daub of black in the sky; for a blessed moment we made our slow, inexorable passage across it unchallenged. Seconds passed. When it came, it came like a mighty shout, a malediction hurling up at us through four miles of twisting wind. They were everywhere; the dark flowers of flak were everywhere. Four successive shells exploded in front of my right wing, and I felt the wheel tremble in my hands. An orange core glared out of a shroud of smoke in front of me. Our plane shuddered against the concussion of two bursts underneath us. A wall of smoke was smeared over my windshield, and for a terrifying instant, I couldn't see the flight leader's tail guns. Again, I couldn't see the guns; a sheet of flame swept over them, and when it cleared one gun barrel was gone, the other flapped against the end of the fuselage. There were four ragged holes in the horizontal stabilizer. My left wing dropped away from me, and I drove my foot hard against the right rudder to bring it up. I didn't pray. I didn't curse. I didn't think. I crouched in my cave of instruments, tubes, and wires. I lived as it was given to me to live, moment by moment, again and again, as each explosion released me to the next, and to the next.

The storm reached for a climax; it reached for us with all its passion to sweep us away, to end our brazen journey in the sun. We were clothed in the miracle of grace. We went on. Not one plane was down. The barrage of flak followed us with unrelenting intensity, and black shell bursts engulfed us. We couldn't last. We would never make it. A series of explosions directly over my plane drove us down away from the flight leader. I eased her back up into her position and waited for the next blow, and maybe the last one. It never came.

"Bombs away."

The bombardier's voice was our deliverance; with it the flak eased, lifting to our right as we rallied north and down in a shallow dive to twenty thousand feet.

"Tail to pilot. Over."

"Pilot. Go ahead."

"There's a group behind us, about a mile or so over at four o'clock. They're catchin' hell. Two planes are down. I saw five chutes."

"Okay, tail. Any fighters?"

"No. Nothin' yet. Out."

We waited. We searched the sky for them. The bombardier kept asking each gun station for sightings.

"Ball. Anything?"

"Nothin'."

"Tail?"

"Nope. All clear."

"Turret?"

"Nothin'."

I couldn't understand it. The group, the stubborn, plodding group, was heading home to Longskirt, and there wasn't a fighter in sight. We had hit Ploesti, and we had got away with it. Every plane was sitting in its spot in a perfect formation. We had got away with it; by some fluke, or by errant gunnery, or by the effect of the twisting ballistic wind, the one variable that flak batteries could not control, we had got away with it. I accepted the gift churlishly, looking over my shoulder for fighters, grudgingly yielding to the reality that we were going home without a loss. My dour conscience took little comfort in the one plane in the high-right squadron with a feathered engine, and the image of my flight leader's damaged tail standing steady in my windshield. I was wary of the clear sky. My Calvinist soul cautioned me: don't be happy; you'll pay for it tomorrow, or some day after tomorrow.

"Little Friends. Six o'clock high."

Our lost fighters, the P-38s, had returned. There were eighteen of them heading west on our course. As they passed over, the leader rocked his wing in greeting.

The bombardier came on the intercom. "The bastards. You'd think they'd hang around—at least until we got to the coast."

I didn't like Nick McDaniels. He was a good bombardier and a dependable gunnery officer, but he irritated me. With the terror of the bomb run behind me, I was able to indulge again in my array of trite prejudices. Nick was one of them. I answered him, and I didn't try to keep the irritation out of my voice. "They've had a busy day. They're probably low on fuel."

"Low on fuel, my ass. They really got it made, those guys."

"Yeah, Nick. Out."

The group moved on. It crossed the tip of northern Bulgaria that probed up between Rumania and Yugoslavia, an old land of Thracian kings. Some of the mountains were white with snow; where they were bare, sullen boulders pushed out of the earth and stretched out along the slopes like great red dogs sleeping in the sun. There were no towering peaks reaching up to us; the tops of the mountains were worn; the ridges were not sharply defined but were coarse and as rough as an old gnarled fist. A frozen stream gleamed between two of the ridges, and on the lower hills it widened into a tumbling river that rushed into the valley. There it wandered on the green flat land, seeking the companionship of a few small houses along its banks. The sun made the river as bright as shining silver. It was beautiful to look at, and if I had been an old Thracian king, this is where I would have lived.

The group leader began a gentle letdown. I reduced power on my inboards and locked the throttles, continuing to control my position in the formation with the outboards. I reduced our engine speeds and trimmed for nose down. The copilot took over the controls. I returned to my window, watching the Yugoslav countryside roll beneath me while I patiently waited to reach an altitude where I could take off my oxygen mask and have a cup of coffee with a cigarette or two.

I was dulled by peace and contentment. Our small armada filled me with pride, and I looked at each of the four squadrons, awed by their steadfast symmetry. I was one of them. I would never be in better company. The flak was forgotten, the fear, and the terrible tension waiting for a fighter attack that never came; it had all gone back deep in my mind, to be buried there with all the other primal horrors for a long, long time. We were at fourteen thousand feet and nearing the coast. The copilot had returned to fiddling with the RPM toggle switches. I didn't interfere with him but drowsily half listened to the steady roar of the engines. At last I could see it ahead of me, the serene blue surface of the Adriatic was framed in my windshield. We were nearly home.

Five bursts of flak appeared a hundred yards ahead of us! More bursts were blossoming on our right!

"For Christ's sake! He's taking us over Split! The stupid asshole!" The navigator kept yelling into the intercom. "Left, you dumb shit! Take us left!"

The colonel must have felt the rage of every man in the group, for he took us to the left and down in a precipitous dive to twelve thousand feet. We were all near panic, and planes were scattering in every direction to avoid collision. The flak bursts trailed away, high and to our right. It was a very close thing. If the flak batteries had held off for five more minutes, they would have had us cold at fourteen thousand feet.

We pulled the formation together in shocked silence. There was not a murmur on the command frequency. As the planes maneuvered back into their positions, it was done with sheepish politeness. We yielded to one another with idiotic deference, like comedians going through a revolving door. We were embarrassed because we had panicked, and now we made a great show of being without haste to return to the security of the formation. I felt sorry for the colonel. He would never live it down, although every navigator in the group should have been aware of the seaport city of Split, a flak haven on the Yugoslav coast, dead ahead of us, and one of them should have warned him.

I took off my oxygen mask and lit a cigarette. Looking up at the high-right squadron, I saw the plane that earlier had one feathered engine now had two; number one and number three were shut down. Sgt. Sam Jaors had come out of his top turret, and was standing behind me with a cup of coffee in his hand. He reached forward and placed it on the control pedestal where I could reach it. He lifted my right earphone away from my ear and brought his face close to mine.

"Everything okay, Lieutenant?"

"Yeah, everything's okay, Sam. Too bad we fucked up back there."

He nodded, but didn't say anything. Sam had not flown with me before, though I knew him quite well. He had been with the squadron for a long time, and I had often talked with him at the club where his tall, stoop-shouldered presence assured me things were as they should be, and his constancy among the ever-changing faces made me believe survival was a possibility. He stayed beside me, staring through the windshield. The group kept letting down. We were now at eight thousand feet. Sam tapped my shoulder and pointed toward the horizon. The coast of Italy was there, at the edge of the sky and sea ahead of us, a faint shadow, but it was there.

I was tired. We had been flying for over seven hours, and we still had an hour to go. I handed my cup to Sam for a refill. When he handed it back to me, I noticed his hand was trembling. I motioned to him to bring his head down so I could speak to him.

"How many missions, Sam?"

"This is my last one. I got my fifty."

"Hey, that's great! Congratulations." I reached back and shook his hand. "Hey. That's really great."

Sam grinned, and then brought his mouth close to my ear. "Lieutenant, do me a favor, will ya?"

"Yeah, sure, Sarge. What'll you have?"

"Just make a good landing—please. Just one good one for me."

"Jesus, Sarge, give me something easy. I haven't made a good landing in months. But I'll tell you something. In fact, I'll promise you something."

"What's that?" Sam asked. He looked worried.

"You'll walk away from it."

Chapter XII

PRACTICE, QUESTIONS, AND PIOMBINO

All is at peace. Ah, never, heart, forget
For this her youngest, best, and bravest died,
These bright dews once were mixed with blood and sweat.

—WALTER DE LA MARE

It would be his last landing, and the end of the whole bloody business. The sergeant would not want to see or smell an airplane for a long time. I should not have been so cavalier about his concern. He was serious about wanting a good landing, fearfully serious. It was perverse of me to see his vulnerability and to take advantage of it with my absurd arrogance, pretending his request was a joke, a contemptible timidity not to be taken seriously. His whole life was ahead of him, within his grasp only minutes away, and I could take it from him. I could take it from him with one stupid move; in one second of indifference, I could deny his survival. He was precious cargo, one of the few who would walk away. I had to be absolutely sure that he did; I had to nail this one.

Since Sam had not flown with me before, there was no way he could have known that I was not careless about my landings; many pilots were, and considered one or two hard bounces as good a way to meet the ground as any. He didn't want that; he wanted a gentle, feathery touch. I was sure he would faint, or worse, if he had to endure a shattering collision with the steel mat and a wobbling wing nearly touching the ground while the brakes screamed and the plane reeled drunkenly down the runway. Fifty missions had stretched Sam too thin. He needed to be brought home easy, very easy.

The other three squadrons had already gone in. We were the last squadron coming up over the runway for our peel-off. Our plane would be the last plane down. Sam was sitting in the jump seat on my right. We had circled the field four times, and I could feel his tension. I could hear the words pounding in his head. "Oh, God. I'm so close. Don't let anything happen now. This guy's a good pilot. I know he's a good pilot. Don't let him fuck up. Jesus, don't let him fuck up now."

I banked to the left, following the six planes ahead of me. I eased back the throttles.

"Flaps."

"Flaps. Twenty degrees, coming down."

I took a quick glance at Sam. His eyes were fixed on the windshield. I didn't think he was seeing anything. I nodded to the copilot.

"Gear coming down." The copilot looked out of his window to confirm the landing gear was secure. "Gear down and locked."

I went a bit farther downwind than usual before turning on my base leg. It would give me a longer approach, a little more time to set up my landing. I held my airspeed and turned on the final approach. I looked at Sam, then tapped the airspeed indicator to call his attention to it. He was supposed to be calling out the readings to me so I could keep my eyes on the runway. He responded with a weak smile and began to call the indicator readings. All I could hear was a faint croaking noise.

"C'mon, Sam! I can't hear you!"

Sam's head shot forward like an arrow. He glared at the indicator. He began to yell. "One forty! One forty! One thirty-five! One thirty . . ."

I didn't want to laugh, but I couldn't help it. I put my hand on his shoulder and gently pushed him back in his seat. "Relax, Sarge. I got it. Just sit back and relax."

As we neared the end of the runway, I chopped the throttles and the copilot set the friction brake to hold them. As she started to settle, I came back very easy on the wheel. She paused, then started to drop, slowly. I had just enough slushy response left in the elevators. I came back all the way with the wheel. She touched tail low. There was no sound. Sam looked puzzled and apprehensive until he heard the faint rattle of the steel mat underneath us as it absorbed the full weight of our plane rolling down the runway. He put his face in his hands. I concentrated on the brakes, lightly touching left and right to keep the plane straight in the middle of the runway. I didn't speak to him or look at him. I knew he was weeping.

.   .   .

At the hardstand, after we had secured the airplane and were ready to leave the flight deck, I turned to Sam. He was under better control, but he was vague, like a man who found himself suddenly in a strange place. I shook his hand again. "Good luck, Sergeant. All the best."

He looked puzzled. "Oh, yeah. Uh—thanks. Thanks, Lieutenant. Uh—thanks for the grease job. You brought her in nice—real nice."

I grinned at him. "Hell man, you gotta hit one once in a while."

I put my gear together in my B-5 bag while he watched me. He didn't seem to know quite what to do.

"Well, Sarge?" I asked him. "What do you say? Let's get the hell out of this airplane."

"Oh, yeah. Right." He turned aft and went through the bomb bay. The catwalk was narrow and he kept bumping into the racks on either side.

I went forward through the nose hatch. When I dropped down on the mat, the crew chief was waiting for me, looking worried. "How'd she go?"

"Good, chief. No problems."

"You got some holes," he said mournfully.

"Yeah, I guess we have, chief. I'll see you later."

When I walked away, he called after me. "Did you write anything up?"

"No. She was okay," I called back to him without turning around.

The crew were mauling Sam. They were pounding him and shouting, exulting in his survival as though it were their own.

"Hey, Sam baby. You made it! You lucky bastard, you made it!"

"Way to go, kid!"

"Touch me, Sam! Put it there, baby!"

"Atta boy, Sarge! Atta boy . . . !"

I could still hear them when I was fifty yards up the road. Their celebration would go on long into the night, and they'd have brutal hangovers in the morning.

None of it meant anything to me. Everybody died. What difference did it make? We were trifles in time, a flicker of an eyelash in a million light-years. Death came, sooner or later, and there was no perceptible difference between the two. I didn't think I feared it, but I feared the dying; that would be the hard part. I wondered what death would be like. Dante said in heaven we would sit around all day adoring God. I wouldn't care for that. If there were a heaven, and I could have it as I wanted it, it would be the same as here, only without the sadness, without the pain. There would be dogs, of course, and I would have a red house on a beautiful river. I would learn to play the cello. Not far away, on a field near the river, there would be a perfectly groomed baseball diamond with grass as green as Fenway Park's. I would play errorless third base and hit four-fifty every year. In the afternoons of warm summer days, I would swim or take long walks in the woods. In the winter my house would be near-buried in snow, and I would live with books and music. Perhaps I would plan a garden for spring. In time Jean would come to live with me. We would have three kids, and I wouldn't play the cello as much. . . .

"Hey, Muirhead. Get in." Major Billings had pulled alongside me in his jeep. He looked well. He must have gained ten pounds.

We drove without speaking for a time until I ended the silence and tried to start a conversation. I wanted to find out what he was going to be doing. "Good to have you back, Major. Captain Ewell will be mighty glad to see you."

"Thanks," he said. "I've already seen Ewell." He glanced at me. "He said you were very helpful."

I felt the blood rush to my face. I didn't know what to say, but I hoped he would keep his eyes on the road and not look at me. It was so typical of that damn fool, Jim, to believe that I had helped him. Like a good liar, I spoke the truth deceitfully disguised as modesty. "Oh, I just hung around—a little moral support, that's all."

"How did it go today? Rough?"

I was relieved he changed the subject. "We were lucky," I said. "The flak was heavy. Only a brush by three fighters—I don't know where the hell the rest of them were. We were lucky—no losses."

"Well," the major said, "don't let that worry you; you'll have a chance to go back and try it again."

I didn't respond to his dismal words. I didn't want to think about it; instead, I began to pry. "Sergeant Chambers didn't expect you back so soon. He thought you'd be away for another week."

The major pulled the jeep off the road at Operations without answering me. "You're going to debriefing, aren't you?" he asked.

"Yeah, I guess so."

"Well, here you are. I'll see you later." As I was climbing out of the jeep, he added, "I hear you went over Split today."

"Yes," I said. "I'm glad you didn't see us, Major. We scattered all over the bloody sky. It was a mess."

His response surprised me. It didn't sound like him. I expected a harsh, contemptuous comment about our lack of discipline, but he spoke quietly in a detached way. "Those things happen."

He wasn't looking at me. He was staring at something over my head, something far away that only he could see. After what seemed to be a long, strange silence, he spoke again. "I did the same thing once, coming back from the refineries up around Vienna. . . . Took the squadron over Pola at twelve thousand feet. Lost one plane—ten men. Didn't see any chutes. Three more were wounded; one died the next day. . . . Stupid. Jesus Christ, how stupid." His eyes were still gazing past me, fixed on the tormenting vision of that day.

I didn't want to be with him any longer. I wanted to leave. I backed away from the jeep, mumbling my excuse. "Look, Major, I've got to get going. I'm late as it is." I waved to the lost man and turned away from him.

Before I reached Operations, I cursed: I cursed the sergeant's fifty missions; I cursed the major's worn and tired soul; I cursed Ploesti, Split, Pola, and all the other goddamned places; I cursed the Germans, the Italians, the English, the Americans; I cursed the air, the sun; I cursed the world; I cursed at God. . . . I waited. Nothing happened.

There were only a few men still in the debriefing room; most of the desks were unoccupied. Six officers were grouped around a long table drinking coffee and talking quietly. I looked for Captain Stoner. I finally spotted him walking across the room with some papers in his hand. When he saw me, he waved his arm motioning me over to his desk. After we were seated, he poured a splash of brandy into a paper cup, hiding his movement of pouring it with a purposeful fumbling of papers in his lower left-hand drawer. He handed me the cup, peering at me in a concerned way. "Welcome back, comrade," he said. "Are you all right?"

"Yes, thank you, Ilyich. How goes the revolution?"

"Not so good. Not so good." He sighed, and then asked, "Are you flying tomorrow?"

I sipped the brandy before I answered him. "Ah, that's good. No, I don't think so."

"I've got a jeep. Let's go down to Manfredonia for the day. A long walk on the beach—stretch your legs and all that. The weather's supposed to be fine."

"I'm sorry, Ilyich, I can't. I've got a chore to do for Captain Salinas."

"Oh, well, another time," Stoner said. He seemed disappointed. Perhaps he had something on his mind he wanted to talk about. Whatever it was, I didn't want to hear it.

"Do you need anything from me?" I asked him.

"No," Stoner replied. "I have all I need to fill out this shit." He pointed to the forms on his desk. "Unless, my boy, you have some special intelligence you want to reveal to me." He leered in his best Lenin style.

"No, nothing you don't already know," I said. "They've got a helluva lot of guns at Ploesti."

"Yes, I know," Stoner replied. He looked at me curiously. "What's it like?" he suddenly asked. "What's it like? Getting your ass shot off."

Jake Stoner and I had talked many times: at the squadron club over a drink; in Foggia, at an Italian family's house where we occasionally brought small gifts of soap and cigarettes for a dinner of spaghetti and sausages; and sometimes at evening mess after most of the men had gone while we lingered, coiled around mugs of coffee and a butt can, gossiping in the dim light like old women clutching comfort after a weary day. His question startled me; it was abrupt and intrusive. It was so unlike his usual sardonic banter, which ranged from a grudging but intense admiration for Tolstoy and Chekhov to his amusing assessment of his life in New Jersey and the foibles of its citizens whom he encountered in his law practice. He had rarely questioned me about myself in any probing way, but had seemed content to accept my superficial accounts of what I had done here and there as reasonable gestures of candor in support of our friendship. Now he wanted something more.

I sipped my brandy again and lit a cigarette while I tried to think of what to say. "I have to think about it, Ilyich," I finally answered.

Stoner wouldn't release me. "There must be something," he said. "What about the war itself? The compelling reasons for it? Your reasons?"

I handed Jake my paper cup. "Just a little snort, Ilyich. You're giving me a hard time."

He took the cup, repeating his furtive fumbling with the pint in his lower left drawer, and then he returned it to me. "Well?" he asked.

"Ilyich, please," I said. "You're asking me things I can't answer. I have no reasons that I can remember. I've forgotten the war, what it's about. I work in this little parish. I'm employed to fly a bomber from here to there. I drop some bombs there, and then I come back here—if I'm lucky. That's my job; I'm used to it."

"You're used to it! For Christ's sake, how can you say you've become used to it?" Jake was intense, and becoming more agitated.

He was driving me to the wall. Why was he doing it? I tried to keep my temper. "A man can get used to anything—anything. What I do scares the shit out of me, but this is what I do—today, tomorrow, the week after that . . . What the hell have you got me talking about? What the hell is the matter with you? Are you going bonkers? Or is this some new asinine psycho-testing crap?"

"No," Jake said. He looked sheepish. "I'm going home. New assignment. Got my orders yesterday. I wanted to talk with you; that's why I thought we might go down to Manfredonia for the day. Look, Jack," he went on. "I'm sorry, I'm sorry about my bad timing. I know you've had a rugged day. But . . ."

"But what? For God's sake! You're going home! What the hell are you bugging me for?" I tried to control my rage.

"Now don't get pissed," Jake pleaded. "When I got the news I was going home, all I could think of was I was going home empty, without the slightest grasp of what has been going on around me. I know nothing. I understand nothing. I've been in Intelligence for almost a year, and I've been asking combat men questions—in North Africa, in Sicily, and now here—and all I have is a memory, a blurred memory of faces, dull, staring, indifferent, vacant faces looking at me with such impatient contempt." Jake smiled, a tired, defeated smile. "It's foolish, isn't it? Trying to understand? You're my friend; I thought we could talk. I thought maybe you could tell me . . ."

"Ilyich," I said softly, "there's nothing I can tell you. We're bloody well in it now, and what each of us wants is to survive. Nothing more. When we're old men we'll sit and talk about it. We need time, Ilyich, time to see it clearly. We are all blind men here, following a fragile thread of duty, or routine if you choose, to some destination. You're lucky, my friend; yours is home."

Stoner sat quietly. The shafts of sunlight coming into the room from the side windows made three paths of gold that reached almost to the opposite wall. He began to arrange the papers on his desk. "Would you like another brandy?" he asked.

"No," I said. "But I could use a ride. Could you give me a lift back to the squadron? I'm tired; I could use an hour or so in the sack before chow."

When I entered the tent, I found Paul sitting on his cot in his long olive-drab underwear, staring into a small hand mirror.

"You're an ugly kid, Paul," I said. "No doubt about it, you're ugly." He ignored me and continued to examine his features in the mirror. There were no letters on my cot. "No mail, huh?"

"Nope," Paul said, and then he asked me, "Did you check the battle orders?"

"No, I didn't."

"Well, you should have. Practice mission tomorrow—you're especially invited." Paul smiled, pleased with his little joke. "Big briefing at seven. Chow between five-thirty and six-thirty." He looked back into the mirror. "I think I'll grow a mustache," he said. "It'll make me look older. . . . Oh, yeah. I almost forgot. Captain Salinas said to forget about the bomb racks. He thinks he's found the problem."

"Okay. Thanks. A practice mission—what the hell for?"

"I don't know."

We rose an hour later than we did for a mission, which was usually about four o'clock and before the sky was touched by light. It was always a time of explicit solitude, a time when we were shadows and most alone. A dome of perfect darkness then held the stars. Now the cobalt dome had faded, and the sky had changed to a lighter blue that stretched away from the glow of the sun and the burning ridge of the horizon. The stars were gone except for two giants that shone in the northwest where the edge of darkness held. I tried to see it all. I tried to gather it into me. I had to hurry. Paul was waiting for me.

The briefing was an interminable critique of our performance over the past month and, according to the briefing officers, we had been on the shoddy side. We were guided through all this nonsense by one intelligence officer after another quoting from mountains of supporting documentation piled on a long table near the podium. There was much tapping of the pointer against charts, maps, and photographs of rubble, accompanied by the droning voices of colonels, lieutenant colonels, majors, and one particularly pompous master sergeant. "Now, gentlemen, if you look closely at this strike photo, you'll see you were short on your Aiming Point; as a result, the whole bomb pattern was short. I might also point out, your formation could have been better. Notice the scattered patterns at the left of the photo—right there." Tap, tap went the pointer. Another voice had been fatherly and patient. "Fellows, I know it's rough up there, but we've got to get the job done the first time. . . . If you will, Sergeant, the next slide, please. . . . Now look at that formation, boys. Look at it. An invitation to a fighter attack, that's what it is. You fellows are better than that. I know you are." The major drove his right fist into his left palm, and it made a good smacking noise. Very impressive. A few of the men could not resist the opportunity to doze, but most stayed awake. Thanks to a long sleep and the three cups of coffee I had with my breakfast, I managed to appear attentive. I even managed, though chastised and contrite, to nod politely when one of the officers stared straight at me as he offered an indulgence to relieve us of our sins. "Let's wipe the slate clean, gentlemen. Let's get back to basics. Keep your formation tight. Hit your Aiming Point. Be sure and pick up your IP, clean and fast. You do that, gentlemen, and you'll shorten the war by six months."

This sort of thing went on for a long time, until everyone who wanted to talk did so. All of the incantations were finally complete, and word could be carried back to some petulant staff general who now could be advised that his will had been done: we had been reminded of our frailty and put back on the path of the righteous. We wandered off in groups, chatting about things of little consequence while we waited for the trucks to take us to the flight line. I looked at my watch; it was ten past nine. It was to be a wasted day, a delightfully wasted day. If we could get this practice mission out of the way by noon, I would have the rest of the day free. Perhaps Ilyich and I could make the trip to Manfredonia.

Two days after the practice mission, we were back to work, heading for Piombino on the west coast of Italy, a small city isolated on a promontory that faced the sea and the island of Elba. We flew northeast from Longskirt toward the coast near Lake Varanov. We would cross over to the west after we reached the coastal city of San Benedetto. The weather was fair, though the sun was veiled by a thin overcast of cirrus that presaged some frontal weather moving in, probably within the next twelve hours. Looking over the leading edge of my wing between the number-two engine and the fuselage, I could see a narrow wake of white water trailing behind a small boat moving north along the coast.

We were at eleven thousand feet and climbing. It was time for my last cigarette before putting on my mask and going on oxygen. I lit up, and as I smoked, my thoughts drifted back to the practice mission. It had been a break in our routine, a welcome departure from the tension of operational flying. For a few hours I had been persuaded that I was a student pilot again, which had been a time of abysmal ignorance for me when I believed all instructors were infallible and everything they said was true. . . . Why was it, I wondered, that every time they laid it on us at one of these morale-building briefings, they always said if we did thus and so, we would shorten the war by six months? It was always six months; never five or four, or three. It was always six.

·   ·   ·

Our attack on Piombino was made from the east, and we approached the target in a column of four squadrons of seven planes. The flak put up against us was intense and accurate, but not prolonged; there were not enough guns for a sustained barrage. We took only minor battle damage. It was later, when we were making our passage back across Italy to the east coast, that we had our trouble.

To a combat pilot, the sky became, in time, as familiar as any habitat of sea or land; he came to know its illusions, its deceits, its beauty, its power, and its dangers. It became the familiar turf of the battleground. And he came to know it well through a sensitivity learned from peril; it was a primitive awareness that often transcended his perceptions. We were halfway across the peninsula when I felt it. I knew it. There was something ahead of us, some threatening presence. The sky was clear; the rolling land beneath us revealed nothing but occasional farms scattered along the boundaries of fields or orchards. There was not a sign of any military activity. The roads were empty. I stared hard into the air around my plane, looking for traces of smoke or for any wisps of vapor trails from fighters' wings. There was nothing. I couldn't wait. It was very near, very near. I switched the intercom to the command frequency and broke radio silence. I was abrupt, and I didn't identify myself.

"Group leader. I smell flak."

I half expected the group leader to blast me for breaking radio silence, if he acknowledged my warning at all. But his answer confirmed my fear. "Yes, I smell it too. I think it's up there about one o'clock. I'm moving the group north. Out."

The group had completed its turn to the left and had come up on the new course when the flak hit us. Most of it was concentrated around our high-right squadron. The colonel's turn had been too late to clear us completely. Three bursts exploded directly over us, and a spray of Plexiglas splattered against the instrument console. My left wingman was hit; flame was streaming from his right wing and it was beginning to envelop the forward section of the flight deck. There was no alternative for him: he pulled away from the formation, and the crew began to bail out. Before his plane fell below us in a banking dive to the right, I counted four chutes. I called the ball turret to follow him down.

"Pilot to ball. Watch him as he comes underneath us. Watch for chutes."

"Wilco . . . there he is. I've got him."

"Any more chutes?"

"No. He's all fire now . . . Oh, Jesus! The wing blew! Christ, he's bustin' up! He's busted in two! No chutes. Nothin'."

"Okay, ball. That's it. Out."

The flak couldn't have lasted more than a minute, and was probably the work of only one battery of from four to six guns. Eight hundred guns up at Ploesti hadn't touched us, and today one battery, in a matter of seconds, had taken Joe Carlson down. And it wasn't over yet.

"Tail to pilot. Over."

"Go ahead, tail."

"They've switched their fire over to a B-24 group behind us at about four o'clock. There's one plane down. No chutes. He took a direct hit. . . . Okay; it looks like they're clear now."

"Okay, tail. Out."

The group leader brought us back on our original course, and we continued on toward the sea. The high cirrus overcast had thickened; layers of stratus clouds were stretching into flat patterns of mist below us. We were beginning to pull thin vapor trails from our wingtips. I began to wonder about ice, and I checked the outside air temperature. It was two degrees below zero. I spoke to the copilot on the intercom. "Take it for a while, Jerry. Watch for ice."

"Roger. Want a little carburetor heat?"

"Yeah, put it on for a few minutes."

The gray sky closed around us; we flew between layers of clouds, and traces of frozen sleet raced over the top of the wing. As we flew south along the coast, the undercast thinned to shreds of mist, and the sea could be seen through it, wind-swept and troubled, beating against the land.

It had become a day without light, a drab leaden day where we were caught among flat broken clouds; shadows of rain hung below some of them like soiled curtains in the windows of an ill-kept house. Our engines roared against the wind that was striving to drive us back over the land. The city of Ortona drifted past off the tip of my right wing; low scud and fog tumbling in from the sea swept over it as I looked down, and it vanished. We followed the group leader in a gentle descent toward Lake Lesina. At twelve thousand feet we encountered turbulence, which was not severe but was enough to make me mindful of my wingmen bobbing up and down on either side of me. My left wingman, who had been flying in the seventh spot as tail-end Charlie, had now moved up to take Joe Carlson's position. I watched him for a moment with some resentment, as though his intrusion had driven my friend away. I wondered if Joe had made it. Probably not. There had been only four chutes. Joe would not have left the controls until all men were clear. . . .

"We're losing oil from number four." It was Jerry, the copilot, on the intercom. "No pressure drop. Do you want to feather it?"

"Is she running hot?"

"No. Not yet anyway."

"She must have ate some flak, but it may not be too bad. Let's see if we can get her in the way she is. If she starts to get hot or if the pressure drops, we'll shut her down."

"Roger." Jerry didn't say anything else but began to wipe the fragments of Plexiglas from the control console with his gloved hand. His oxygen mask was dangling free from his face. I could see his mouth moving. He was singing. When he saw me watching him he grinned, and he touched his throat mike to hold it secure before he spoke. "I can't compete," he said. He waved his arm in a sweeping gesture out toward the engines. His motion summoned them, and the sound around us seemed to swell in power. Even number four was in good voice, paying little heed to her wounds and the trailing streak of smoking oil behind her.

.   .   .

I have heard my engines since that day, down through all the years when a trick of time or memory catches me. I have heard them in an empty sky. I have heard them in familiar rooms. I have heard them coming in from the sea, roaring above the tumult of the surf. I have heard them in the night. I have heard them thundering over the land. I hear them still.

Chapter XIII

THE PO VALLEY, THE AZONS, AND A HOLIDAY

Does the road wind uphill all the way?
  Yes, to the very end.
Will the day's journey take the whole long day?
  From morn to night, my friend.

—CHRISTINA GEORGINA ROSSETTI
Uphill

Perhaps we needed some luck, or perhaps we needed another practice mission. We were making mistakes. Coming back from Ploesti over a week ago, we had carelessly wandered over Split and had been hammered by flak. Four days later, on our return from Piombino, we had blundered into a barrage south of the target, a flak area that Intelligence had failed to note on their charts. And two days after Piombino, our luck went sour again, although I thought it was not so much a matter of luck as it was a repeat of sloppy intelligence work that sent us on a course down the Po Valley after we rallied off the target.

We had attacked the marshaling yards at Brescia, a city east of Milan, to interdict transport being moved through to support the German Tenth Army. Flak over the target had been moderate, and after bombs away we had proceeded on a southeast course to the Po River Valley where we turned east to the delta and the safety of the Adriatic. We had entered the valley south of Verona when we encountered the first bursts.

It was accurate fire from heavy batteries, probably eighty-eights. The squadron leader broke our course to the left; at the same time he took us down in a shallow dive, trying to evade the flak. His number-three engine was smoking and it left a curling greasy banner behind him. The maneuver was successful; the explosions trailed off high and to our right. We were at sixteen thousand feet when we leveled off. We were too low, much too low.

The next minutes of flight were excruciatingly tense. We were approaching Ferrara and heading for the delta, that pristine land where there were no guns to challenge us. But between us and that haven was a wide belt of flak that extended south to Ravenna and as far north as Venice. I cursed the stupid bastards who had planned our return. We could have gone southwest over the Apennines to Leghorn and down the west coast. It would have been longer, but it was well within our range. As I stared through my windshield waiting for the first black explosion, the question raged in my mind: Why? Why had they sent us down this damn valley?

Flak sometimes rose with a certain languor out of the oppressive stillness of an empty sky; it appeared sometimes before you, black and ominous; it appeared sometimes above you or alongside, unhurried and indifferent to your presence, like a prowling animal without hunger; then we would pass by, wary but without fear. When we were caught in the Po Valley, it was not like that; it stormed out of the clear sky, ravenous and insatiable; black bursts were everywhere. We were consumed in an onslaught of flame and smoke. The squadron leader was now showing fire streaming out of the cowling of his number-one engine; number three had been feathered and was still smoking. "Break! For Christ's sake, break!" I shouted into my mike. I didn't have my button down so I knew no one heard me, but the squadron leader must have had the same idea.

"Second flight, break right," he yelled.

I took my flight down in a diving turn, heading for the hills on the south side of the valley. The leader headed north in a steep banking turn; his wingmen were shaken loose but they followed. The flak chased after us, adjusting to our evasive action.

"Tail to pilot!"

"Go ahead, tail."

"Charlie's in trouble!"

Three successive explosions erupted in a pall of black smoke over our number-two engine. The left wing shuddered in the concussion.

"Tail to pilot. He's breaking up! There's stuff comin' off his wing!"

Against the green background of the hills ahead of me, I could see the flashes of gunfire along the lower slope. I held the flight in a dive, heading for the crest of the high ground. When we reached it, I turned east, following the ridge. We leveled off at four thousand feet. The flak was falling behind us; two bursts blossomed off our left wing about three hundred yards away. We were out of it. I called the tail gunner on the intercom.

"Pilot to tail. Over."

"Tail. Over."

"Is tail-end Charlie still there?"

"Yeah, he's going to make it. . . . I think he is. Number one's feathered, and he had some fire from his right tip tank. It's out now. He looks okay."

"Okay, tail. Keep your eye on him."

"Roger. Out."

Across the river on the north side of the valley, I spotted the lead flight heading east. They were higher than we were at about five or six thousand feet. I made an easy bank to the left, holding my wingmen close, and boosted my manifold pressure and RPM. I trimmed nose high for a slightly climbing altitude. We were still four hundred yards behind the lead flight when we came to the delta, but we were slowly closing the gap. The copilot took the controls while I looked around, ostensibly for the rest of the group. They were nowhere in sight.

After the terror of an attack, whether it was fighters or flak didn't matter, there was a sublime peace, and I was always possessed by an unbounded serenity. There were no threads of fear clinging to my consciousness. As I accepted life again, I took it back in small draughts, which were of such savor and sweetness, I could not bear more than one small taste at first. If we were low enough, as we were today, there had to be a cigarette for ceremony, and then the flame of the lighter to begin the moment of celebration. I flavored the safe air with smoke, and blew it out in front of me with deep satisfaction.

Below me, the great alluvial plain, formed where the Po entered the Adriatic, stretched as far north and south as I could see. Far ahead it floundered into the great depths, and white-topped waves washed over it. Inland, away from the edge of the deep, the lush green land was veined by glistening streams branching away from the main course of the river. There were wide pools and lakes; some were shallow, and I could see long barriers of sea grass waving back and forth in a tireless rhythm beneath the surface.

We made our way out over the sea, away from the hostile land. We turned south for home. In the distance, although I could not see them clearly, I could make out what appeared to be three squadrons in a loose formation. If it were the group, we made no effort to catch up. Our squadron leader had two engines feathered; my number two was running rough and beginning to heat up; tail-end Charlie was

pretty well battered with his number one shut down and his right wing
damaged. We labored on a long journey down the coast until at last
we turned in over Lake Lesina toward Longskirt.

After Brescia, Paul and I had a week off. We caught up with our
letter writing, and Paul resumed his Italian studies with Tony, or with
Anthony, as Paul preferred to call him. When Tony came in the
morning to clean our tent, which was always about eleven o'clock,
Paul would be waiting for him and would plague him with questions
about pronunciation or grammar. For a sixteen-year-old boy, Tony
was remarkably patient. He did, however, sometimes turn to me,
rolling his eyes in desperation at Paul's tedious inquisition, or he would
kiss his hands and then throw them wide over his head as if to appeal
to heaven to save him from the relentless attention of my importunate
friend.

Tony was an exceptional boy: quick, and as intelligent as he was
persistently brave. He had been orphaned by the war. His father had
been killed in North Africa; his mother had been killed in an air raid
on Foggia a few days before the allied invasion. He had endured
tragedy; he had endured hunger and violence, but he would survive.
He had a warrior's soul.

He lived with a little girl about his own age somewhere in Foggia.
I had seen them on several occasions outside of the Red Cross Club
where Tony also worked in the late afternoons after he finished his
chores with the squadron. His girl washed our clothes and ironed our
suntans like a professional for only a few lire, which weren't worth a
damn anyway. She and Tony made their real profit from us in the
soap, cigarettes, and chocolate we gave them. When I had first seen
them together, shortly after Tony came to work for us in the squadron,
they had both been wretchedly thin and their poor unwashed bodies
had smelled rank and stale. Now they were prospering. They were
sleek and shining, and irrepressibly optimistic about life. Tony's girl
particularly manifested her hope for the future: she was pregnant. Her
young belly pressed out against her dress, and her large brown eyes
were bright with happiness.

Tony and his child inamorata were marvels. They could not wait
to live; they could not wait to embark upon the misadventures of passion
and enterprise. Through them I began to see Italy, not as a devastated
land, but as a renascence following the wake of the British and American armies in their agonizing journey up the peninsula. Where the
blood and pain of the armies passed, green shoots sprang from the

earth; out of the rubble and havoc of a sterile tyranny, life began again.

Paul, Jake Stoner, and I spent a day at the beach in Manfredonia where we didn't swim but walked a long way along the water's edge. We watched the sea foam up over the sand, flattening it smooth as each wave gave itself to the task. We watched gulls and terns. We idly picked up shells, then threw them away. We talked, and at the day's end we drank red wine with our pasta, listening with amazement to Paul's persistent attempts to converse in Italian with the old man who owned the café and the small flagstone terrace where we sat in the cool wind to watch the sea birds and the surf. The old man also owned our torn red canvas chairs, the uneven metal table that precipitously held our bottle of wine and our food, and the orange-and-white awning that flapped over our heads. He was a kind fellow; he smiled at Paul and pretended he understood him, nodding seriously when he thought he should.

There was one couple sitting on the terrace with us three tables away, a middle-aged man and his wife, who quietly sipped small cups of coffee, one after the other, while they stared out across the beach toward the sea. Their presence was a gentle one; a kind of courtly shyness held them from us, probably because we were strangers. There seemed to be a contentment between them so sure and serene that words need not be said. Or was it sorrow I sensed? The tired end of an old sadness they sought to wear away with peace and silence. I could not know. I was only sure they had been together for a long time.

On another day, Paul dragged us to Lucera where we wandered among the ruins of an old castle that had belonged to Fredrick the Second, a fact Paul made a point of stressing in case we should ever be asked about it in the future. He also showed us a cathedral which, he proudly announced, after puzzling over the words in a battered Italian guidebook, had been built in the very early years of the fourteenth century. He rattled on about the water supply in the town, and how it came from cisterns and wells built by the Romans. He was becoming tiresome; I didn't want to listen to him anymore.

I turned to Stoner. "When are you leaving, Ilyich?"

Before he could answer, Paul interrupted. "Why do you call Jake 'Ilyich' all the time?"

"Because he's a goddamn Communist," I answered impatiently. "Didn't you know that? His real name is Vladimir Ilyich Ulyanov. He's a big-time Russian spy. He's going to blow up Newark."

"No kiddin'," Paul said. "You've always got to be such a wise guy.

You could get Jake in trouble talking like that. What if somebody heard you that didn't know you were trying to be funny?"

"I don't know, Paul. I'd guess they'd have to line him up and shoot him."

Paul grinned. "They ought to shoot you, that's what they should do. You're so full of B.S." That was as close as Paul ever came to swearing. I was getting to him. Maybe I'd get a *damn* or a *hell* out of him one day.

Jake stopped our bickering by answering me. "I'm waiting for an ATC flight. It'll take a week or ten days, I guess. C'mon, let's go back to the jeep. It's getting late; besides, I'd like a belt." He looked up at the sky and said, "Yep, sun's over the yardarm."

We sat in the jeep for a while, taking turns with Jake's bottle of brandy. Paul had three drinks, and immediately became mellow. He put his arm around my shoulder and pronounced to the world, "This here is a good old boy, a good old boy—for a Yankee." He fell back in his seat, laughing uproariously at his performance. He took another swig from the bottle. On the short drive back to the squadron bivouac, we couldn't shut him up.

Our holiday ended on the seventh of May when we were sent to Bucharest to bomb the rail yards where a large number of tank cars had been assembled for shipment to Germany. Oil, whether it was transport, refineries, or storage, had become one of our main priorities. The target was well defended: flak was heavy, and we had a brush with thirty fighters. Although we sustained casualties, we were better off than the bombers that, two days prior to our mission, had gone to Ploesti. They dropped thirteen hundred tons on the rail yards and pumping stations, but it was not done without sacrifice. They lost nineteen bombers.

Three days after Bucharest, we went to the Wiener Neustadt area to hit the ME assembly and component works. The weather was poor with thick cloud formations and rain squalls hammering us all the way to the target. Over three hundred bombers, out of a total of seven hundred, never made it, and had to turn back. Those of us who were able to press through the towering cloud banks were met by German fighters about thirty minutes before we reached the IP. The fighters broke away when we entered the flak; they pounced on us again as we rallied after bombs away, persisting in their attacks all the way to the coast, where P-38s assigned to take us out joined us and took the MEs off our backs. The bomber groups that had made it to the target lost twenty-eight planes. The losses at Ploesti and Wiener Neustadt on the fifth and tenth of May, not counting severely damaged planes, were equivalent to a whole combat group.

The day after Wiener Neustadt, I was called to Operations to attend a special briefing. I had no idea of what it was about; I was certain it would be something unpleasant, and I reluctantly left my sack and my book. There was only a small group there: four pilots, four copilots, four flight engineers, and two briefing officers; one of them was Capt. Mike Salinas. The other officer, who was introduced to us as Major Corey, was a tall, diffident young man who peered at us over his coffee cup and through a haze of smoke curling up from a cigarette that dangled from the corner of his mouth. We all took coffee, and Mike began the briefing.

"We got a special assignment—for which you boys have just volunteered." He smiled. They always smiled when they were going to give you bad news. "We have a new gadget we're going to use tomorrow, a special kind of B-17 called an Azon. That's probably misleading because the plane's not special, just the bombsight and the six bombs, thousand-pound regular-purpose bombs. I'll let the major explain it. If you will, Major?"

Corey took the cigarette out of his mouth and placed it in an ashtray. He held his coffee, sipping it occasionally while he briefly outlined what Mike referred to as a gadget.

"All you fellows have to know is that we have a device that can control—to a limited degree—the azimuth track of a thousand-pound bomb after it leaves the airplane. We can't control the forward rate; that is still a function of your airspeed. The Azon transmitter, responding to the bombardier's adjustment to his sight as he observes the falling bombs, can, by its electrical signals, vary the pitch of the bombs' stabilizing fins, causing the missiles to drift to the left or right. With this device, your bombardier can reduce your deflection error— not by much, but enough to be very effective on a narrow target that you're likely to straddle . . . like a bridge." Major Corey grinned and paused to light another cigarette before he went on.

"Now, as I understand it, you fellows have been assigned to fly lead for your respective squadrons tomorrow. Everything will be the same for you except one thing: instead of an immediate rally after bombs away, you must hold your course steady for a number of seconds equal to the actual time of fall of your bomb. This will give your bombardier the opportunity to control the lateral movement of the bomb on its way down to the target. The other planes in your squadron will, as usual, drop when you drop. Only the squadron lead planes will be carrying Azon bombs. Your bombardiers, who are not present this afternoon because they have already been briefed on this technique, will advise you tomorrow, after your mission briefing, on the length of time you must hold your heading after bombs away. Any questions?" There were none. What we were required to do seemed plain enough. I would have liked to ask what the target would be; those extra seconds on a straight and level course could be bad news over a tough target, but I knew such a question would not be answered.

Mike took over for the major. "There's one more thing," he said. "There's another wrinkle, a job you've got to do before tomorrow."

A captain from one of the other squadrons standing beside me said dryly, "There always is."

Mike ignored the captain's remark and carried on. "For security reasons, the Azon planes are kept at Foggia Main Airfield, where they have been loaded and preflighted. Now we'll have to truck you fellows over there to fly them back here to Longskirt—this afternoon. I don't have to spell it out; the planes will be heavy, very heavy for your landing." He added grimly, "If you never made a good landing in your life, you'd better make one this afternoon." He smiled that damn smile again. "Anyone who busts up one of these planes is going to be in serious trouble." Nobody laughed. "Okay," Mike said. "The truck's outside. Let's go."

We brought the four Azon planes in around six o'clock without incident. They were beautiful new machines with new unscarred tires, which made me feel more secure about landing, though I made every effort, combined with prayer, to touch down on the steel mat as gently as possible. I touched tail first and held the main gear off as long as I could, letting the tail wheel assume some of the load while the wing still had enough lift to ease the balance of her full weight onto the runway. When the main gear hit and we began to roll, I held my breath. A blown tire now, with ammo and fuel and six one-thousand-pound bombs on board, would be disaster, one that I would only briefly be aware of before my parts spectacularly joined the universe to whirl around until God's whim might put them together again. She rolled smoothly to the end of the strip, and I taxied to the stand where a concerned crew chief took her from me. I went to evening mess happy and hungry; something else had been put behind me.

On the following morning of what promised to be a clear day, we headed for the Avisio viaduct, a target a few miles north of Trento, an inaccessible place buried in the Dolomite Mountains. The viaduct itself was a long, narrow structure and a vulnerable link in the rail transport system coming down through the Brenner Pass. We had been there before with mixed results. It was a difficult target to hit; even with a tight intervalometer setting or a salvo, the bombs seemed inclined to straddle the bridge. On occasions when we did hit it, we apparently didn't hit it well enough to knock it out; the Germans always had it back handling traffic within a week or two. But today would be different; the Azon bombs would do it, or so they told us at briefing.

Our group was alone; the other four groups of the Fifth Wing and the B-24s were standing down. It was a 301st show; the Azon bombs were dedicated only to the Avisio viaduct. The sun was strong; its rays slanted down through our formation to the sea below us, where its light struck the spray and was shattered into fragments of fragile iridescence. Over our heads, the sky was a pale blue pavilion that stretched as far as we could see. But we were unmindful of the day; our vision held something else; an image of a long bridge hiding in the mountains.

After three hours of flight, we reached the IP. There were no fighters. A black cloud of flak came up on cue, as we knew it would; it drifted over us and and then with deliberate malevolence it adjusted to our altitude. Four bursts exploded off my left wing, following me like the rage of a vicious black dog. We made our run in a column of four squadrons so each Azon lead plane could aim and bomb the target independently. The mass of flak moved off to our right, and each of the squadrons completed its run by the grace of indifferent gunnery that floundered around the sky vainly searching for us. When my bombardier released me to rally, I took the squadron down in an easy turn to the left. Below I could see plumes of smoke rising from the gorge under the center of the bridge. The bridge itself was obscured by the smoke; I could not tell whether we had hit it or not.

The journey home was peaceful, a long letdown with the engines purring softly in air as smooth as glass. It had been a good mission without much trouble, which in my measure of victory, was a glorious one. As it turned out, and in spite of my uninterest in the results, our Azon bombs had made four direct hits on the viaduct; we had put a seventy-foot gap in it. Intelligence told us the Avisio bridge would be out of service for a long time; of course this didn't prove to be the case. The Germans had it back in operation in ten days.

Chapter XIV

OLD FRIENDS REMEMBERED

We are but warriors for the working-day;
Our gayness and our gilt are all besmirch'd
With rainy marching in the painful field;
There's not a piece of feather in our host . . .

—WILLIAM SHAKESPEARE
Henry V, Act IV, Scene 3

The squadron had changed. The old men were gone; I knew very few of the new men. Major Billings had been transferred to a staff job in wing headquarters. I seldom had a chance to talk with Jim Ewell; when he wasn't flying he was buried with routine chores in Operations. My friendship with Paul had its limits: as much as we depended on one another, we could not refrain from endless disagreements, which were about trivial things we mutually used to nag the peace and the affection that bound us. Jake Stoner would be leaving soon. Mike Salinas was totally occupied with his engineering work and the endless labor required to keep us in the air. Whether I preferred it or not, I found myself alone much of the time.

I wandered in the streets of Foggia, or I sat in the Red Cross Club pushing a spoon around in a dish of tasteless ice cream, finally leaving it untouched to return to the street. On many of the days when I wasn't flying, I never left the squadron area, and it became less and less of an imperative for me to spend my time in any particular way. Books that always had been a comfort to me were a burden to read; I looked at the pages, and the words, which once had been so wise, so full of beauty and meaning to me, were now unable to lift me from the obscene trough where I plodded in a montonous pilgrimage. What destination I would come to no longer mattered. Even letters from home awakened nothing more than a vague recollection of the past, a past that was fading from me; it was as though they were speaking of someone else, and I had no right to read what they had written down. Sometimes I thought about the old men who were gone: Mac, Coursey, Bernie, Turner, and all the others. I didn't think about the new men who were killed, or of their flaming falls to earth, although I pretended to for form's sake. I never knew them and I could not remember their faces or their names. It didn't matter. I had become a good soldier, worn and hard at last. I remembered nothing. I wanted nothing. I believed in nothing. I lived as they told me to live. All they had to do was to tell me where to go, and I would go there. I would do what they told me I had to do.

After our activity in the north where we had worked over tactical targets to harass German transport moving down into Italy, we returned to our strategic tasks in the east. We went back into the oil business. On May 18, seven hundred bombers started out from their bases for Nis, Belgrade, and Ploesti. Only two hundred and six got through. The weather turned out to be in the enemy's favor, and the larger part of our force had to turn back. There were dense clouds towering up to thirty thousand feet. Rain squalls, severe turbulence, ice, and very limited visibility raised havoc with the group and wing formations. The groups that reached their targets made their bomb runs in the adverse circumstances of rough air and gray mists streaming across everything below them. We had hoped the weather would keep the German fighters from us, but they were there. The radar-controlled flak batteries were hampered little by the lack of visibility, and they took their toll. Between the two, our groups lost fourteen bombers; two more, we could not verify, were presumed lost in a collision somewhere around Nis. It was a high price for what we did that day. All in all, we dropped less than five hundred tons. At Ploesti the 463rd claimed they had some luck with hits on the Americano Romano Refinery. At Belgrade and Nis, I didn't think we hit a damn thing, except perhaps for a few cows and some foolish civilians who may have thought they were safe ten miles from the target.

I had five days off before we went back to Avisio, the enchanted viaduct that like the phoenix rose from its ashes every time we bombed it. This time there would be no Azon planes, though I didn't believe it would make any difference. It was too narrow a target for high-altitude work. I felt it should have been put on hold until the low-level fighter bombers from the Twelfth could have been put within range to pound it around the clock. Besides, fighters were fond of trains and bridges, particularly trains. Even our escort, although they would deny it, sometimes yielded to the temptation to abandon us for a quick dive on a train caught in the open.

The evening before the Avisio mission, Major Devereaux called Jim Ewell and me to his hut where he startled us by announcing, in an abrupt and arbitrary way, that we were to complete our tours in thirty-five missions rather than fifty. Knowing I hadn't heard all of it, I waited for the major to drop the other shoe.

"You'll go home after thirty-five for a thirty-day leave," he said. He watched us for a few moments, looking for a reaction.

Jim spoke quietly. "And then what, sir?"

"Well, then you come back and finish your tour—but for the last fifteen, you fly squadron lead only. Probably no more than one mission a week. I need experienced squadron leaders. You know that better than anyone, Jim. That botched-up mess at Belgrade was a disgrace—an absolute disgrace."

Jim and I were both silent. We couldn't decide whether what was happening was good or bad. We had been in the Army long enough to be wary.

The major went on. "Let's see. Lieutenant Muirhead, you have completed about twenty—right?"

"Yes, sir. Something like that."

"And, Jim?"

"Twenty-two, sir," Jim said.

"Very good." The major smiled and reached out and shook hands with each of us. "I know you can do the job. We'll discuss it later in more detail. That'll be all for now."

After we left and were outside, I asked Jim, "What do you think?"

He hesitated before he said, "I don't know. I guess I hate the thought of going home for thirty days, and then coming back to this." He waved his arm to include everything around us and beyond us.

I knew what he meant. This was a special place, a world apart from the one back home. We would carry it with us; we would be unable to leave it. It would be a haunting presence that would foul every moment: every kiss, every embrace, every minute of what might have been joy or peace would be soiled. Those we loved would be saddened and would wonder why we drank so much, or why we laughed at such strange things. They would try to understand, but they would not see the specter following us, brooding and waiting for us to turn back so it could settle its claim.

As Jim started to leave for Operations, I called after him, "Just who the hell was leading at Belgrade anyway?"

"Oh, some asshole from wing staff," Jim yelled back. "A guy named Barnard, Major Barnard. He wanted a silver star or some goddamn thing, so they set it up for him to lead. That's what I heard. See you later." Jim waved and walked away.

The Germans were not surprised when we arrived at Avisio. They were waiting for us. The flak was murderous. We didn't lose a plane on the bomb run, but we had one man killed and four wounded. On the way back, one of our planes that was badly shot up gave up the ghost between Rimini and Anconia; it ditched in the sea. Two P-38s circled low over the downed B-17 and confirmed that eight men in two life rafts were paddling toward the shore. If they were lucky, they would end up with the partisans.

Two days after Avisio, we went on a long haul to Avignon in southern France. It turned out to be a routine mission, but an intolerably exhausting one. Nine hours of formation flying, and the last three hours in very rough air, wore me into a stupor of fatigue. My flight suit was stained with sweat; my eyes burned, and my arms and wrists were responding to my mind's command in a sluggish way I could not control. I watched in listless horror at my wingmen bouncing up and down on either side of me, knowing they were as tired as I was. What a stupid way to die, I thought; just too damned weary to get out of someone's path. The last hour was interminable. When I was finally on my blessed approach to the runway, I knew I would make the worst landing of my life. I did.

Chapter XV
D DAY AND FALSE HOPE

Soldiers are citizens of death's gray land,
  Drawing no dividend from time's tomorrows.
In the great hour of destiny they stand,
  Each with his feuds, and jealousies, and sorrows.

—SIEGFRIED SASSOON

Before Paul and I went to our tent, we stopped by Sergeant Chambers's office to pick up our mail. I had a letter from Jean, one from my mother, and one from my brother Bruce. Bruce was my second older brother, and from the time when we were all very young, Bruce was the talented one; Sandy was always the intellectual, while my claim to notoriety as a boy was pretty much based on my bad temper and a penchant for trouble. As one of Sandy's friends put it, "Jackie's got more nerves than brains. He'll never live to be twelve." This particular assessment of my early character was made after I had picked a fight with an older and stronger boy named Pete Kelsey. The fact that I was impudent enought to challenge Pete in a way that left him no alternative except to pummel me was typical of my rashness then, and was only one of many incidents that made my boyhood precarious. Sandy scorned my folly; my mother prayed I would mend my ways; my father shrugged his shoulders, knowing time would ease my madness, and I would change; my younger sister giggled at my misdeeds, but would cry when I was hurt. Only Bruce would indulge me. He patched me when I was bloodied; when I was made outcast by the others, Bruce would comfort me by drawing pictures, especially of horses. I loved horses.

Although Bruce still enjoyed painting, when he could find the time, he was now fully committed to his work as an electrical designer at the shipyard. But when he wrote me a letter he returned to his old kindness, and his letter was always in the manner by which he had charmed me out of my misery and tears when I was a very young boy. He knew my troubled spirit now as he had known it then. He drew pictures for me.

When I was in the tent and settled on my cot, I chose to look at Bruce's letter first. After the long trek to Avignon, I knew I would not be able to concentrate on Jean's letter or my mother's before falling asleep; I would save them for after evening mess; then I would be able to take my time reading them while I sipped my second cup of coffee. I opened Bruce's letter for a quick look: there were two white sheets of paper covered with small drawings, all sequenced to remind me of the unchanged patterns of home. Bruno, the cat, was there, troublesome and spoiled, and so real I wanted to put out my hand to stroke him; my father was in his special chair reading the paper, as he always did in the evening after dinner; Sandy was grumbling about something, and Mary, Bruce's wife, was smiling at him; my mother was in her domain, the kitchen, squinting in a concerned way at something cooking on the stove; my young sister was sitting primly in a chair showing off a new dress. . . .

"You got some pictures from your brother?" Paul asked.

"I thought you were asleep," I said.

"Naw," Paul answered. "Not yet. Can I see them?"

"Yeah, in a minute."

It would be the same as it always was with Paul. He would look at the drawings, and I would have to tell him about each scene, who each person was, what they were doing, how old they were, and on and on. He would then say precisely what he said the last time, "I wish I could draw like that." I gave Paul the two sheets from Bruce's letter and closed my eyes. Before I fell asleep, I heard him. "Now which one is this? Is this your father?"

We had a day off after Avignon, a quiet day I spent writing letters in the morning and playing bridge in the afternoon. Though I played bridge, I didn't play well and was always a reluctant choice to fill in to make a foursome. I had a poor memory for cards, or an indifferent one, which put a strain on a series of partners who swore they would never play with me again. The Culbertson point system for evaluating one's hand was never entirely clear to me; neither was the Blackwood convention for bidding slams. I chose a cavalier approach to the game that always ended up provoking a violent reaction from across the table.

"Jesus! What are you leadin' spades for? He hasn't got any! He's goin' to trump it! Can't you count, for Christ's sake?" Or when I was dummy and put my cards down on the table for my partner to play. "Holy shit! You bid two hearts on that? We're goin' to go down! We're goin' to get set! We coulda' made three no trump! Why the hell didn't you bid no trump? Look at the distribution, for Christ's sake!"

Paul used to kibitz when I played; he enjoyed my humiliation. On this particular day, he was so pleased with my poor performance he bought me two drinks. When I finished my second, I said to him, "C'mon Paul, let's check the orders. If I'm not flying tomorrow, I think I'll go down to the RAF club tonight. They owe me some scotch; I gave them a gallon of grapefruit juice a couple of days ago."

We were both on the orders for tomorrow's mission. We went to early mess, and each of us was silent afterward as we read our letters with our coffee. When we were back in the tent, I read a few pages of Carlyle and became lost in the long sentences. I kept reading the same words over and over again. It was very quiet. A light breeze brushed across my face. I wondered for a moment where we would be going in the morning. Sleep took me into a deep and still place. There were no dreams. There was nothing . . . nothing.

When we were to fly a mission, morning came in its ordinary way; it came at the end of night in the darkness, in the fumbling of rising, of pissing and grumbling. It came in our pitiful challenge to this dreary beginning with the probing glow of our cigarettes that marked each shadow moving toward the mess hut. It came with the clatter of plates, with vapor swirling up from coffee mugs; it came with the rustling, murmuring sound of sullen men moving. It came with the rumble of trucks and with the whining protestation of engines in low gear. It came with the bang of tailboards dropping, with the cheerful curses of drivers, and with the slap of a cloth escape purse being placed in your hand. It came with urgent pleas to hurry. It came with the lurching, bouncing ride to a briefing. When you looked up at last from your quaking misery in the truck and saw the first light in the eastern sky, it was then you knew the night had ended and day was at hand.

It was to be the Wiener Neustadt area again. Over one hundred B-24s were to hit the ME assembly plant; another force of B-24s of equal strength was to hit the ME component factory at Atzgerdorf. Our group, which was to be part of a third force of three hundred bombers, would attack the Wollersdorf airdrome. At briefing they warned us we could expect German fighters to be around the targets in strength, particularly at Wollersdorf. The Germans knew we wanted to finish the destruction of all of the manufacturing installations around Wiener Neustadt; they were battered now, and perhaps this mission would close them down, though I had my usual reservations about such optimism.

The weather was fair. We climbed slowly on a northern heading, reaching twenty-two thousand feet before we made our landfall west of Pola. We were over two hours on course when we passed the city of Graz and picked up some light flak. The bursts were off to our right. Our formations were untouched and we pressed on to the IP. The first pass from German fighters came in high over our squadron; they were heading for a B-24 group ahead of us. There were more fighters swarming at ten o'clock. We reached the IP without being attacked, and we entered the alley for our run.

A barrage of explosions leaped up in my windshield. Suddenly there was something else: a flaming ME-110 was sitting in front of me! His left wing began to lift and it separated from the fuselage. The plane disappeared; where it had been an instant before was now a twisting torch, a violent incendiary blasting the air with fire and black smoke. The burning mass fell beneath us. The left wing drifted down after it like a benediction following the pyre; it fell in a gentle, spiraling pattern of unhurried motion that repeated itself again and again.

Shreds from the dark clouds of flak blew past us. I watched the group leader, waiting for his bombs to drop; the gleaming metal of his plane seemed to shield it and it scorned the black bursts. My usual stream of sweat was blinding me. With my right hand on the outboard throttles and my left hand holding the wheel, I couldn't rub my eyes. I squinted and blinked to ease the irritation. The bombs dropped from the leader's plane, and I heard my bombardier's voice on the intercom. "Bombs away! Let's get the hell out of here!"

We rallied left off the target, and I waited for the fighters to hit us. We flew on toward the towering mountains between us and the sea. Six MEs came in from twelve o'clock, but they broke away beyond six hundred yards. Their tracers drifted in lazy curves down toward two o'clock.

"Hey, see that? Over about eleven o'clock?" It was the top turret. "Those bastards are going after that straggler, the sons of bitches."

I could see the B-24. It was alone with one engine feathered, and it was trailing smoke. It was like watching an execution. The German fighters attacked in pairs, setting up a leisurely pattern as though they were on a practice range lobbing shells at a lone target. The bomber began to flame; fire was streaming out of the port wing.

The top turret's voice was pleading. "Get out! For Christ's sake, get out!" As if in answer to him, a white chute blossomed below the bomber. Then another, and another. Two ME-109s were boring in to finish the job; this time they went in all the way, slamming shells into the crippled plane at point-blank range. The fighters flipped over in a half roll as they broke away, and headed down in a straight dive to the deck. They cleared just in time. The B-24 blew, a staggering blast of flame and smoke. Pieces of burning debris fell out of the dark spreading cloud that now loomed before us. There were no more chutes.

Our group continued on its southward journey. The formation was tight and in good order. There was one plane missing from the high-right squadron; there was an empty spot in the second flight of our squadron. The group deputy leader was showing a brown string of smoke from a feathered engine. But we were still very much in business, and I could feel every gunner's rage as I watched the departing ME-109s turn to small dark specks in the west. I could understand why they had gone after the straggler; it was an easy kill. Had they come at us, we would have made the bastards earn their pay.

The top turret's voice came on the intercom again. "Little Friends at three o'clock, coming in. Boy, ain't they pretty!"

They were P-51s, the new long-range models, and they were pretty. They flew over us, crossing our formation in graceful turns. They stayed until we were near the sea, and then they turned back toward the northeast, probably to look for other stragglers who might be summoning them with their prayers, and who, if found, would bless them every day, even to the day when they would be old, old men.

When we were back at our base, I didn't inquire about the plane that hadn't returned, except to verify that I didn't know the pilot or any of the crew. I sought to isolate myself from such things, which was a hopeless posture of evasion I persisted in trying to maintain. If I didn't know them, I would not grieve. If I didn't speak to them, I would not remember or recall whether they were fair or dark, or whether I liked them or disliked them. I would not remember. Today twenty bombers in our combined force had been shot down; two more were missing. To a military statistician, these might be acceptable losses; those of us who flew the mission saw them in a different way. If all the men on a mission were killed except oneself, the losses would be acceptable; if all survived except oneself, they would not be so. For if I died, the whole earth died, the sun, the stars, the sky, and every living thing. Each one of us saw the game that way. It was a kind of Russian roulette we played, and we pulled the trigger fifty times, or as many times as we could.

In this strange life, we lived in the narrow dimension of the present. We didn't seek the future, for it was not there; and if we could not move into it or beyond it, we could not return to our past. We were dull and listless, but we did not have the true languor of young men whose dreams were of worlds ahead of them, and who saw the present only as prelude to it.

If we were without dreams, without a past or a future, and were caught in the stillness of the present, our vision then became wise. There was peace in the absence of clamor; there was serenity in the days without battles. If this tattered place where we lived were to be the full measure of our lives, we would find some sweetness in it. A small mouse nibbling a piece of biscuit in my tent was as wondrous as a unicorn. The soiled streets of Foggia were full of light, and one time when I was walking there, I heard the pure voice of a woman singing. I learned each day of the goodness of life. I cherished what was given to me, holding it just for the moment it was given, for I knew it was fragile and could not be held for long.

The day after the Wollersdorf mission we joined a small force of fifty-six bombers and flew to Zagreb to bomb the marshaling yards, while a large force went back to finish off Wiener Neustadt, that stubborn place like Avisio that kept rising from its ashes. Three missions in four days was wearing, on my shabby mask of courage and on my buttocks and back as well. I had two painful creases on my bottom where my chute harness had grown into my flesh; my lower back in the area of my kidneys was sore and sensitive, which was aggravated by long hours of formation flying in subzero temperatures but was initially caused by a violent spasm of fear at Avignon when my body tried to twist itself inside out to get out of the way of a flak burst in front of my plane.

After a few days of rest, the squadron went up to Vado in northern Italy, and on the next day we went to Turin Severin in Rumania. On the way back from Turin, halfway across the Adriatic, radio silence was broken, and we received the heartening news of the invasion across the English Channel and the landings on the Normandy beaches. It was the sixth of June. The second front had opened up at last. We were flying loose at the time, relaxed and pleased that the mission had gone well. The Italian coast was within sight. The news shook us out of our sloth, and we began to pull the formation together. The radio was blaring martial music over the command frequency. When we crossed the coastline and I felt the thermal bump that marked the precise point where the land met the sea, the formation was in splendid order. Every plane was in its place, holding steady in its position as a matter of great pride. For the first time in months, I felt the overwhelming sweep of an emotion other than fear. Through my exultation and joy, I felt a surging pity for their pain. I saw them coming out of the sea; I heard the piercing cries of men dying on the beaches. Another day, another long sorrow of marches and battles, another had begun.

After landing, Paul and I headed directly for Squadron Operations with Captain Salinas, who picked us up at our planes. I gave my B-5 bag and my gear to the crew chief, asking him to turn it in for me as I ran toward Mike's jeep. We didn't go to debriefing and Ewell would probably ream us for our sin, but that didn't seem important. We needn't have worried; Ewell was in the hut with Sergeant Chambers and both were listening to a large liaison radio that sat like a squat deity of gleaming knobs and lights on a conference table in the center of the room. We were devout and crouched in front of it, but not before grabbing mugs of coffee as quietly as we could, taking a quick sip as we settled down to listen for news of our comrades in the west.

The information was sparse, and probably it was deliberate at this early stage of the operation. The American First Army had established beachheads somewhere, we guessed, in the area of St. Laurent; the British Second Army was somewhere on their left. Both British and American airborne divisions were in the action, but they were not identified. The allied air forces were maintaining complete air superiority; at this, all of us in the room cheered and banged our coffee mugs on the table. The invasion had been preceded by a massive naval bombardment, and that was about all the information we could get. The same words were repeated at regular intervals, and these intervals were separated by the prolonged crackling din of military music that started my back aching again. My coffee was cold; I kept lighting one cigarette after another.

I finally said to Paul, "Let's go. We won't hear anything new for a while."

Paul followed me outside, and we started to walk toward our tent. He looked at me curiously and asked, "Did you see that plane go down today up in the lead squadron?" Without waiting for my answer, he added, "That was one of ours—Jesse Lacky. He was a spare. He filled in for some guy who aborted just before we rendezvoused with the wing."

"I didn't know him. Was he new?"

"No," Paul said. "He was around for a while. It didn't look like anybody got out. You don't seem to know anybody anymore."

"So?"

"It's not right. Have you seen Pete around lately?"

"No," I said. "Come to think of it, I haven't."

"He was killed at Bucharest—over three weeks ago."

"Pete? Sergeant Petrosky?"

"Yes."

"Jesus, Paul, I didn't know."

"Did you know we got three men in the hospital with malaria?"

"No."

"Are you taking your Atabrine?"

"Yes—well, most of the time."

"You flew a good lead today. Did you know any of your crew?"

"Nope."

Paul shook his head. "You're bonkers," he said. "You're bonkers."

"Yeah, but I'm a helluva bridge player."

"Yeah," Paul grunted. "Sure you are."

The men who had flown with me had all done well, and it was to my satisfaction that I didn't have to know them. It allowed me some imagined freedom of conscience. But perhaps Paul was right; perhaps I was becoming pathological about it.

It didn't matter. It would be over for me soon. The idea of flying thirty-five missions and then going home for a thirty-day leave had become agreeable to me. To come back to fly fifteen more as squadron lead shouldn't be too bad. It always took time for orders to come through, and there were always delays in transport. Maybe they'd send me back by boat—a slow boat. I'd be much better when I came back; Paul wouldn't have to worry about me. Things would be quieter. All I had to do was make the thirty-five. Only eight more. I should be able to do it by the end of June surely. . . .

The Pola sub pens needed our attention again. We went up there with a small force of fifty-two bombers, escorted by P-47s, or Jugs as we called them. They were a freshmen fighter group, the 332nd, an all-Negro outfit new to escort duty. When they joined us, precisely at the time they were supposed to, it was a spectacular rendezvous. I had just looked at my watch wondering where they were, and I was considering the likelihood they were chasing trains or engaged in some similar frivolity that fighters preferred to sharing our plodding progress, when suddenly the air was full of P-47s, diving and whirling through our formations. They were under us, over us; they were ahead of us, peeling up in lazy aileron rolls. They were everywhere. But within minutes, they were formed about five hundred feet above our planes, throttled back in a prim, decorous line that crossed back and forth in a serpentine pattern with each Jug's monstrous Pratt & Whitney engine sniffing the tail of the plane it followed. Once established in their positions, the 47s never left us. When we reached the IP, they showed no inclination to turn away from the flak rising up ahead. I couldn't believe it.

If we were fortunate and had fighters escorting us to the target, we would have thought them mad if they followed us down the bomb run. They never did. They sensibly left us before we reached the IP, and gave the alley between the IP and the target a wide berth. But these fellows stayed. They flew through the clouds of bursting shells with deliberate aplomb, sharing the fearful passage with us as though they were performing a routine duty guarding us from any German fighters who might dare to presume we were vulnerable. It was a grand gesture, for they must have known that enemy fighters would no more enter into the barrage than would our own; they would always wait for us to come out of it, and then they would greet us. Perhaps the rashness of our black friends stemmed from their not being totally familiar with bombing procedure or with the precise extent of their responsibilities as escorts, although I did not think either was the case. It seemed to me they knew what they were doing. Their insouciance was too brazen, their contempt for any part of the sky, except the corridor directly over our bomb run, was too brave a choice for me to remember them in any way but as the best of the shepherds.

We were on our way up the Adriatic again. It was a perfect day, and the forecast for the Munich area was for an open sky, which meant the fighters would have every opportunity to play their games. I would have been pleased to see the 332nd P-47s overhead, but that was our luck yesterday, a century ago; today we were on our own and it didn't appear we would have cover going in. Three squadrons of P-38Js streamed past heading north, going somewhere in a hurry. I watched them for a long time, until I could only see the shimmer of sunlight reflecting from their belly tanks, and then they disappeared. It was

going to be a long haul; it would take at least four hours before we reached the target.

The great harbor of Venice went under my left wing, and we crossed the coastline east of Lido di Lesolo, holding our heading until we passed Cortina. The mountains below us were magnificent, great towering wind-swept crags that invited us beyond them to the west where they held the quiet haven of Switzerland. Many crews had gone in there to be interned for the duration; a few of them had to, but many were men who sought to live another day by any means and had no compunction about feathering a good engine and limping down in this pitiful deceit to live forever among the lotus eaters. Although they received their full pay and had the run of the place, it wasn't quite heaven. There was an eleven o'clock curfew, and the poor lads and their girls had to be in their apartments by ten or they were punished by having certain privileges taken from them. Probably they were not allowed to screw on Tuesday nights, or some other equally austere denial was imposed upon them.

The attack on Munich was to be made from the north. We were to pass east of the city and then wheel in a one-hundred-eighty-degree turn to begin our bomb run. As we approached the Munich area and adjusted our heading north to reach the IP, I had a clear view of the target. What I saw over it terrified me. There were fifty or more dark shapes prowling through the sky around the city. They were ME-109s. They were waiting for us. But what the hell were they waiting for?

The top turret called me. "Turret to pilot. Over."

"Yeah, go ahead."

"Are those MEs, sir?"

"Yes, I'm pretty sure."

"Jesus."

"Left waist to pilot. Over."

"Go ahead."

"Hey, they ain't 109s! The're P-51s! They're 51s, for Christ's sake! Yahoo!"

I stared hard across the sky at the fighters, cursing myself for again not having binoculars with me. I caught the flash of a square-tipped wing, and then the unmistakable configuration of the tail. The waist gunner was right. The silhouette was similar to the 109, but he was right. They were 51s! They were covering the target!

We began our long sweeping turn back toward the city. Below my low wing on the inside of the turn, I saw a gleaming pattern of light falling slowly down between us and our target, the airfield on the eastern edge of the urban area. I was puzzled for a moment, and I thought it was some phenomenon of sunlight refracting in the cool, dense air. It was chaff. Of course, it was chaff: thousands of strips of shining silver paper used to confuse radar impulses from the flak batteries were twisting and tumbling in the path of the radar signals and shielding us from their search. Some brave boys had made a run ahead of us, and had dropped tons of the stuff. The group came level and straight out of its half-circle turn; we began our attack.

The first bursts exploded in front of us high and to our left. The copilot tapped my shoulder. He pointed to his side window, and I leaned forward to look past him. There were three groups flying in parallel with us; behind them another wing formation followed. The flak now was reaching across the line of advancing bombers. The sky was crowded with bursts of flame and dark smoke. Fear, my gray-faced companion whose stinking sweat shamed me, was with me again. I could not pray. How could I when we were dropping frags? The explosions wavered on our side of the echelon, becoming more intense in the center of the wing. A B-17 wrapped in flame and black smoke slanted down ahead of us in a steep dive. I felt my plane shudder with relief, and I watched clusters of fragmentation bombs fall past the open doors of the group leader's bomb bay.

My bombardier's voice sounded casual. "Bombs away."

We rallied left. As we came off the target, I could see P-51s. They were high ahead of us, about a thousand feet above our formation. I watched them wheel and soar, waiting like hawks on a summer day, waiting for something to kill.

It was too soon to relax; the gunners tracked every quadrant of the sky. I turned the plane over to the copilot while I listened to the crew check in with the bombardier. There were no casualties. There was no battle damage except for a few holes in the horizontal stabilizer.

A stream of white smoke trailing what looked like a silver projectile shot up through the formation! Christ, they were firing rockets at us! White puffs followed the thing as it twisted in a turn and hurtled down toward the group below us.

"Waist to pilot! Waist to pilot! Jesus, it's one of those new rocket fighters—some new kind of ME! Hey, tail, he's goin' into your zone."

The tail gunner yelled on the intercom, "He's headin' for the group behind us! Christ, he went right through the formation! He didn't hit a fuckin' thing! Jeez, he's almost out of sight!" The gunner's voice was shrill with excitement.

The bombardier came on the intercom. "Okay. Okay. He's shot his bolt. He won't be back."

I called the bombardier. "Joe, what the hell was that?"

"I don't know, Jack. Some new fighter, I guess. Maybe one of those ME-262s they briefed us about." Joe's voice was indifferent; he sounded almost bored. "Don't worry about 'em," he said. "They only got a few of them, and they've got no range. One pass, and that's it. Okay?"

"Yeah, okay, Joe. Out."

We moved on unchallenged in a quiet sky, and in time we reached the sea. We held our altitude until we were beyond the Po delta. A mild turbulence along the coast ruffled our descent; it made me feel giddy, like a boy riding a sled down a hill of hard-packed snow. When we were low enough to come off oxygen, the flight engineer handed me a half-filled cup of coffee. I held it carefully and watched the surface of brown liquid make its tiny storm in resonance with the turbulent air. I considered how I might drink it without spilling any of the precious stuff. It became imperative for me to have the coffee. Suddenly the air became smooth; the liquid in the cup was placid and still. I quickly took a swallow. It hadn't cooled; it tasted fine.

I thought about the mission; it could have been much worse. And the presence of so many of our fighters that far north promised a better future for us. I began to see a budding hope in the events of the day and, like all selfish men, I saw the flowering of it in my deliverance. We had attacked a major German city with five hundred bombers. I found out later we had lost only thirteen. I was charitable enough to feel a brief pang of sadness for the one hundred and thirty men who were gone, but it was truly a brief sorrow and didn't lessen the joy I felt because I was alive. It was the luck of the game. Everything was going to be better from now on. I knew it was. I took another drink of my coffee and lit a cigarette. The weather was splendid; there were just a few shreds of stratus clouds stretched flat across the blue sky. We turned in to the coast and headed home.

Of course I was wrong about everything. In the next six weeks, for the last two weeks of June through the end of July, the Fifteenth lost nearly four hundred bombers, over a third of its force. Over Ploesti alone, in seven savage missions, one hundred and thirty bombers were shot down. In this period of crisis, over thirty-five missions were flown, and all but a few were hard and bloody. It was a bitter time, though I saw little of it, for I was among the first to fall.

Chapter XVI

BAD WEATHER AND JAKE'S LAST DAY

I have been laughing, I have been carousing,
Drinking late, sitting late, with my bosom cronies—
All, all are gone, the old familiar faces.

—CHARLES LAMB
The Old Familiar Faces

After Munich, I completed my thirtieth mission with a sortie to Sme-
derevo in Yugoslavia, where we hit a refinery and tank-car marshaling
yard complex. We left a great column of smoke behind us, so we
presumed we must have scorched it fairly well. I had logged thirty-six
hours of operational time in less than a week, and I was tired. My
nerve seemed to be holding out, but then one could never tell. A man
who developed what we called the clanks often appeared quite well in
the instant before he dissolved into a shaking wreck. I saw a gunner
in the mess hall become comatose while talking with his friends. It
happened in a second, as though someone had snapped a finger and
told him to leave this world. They carried him out rigid and staring.
He escaped from us to become safe in the only way he could, by
entering a secret place where we could never follow.

Between the two virtues of bad weather and our policy of rotating
crews, I, too, escaped for nine days. But there was no freedom. I was
like a dog tied on a rope. I was held fast to the days ahead. The time
stretched endlessly as I occupied it; it was relentlessly dull, and I wanted
it to be that way. Five more missions. Only five more, and I could
go home for thirty days. It would take at least two months before I got
back. Anything could happen in that time—anything.

After two days of this, I began to emerge from my stupor. Perhaps
some of my healing came from long sessions in the shower stalls where
I comforted my burning backside with soap and water that was oc-

casionally warm. These ablutions soothed me. Life in the squadron again appeared as it had been before, as a familiar neighborhood of familiar habits, a place where I had lived it seemed for a long time. My melancholy left me, and like a good citizen, I began to get about.

I played third base in a softball game, and I got two hits off a very hard-throwing left-handed tech sergeant; both hits were solid line drives to right center field. I should have had a third, but my drive went directly to the left fielder who for some reason was playing shallow. He caught the ball without moving a step. The sergeant walked me the fourth time I was up, and as I trotted to first base, he called over, "Hey, Lieutenant, how do ya' get so lucky?" Like all left-handers, he couldn't believe anyone could hit him; if one did, he considered it as divine intervention over which even his fastball could not prevail. After the game, I went to the club and bullied my way into a rubber of bridge. A man with thirty missions could always intimidate one with fewer. My play was not up to its usual standard; that is, I played reasonably well. Even Paul was impressed. All in all, I had a good day.

In the morning, I nursed a mild hangover, the result of too many drinks the night before when I had enjoyed the camaraderie of the club and the memory of my three hard-hit balls. I peered outside the tent; the day promised to be different, with different pleasures. It was overcast, and the cloud ceiling couldn't have been over two hundred feet. A fine mist drenched the area, covering the tents with silver beads of moisture. It suited me. When the sky was covered, it didn't threaten me. It didn't beckon me to it. It wasn't there. Instead, there was this small shrouded world where a soft wet wind grazed about, nuzzling the old trees and the brown, thirsting grass. Fog covered the area and became the substance of the day, which to me was better than the damned sun. It was a day of shadows, of indistinct vague shapes groping for a tenuous presence in a cloud-swept land. Two ghostly forms moved past our tent and disappeared in the mist. I heard Rich Egan's voice. "These cigarettes aren't so bad. You get good stuff with the coupons too. I already got enough for a surf-casting rod—a real beauty. . . ."

The voice faded, and I heard only the rustle of the wind. Paul had finished dressing. He stood beside me considering the hazards between him and the latrine.

"Hurry it up," I said. "I'm hungry."

He stepped out of the tent, holding his raincoat tight around his neck. As he walked away, he called back to me, "I won't be long. I hope the guys have been there." What Paul was hoping for was to enjoy the luxury of hitting the latrine immediately after the morning sanitary crew had treated it with lime and had burned the residual gases with their blow torch. It was a pleasure to have a warm seat, particularly on a cool, wet morning.

The mess hut was loud; it was only half full, but the men who were there were noisy. Bravado and good humor were always evident when the weather was bad; it did wonders for morale when we couldn't fly and had to stand down. The war was put aside like an unpleasant chore we were happy to leave until another day. We would get back to it soon; there was no need to worry. Tomorrow, or the next day, would do just as well. It could wait. We chose not to consider what a blessing this foul weather was for the krauts. It gave them time; it gave the bastards time. I often wondered when we each thanked God for a respite, whose thanks pleased Him more. I was a young man then, and inclined to probe such mysteries.

Jake Stoner joined us. He was carrying his coffee mug; he eased himself down on the bench beside me. "Well, this is my last day," he said. "I leave tomorrow."

"You got a ride out of here, Ilyich?" I asked him.

"Yeah, I got a ride from here to Casablanca, and then I pick up an ATC flight to the Azores and New York."

"Good for you, my friend," I said. "Keep the home fires burning and all that shit."

"Yeah," Jake muttered. "I wish I knew where they're going to send me."

Paul spoke up very seriously. "I thought you were supposed to blow up Newark."

Jake smiled. "I mean after that, Paul."

After breakfast, the three of us drove into Foggia. The drive in the open jeep was cold and wet, but we were convinced that it was absolutely necessary for us to go into town. Paul wanted to go to the PX, Jake wanted company, and I wanted simply to get away from the squadron. In the PX, Paul looked at everything, and finally bought a box of Hershey chocolate bars, although he took forever deciding whether he wanted plain chocolate or the ones with nuts. Jake and I finally left him there, still poking about, pretending he was interested in buying a new dress blouse.

When Jake and I were outside, I had some concern about his mood. I didn't want him to begin a maudlin coversation about the war, about friendship, and all that damned nonsense. He didn't. He surprised me by being cheerful, almost gay, which for Jake was an extraordinary mood. The streets were empty; their old stones were shining, washed clean of silt and dirt. A soft drizzle of rain accompanied us as we walked, like a gentle companion who was somewhat sentimental but still quite agreeable to be with. Jake reached deep into his raincoat pocket to retrieve his omnipresent brandy; this time it was in a silver flask. We stopped walking for a moment while he unscrewed the top. He extended the flask to me; when I took it, I tipped it toward him.

"To the revolution, Ilyich," I said, and I drank.

Jake accepted my toast with a smile. "My name is Jacob, damn you—not Ilyich. And I'm not going to blow up Newark. Not right away anyway. Here's to you, my friend," he said. He took a swallow, and then offered the flask to me again.

I shook my head. I began to walk away. "Come on, Jacob," I said. "Let's go around the block. Take your last look at the grand city of Foggia, the jewel of southern Italy."

We walked in the rain for almost an hour. We talked about baseball; we talked about books; we argued. When we returned to the PX, Paul had progressed to another aisle. He was looking at trench coats. I watched Jake as he chatted with Paul. His face was bright with amusement and pleasure. It seemed as though he had finally shed his burden of guilt about going home.

From the PX, we drove to the RAF club where Paul, after having had two drinks from Jake's flask, ordered a bottle of dark. Jake and I both had whiskey, and we settled down at a small table to pass some time. There were two British officers sitting next to us playing chess who didn't seem to mind when Paul asked permission to join them so he could watch the game. Paul fancied himself a chess player. The room was quiet. There was a soft sound of music from a radio on the bar counter.

"Ah, this is a great spot." Jake sighed. "I haven't been in an English club before." He sipped his whiskey while he looked around. The ambiance pleased him; it was aloof in a pleasant snobbish way. It had the modest comfort of a British pub, and one could tell it cared little for the outside world; it really didn't give a damn. "How come you rate here?" Jake asked.

"Oh, I met a British pilot who fixed it up for me," I said. "He got me what he called a ticket. I earn my keep by bringing them cans of grapefruit and orange juice. The Brits like fruit juice with their gin. International trade and all that, old boy." Jake laughed at my affected accent.

We stayed until late in the afternoon. I can't remember how many whiskeys we had, or how many beers Paul had, but I do recall playing darts. I recall Paul staring owlishly at a chessboard while his opponent, a gray-haired major, drummed his fingers on the table, impatiently waiting for him to make up his bloody mind. I recall singing a solemn dirgelike song, which was particularly obscene. And I recall we paused at one point for a pot of tea with bread-and-butter sandwiches.

It was dusk when we drove back to the squadron. The rain had stopped, and the road was nearly dry. Since we were somewhat drunk, Jake drove at a sedate pace appropriate to our condition and our mood. Paul dozed in the back. Jake was singing "Tiptoe Through the Tulips" in a peculiar off-key monotone, more to keep himself awake than to amuse. Those Brits were splendid fellows, I thought. And good old Paul. Good old Jake. What good old boys they were. Through my haze of scotch whiskey and happy affection, I was suddenly struck by melancholy: Jake was going home. In two days, Paul and I would be back on the battle orders. I looked at Paul, and found myself cheered again. His absurd mustache, which had failed to respond to his constant care, had grown only into a sparse collection of blond hairs that were now stained with dried dark beer foam. It pleased me to see him slovenly; he was always so insufferably tidy.

On the twenty-second of June, we flew a mission to northern Italy, to the railroad marshaling yards at Fornovo di Taro. My days of peace, which were not really so but were only days of waiting, were past me. I was apprehensive and tense when the group formed over the field, flying in a tight mechanical way that made it difficult for my wingmen to stay with me. I turned the plane over to the copilot for a time, and I tried to relax. Tommy steadied us down; the wingmen edged in closer, cautious as cats. By the time we rendezvoused with the wing, which was about thirty minutes after forming, I found my old sullen self again, and I was able to fly calmly with acceptable concentration. The weather was fair with broken clouds drifting below us. The formation was in good order. We made the IP before noon and had a good run in moderate flak. There were no fighters. There were no losses.

Chapter XVII

PLOESTI AGAIN

And if you have lived one day, you have seen everything, one day is equal to all days. There is no other light, there is no other darkness, the whole disposition of the heavens is the same. . . .

—MONTAIGNE

Following the mission to Fornovo, on the twenty-third of June, we were briefed for Ploesti again. There was a question about the weather. Over the field the sky was clear, but there were high cirrus patterns in the east, stretching out from the coast of Yugoslavia. Behind the cirrus, we were advised, there were heavy cloud formations covering most of Yugoslavia, but the target area would be open. Around Ploesti, if there were any clouds at all, there would be no more than a few scattered stratus at about ten thousand feet.

I was to fly tail-end Charlie again, as I had on my first mission to Ploesti. I knew it was probably Captain Ewell's doing; for some reason when he was leading, he wanted me back there. Perhaps he thought of it as a matter of luck. It was an easy position to fly: all I had to do was to tuck up behind and below the second flight and keep alert for fighters coming in from six o'clock.

When I arrived at the hardstand, Tom Connors was already briefing the gunners. They were listening to him with solemn attention. I was glad Tom was flying in the right seat. He was a good man. He had flown with me yesterday at Fornovo, and I was sure he had flown with me before on one of the earlier missions though I couldn't recall which one. Lt. George Hamilton, a tall, scholarly-looking fellow, was our navigator. George had also flown with me before. Like Tom, George was dependable, but sometimes his affected manner irritated me. I

could never get used to him calling me chum, or old chum. I don't
know why it pissed me so. The bombardier, Lieutenant Prairio, and
the two waist gunners, sergeants Coffin and Ramirez, were new to
me. Tom Connors told me the radio gunner and the top turret, sergeants Keisacher and Tibbets, were flying their first mission. Willy
Balcom, the tail gunner, and Jim McNaught, the ball turret, were old
hands and I knew them well. I was sure they would be able to steady
the new men. It was my usual draw for a crew, some green, some
seasoned veterans. Another day had begun.

Flying east in the early morning was always hazardous when the
sky was clear. The low sun then glared into your eyes as it rose on its
western journey, and it made it nearly impossible to see the planes
around you. Today the sun's rays were diffused by the higher layer of
cirrus drifting slowly toward the Italian coast; we were not blinded by
them. We were able to hold our positions in the formation without
fear of collision. But it was even more meaningful to our survival as
we neared Ploesti, to be able to see fighters ahead of us coming in
from twelve o'clock.

We were crossing the Yugoslav coast when Tom touched my arm
and then pointed to the number-three manifold pressure gauge. He
shook his head in a doubtful way; then he spoke to me on the intercom.
"It keeps jumpin'," he said. "Seems to be dropping, too."

"The others okay?" I asked him.

"Yeah, it's just number three."

"I'll switch alternators," I said. "See if that does anything. Any
change?"

"Nope."

"Shit. What's the reading now?"

"It's pullin' twenty-five. It should be thirty-three."

We were still climbing. I had to make up my mind. "Is it still
holding twenty-five?" I asked.

"Yeah, she seems to be holding steady."

I decided not to abort. I could delay that decision for another thirty
minutes.

The forecast had been on the mark. There were thick layers of
clouds; most of them were below us between twelve and fifteen thousand feet, but there were some towering up to over twenty thousand.
We had to change course twice to avoid large masses of gray ham-
merheads that blocked our way. The other groups in the wing were
having the same difficulty finding a path. Our whole echelon was in

disarray. There was no chance now that our attack would be coordinated. We were disorganized. Our group was alone, as were the others, and we were already five minutes late.

When we leveled off at twenty-two thousand, I set my power for cruise at thirty inches of manifold pressure and two thousand RPM. I locked the inboards. The copilot spoke to me on the intercom. "Number three is holdin' at twenty-five. Cylinder head's a little hot. Not bad, though."

I decided not to abort. We were halfway across Yugoslavia, and we were out of our climbing mode. The engines were not working as hard, and we had used up fuel. The wingtip tanks were nearly empty; we were that much lighter. Even if I had to shut down number three, we could still hold our position. We had seventy minutes to go before we would reach the IP.

As our meteorologist predicted, the clouds thinned as we approached the Rumanian border. There were broken patterns of cumulus below us, but they were the end of the cloud mass and would soon trail behind us. We were forty minutes from the IP. The plane was sluggish. I couldn't understand it. Number three's problem at this point should not be having any significant effect on our flight performance. I boosted power on the outboards and number two.

"Manifold pressure's gone on number three! She's gettin' hot as hell!" Tom's voice was tense; he was waiting for me to hit the feathering button.

"Feathering number three," I said. "Okay, Tommy, shut her down."

Tom's hands moved quickly. "Okay. Number three's secure."

I waited a few minutes before I asked him, "How's the temperature?"

"It went up a bit, but it's steady. Yeah, it's okay. It's startin' to drop."

Something went by my window. Christ! Two 109s were breaking toward nine o'clock. At the same moment, I heard Willy, the tail gunner. "Bandits. Six o'clock high. They're comin' in!"

There was something wrong. We were dropping back from the squadron. Almost sixty yards now separated us from the second flight.

"Number one and four are runnin' hot! I'm goin' to crack the cowl flaps and richen the mixture." It was Tom again. He was leaning forward; his eyes were fixed on the engine instruments.

We were still losing ground. The squadron was getting away from us. We were alone. We were a bone for the dogs. I couldn't put more power on number one and four—not until we could get the cylinder temperatures down.

The top turret was firing steady bursts. Tracers were streaming over us and curling down in a spray of white smoke ahead of our plane. The squadron was making a turn to the left, a standard maneuver made to try to bring in a straggler. If I could turn inside, I might be able to cut them off and get back in position. But we had no power; we were too far behind them. Pieces of metal were flying away from my right wingtip.

"Six o'clock! Four comin' in!" It was Willy again.

"Three o'clock level. Two comin' in!"

Two more MEs were breaking away toward nine o'clock to circle behind us for another attack.

We were far behind the squadron now, and we were laboring. With number three feathered and the drag of the open cowl flaps, we couldn't increase our airspeed. The overheated outboard engines were becoming less efficient; they were losing power by the second. I kept nudging the throttles forward, but nothing was happening. There was no response. A pale blue flame was streaming from the top of number four. The fighters had us cold. We were alone. We were at bay, and we had only moments to live.

I pushed the wheel forward. The motion and the decision were one act, an instinctive grasp at the only chance we had. The clouds. We had to get into the clouds. If we could get low enough and head west into their thickening mass, we could shake the fighters; and at that lower altitude, with near sea-level pressures, maybe I could bring back number three and ease off on one and two. We had to break away; we had to. Run, by God! Run! It was better than being slaughtered like some wretched beast standing helpless in the sun.

As we dove, I dropped the left wing to spiral down into a westerly heading. Three MEs who had been coming in from six o'clock overshot us, and I could see white streamers from their wingtips as they desperately tried to recover to follow our dive. The big wing of the B-17 had too much surface, too much lift; the speed of the air rushing over it made it struggle to lift us back into level flight. I had full forward trim, and I was pushing the wheel as hard as I could; but the nose was still coming up. I braced my knees against the wheel and pushed; Tommy did the same. We fought her with all our strength to keep her in a steep dive. We were near twelve thousand feet; the plane was vibrating badly; I pleaded with her, I begged her, not to come apart. We plunged through a thin layer of stratus. Tom and I released the wheel. Her nose came up fast, too fast. I put forward pressure on the

wheel again, trying to ease the pull-out. She got away from me, and she surged up, breeching through the cloud vapors like a great whale leaping out of the sea.

I leveled her out at last. She had taken the dive and the pull-out. We were still flying. The fire from number four had burned itself out; there was a thin trail of smoke, but there was no flame.

"Bandits! Three o'clock!"

"Four more! Six o'clock!"

The crew was functioning. They must have been terrorized during the dive, but now they were back at their stations. Good boys, I thought. Good boys. We'll get out of this. . . .

There was a string of small cumulus about a mile ahead. If we could just hold the fighters off until we could get into the shelter of those white puffs. . . . There was an explosion behind me! A cannon shell had taken out the top turret! There were two holes in the right wing, and I could see fuel siphoning out of the main cells. We reached the cloud bank, and as soon as the white fleece closed around us, I changed course. The fighters couldn't set up for another pass. We were going to make it! By Jesus! We were going to make it!

I called the navigator. "George, our position? Do you know where we are?"

"I think we're into Yugoslavia—or damn close."

We were in and out of the cloud cover, which was getting thicker and darker as each moment passed. We were going to make it. Maybe not all the way, but the coast. We'd make the coast.

Tom pulled on my arm. He was pointing to the right wing. It was wrapped in flame from the wingroot to about six feet from the tip. We had bought it. It was over.

The alarm bell! Find it! Don't miss it. The alarm was operated by a toggle switch buried in an array of toggle switches for our batteries and generators. During emergency practice, I could never find it, but by a miracle my fingers were quick to touch it; I flicked it on, and I immediately heard the shrill ringing in my earphones. I held my throat mike tight. I tried to speak in a loud voice but without panic, "This is the pilot. Hit the silk. Bail out! Bail out." I repeated the command. The alarm was still ringing.

Tom pulled his chute from under his seat, and then opened the access hatch between us so we could go forward to the nose hatch. Before he left the flight deck, he unstrapped the turret gunner and eased him down out of his station. The man was dead. Tom left him and dropped down through the open access to go forward.

I had all the time in the world, or so it seemed to me. Although I was probably moving fast, everything was framed in a slow, deliberate sequence of acts. What took me seconds to do, I remember as interminable dreamlike events. I switched the automatic pilot on to the operational mode, and I waited. The sensitivity and ratio lights flickered on and off in their usual way like the bright beckonings of a small neon sign. The right wing began to drop. I corrected the aileron control, and again watched the lights. I snapped on my chute and squirmed up and out of my seat. For a moment I stared at the dead man whose body was crumpled against the aft firewall. I didn't know him. I would never know him. Smoke was beginning to drift out of the bomb bay, and was being sucked up through the shattered top turret. It was over. What I had feared would come had come. There was nothing now to fear. It was over. If she blew, she blew. It would be quick.

When I went forward into the nose compartment, there was only one man there. The navigator and the bombardier were gone. Tommy was alone, crouched over the hatch ready to dive out. His arms were extended straight down and he was grasping the side coamings of the hatch; he looked like a sprinter in the blocks. Why was he waiting? Christ! He was frozen there! He couldn't let go!

I kicked him. I kicked him hard in the butt. He fell forward through the hatch. I looked for the pull ring on my chute pack. Where's the ring? Where's the goddamned chute ring? I made sure I had my fingers wrapped around it when I tumbled out head first away from the falling plane.

It was quiet. It was so very quiet. I wasn't falling. I was floating in space. There was no sense of motion, no rush of air, no hurtling passage toward the ground, which was a peaceful panorama below me. Mountaintops were ridged with great rocks whose shoulders bore mantles of green moss and lichen; tall trees grew along the slopes; there was a yellow meadow; and all were revolving slowly, gently.

I had to know where the plane was before I pulled the ring. I rolled over on my back. She was far away from me, abandoned and alone in her agony. She was framed between my two boots, and she was falling off on her right wing, yielding to the flames that were now consuming her. When I pulled the ring, I heard a soft flapping sound. I felt my weight eased against the chute harness. The restraint was so gentle I looked up at the white canopy above me to be sure I was tethered by the web of nylon shrouds. The plane had completed her sinking turn, and at the end of a long shallow dive it crashed into a mountain, halfway up the lower slope. A tremendous explosion roared into the silence—her last great cry. A spout of flame and smoke leaped up into the wind. . . . There was no sound except the hushed rustle of the chute. It was a fearful stillness. I was rocked back and forth like a child being soothed and comforted. Below me I could see the smoke drifting away from the mountain. There was a long, black scar rimmed by orange fire marking the place. . . .

The ground was rushing up at me! I was moving fast toward a high ridge! I swept over it, and then I plunged through the upper branches of a giant pine; my chute caught and was held fast while my inertia drove me out over a deep, rocky gorge. My forward motion was violently snubbed, and I was sent rushing back toward a massive trunk. I missed it by three feet, but continued to swing wildly beside it. After a time, the motion ceased. I hung there over the steep incline of the gorge. The base of the tree reached down deep into the slope; it was much too far to drop. The trunk was too thick to grasp. There was no way I could slide down; besides, there wasn't time. I could hear the popping sound of small-arms fire. It sounded very close. There was a half-dead branch extending toward me, and I began an easy swaying motion toward it. After several attempts, I was able to grab it and clamber on. I perched there, trembling with excitement while I unbuckled my chute harness. When I was free, I wrapped the nylon shrouds around my wrists. I had to swing myself out as far as I could toward the high side of the slope. It was the shortest distance to the ground. I held the shrouds tight and pushed hard against the dead limb that held me. I heard it crack.

I threw my legs out hard ahead of me at the beginning of each arc. I rose higher and higher until I began to fear I might drag the chute out of the branches above me; I could feel it loosening. At the top of my last thrusting swing, I released the shrouds, and I flew into the steep side of the gorge. I was stunned, but my hands dug into the loose shale with a desperate will of their own. There was nothing to hold; I began to slide. The slide accelerated into a tumbling fall. I crashed down through the shrub growth with rocks and dirt hurtling along with me. I was shaken but still in one piece when I came to a stop against the smooth surface of a huge boulder.

Cool water was gurgling around me. I was sitting in the middle of a small stream overcome by a feeling of bliss, and I was untouched by any despair. I was alive. A gentle breeze moved through the defile. There was sunlight, but only where thin spears of it could find a way through the trees or down between the steep slopes of the gorge. I leaned back against my boulder watching the water's tumbling journey through clusters of rocks and past swaying ferns that crowded its banks. The shrill, sweet cries of birds pierced the quiet while I sat still so they might never end. . . .

I wanted a cigarette. Where were my cigarettes? My lighter? I found them, safe and dry, zippered tight in the upper pocket of my flight suit. A full pack of Chesterfields: I wondered how long they would last. When I opened the package, I noticed my hands were covered with blood and deep scratches. To my relief, the lighter worked on the first try. I touched the flame to my cigarette, and after two drags, I began to wonder what I should do. I needn't have concerned myself about it. There was fate standing before me, about twenty yards away.

My small canyon opened into a wide glen a short distance from me. There the stream emptied into a pool whose surface was partly covered with green pads, and there were long stalks on some of them holding large white blossoms. On the far side of the pool, ten soldiers were holding rifles pointed at me; one soldier, who seemed to be the leader, was holding a semiautomatic.

The leader made a motion with his hands as if he wanted me to take cover. Of course, I was in Yugoslavia. They were partisans. There was probably a German patrol nearby. I stood up in the stream, and I started to move behind the boulder.

A burst from the automatic shattered the air. The screaming whine of ricochets off the face of the rock about a foot over my head convinced me I had made a mistake. I held my position and raised my hands. Turning slowly, I faced my captors. They were watching me carefully, very carefully. The leader motioned again with his gun. I walked toward him.

They searched me for weapons and found nothing. They returned my cigarettes with some reluctance. I offered one to the officer, and then I indicated to him that he might pass the pack around to his men. I owed them that: it was a way of saying thanks for firing high. This small courtesy seemed to relieve the tension: the men smiled, pleased to have an American cigarette and a prisoner who was sensible enough not to make a fuss. After all, it was a pleasant day. One ran out of luck, but these things happen. No reason for anyone to get killed.

The officer pointed to the pool; then he made a pantomime of washing. His hand reached out and touched my face. He pointed again to the pool. I was puzzled by his action, but when I knelt down and saw my reflection in the water, I understood. My face was covered with dried blood; some of it had streaked my neck. I washed it off as well as I could. The source of the blood was nothing more than a patchwork of cuts and scratches. When I was finished, the officer nodded approvingly. He was satisfied I was not mortally wounded; there would have been no reason to walk me out if I had been.

We made our way up a narrow path on the side of a low hill. After an hour, we came to level ground, and we came out of the trees. There was a large field; in the middle of it a dirt road led to a village about a mile away.

The officer turned to me and made a strange inquiry, or perhaps he was only making coversation. "Boom, boom, Ploesti?" he asked. "Boom, boom, Germans? Boom, boom, Bucharest?"

I guessed he was asking if I had bombed these places, I nodded, and then said, "Yes."

He still kept looking at me. He had something else on his mind. "Boom, boom, Sofia?" he asked softly, and he was smiling. The soldiers were all listening intently now, waiting for my answer.

I remembered Sofia had been bombed in the early part of the year;

I hadn't been on any of the missions. I shook my head. "No," I said.

"Ah!" the officer exclaimed. "Good. Good. Bulgaria good. Sofia good." He patted my shoulder.

I was in Bulgaria! I wasn't in Yugoslavia! Where the hell was Bulgaria?

I was feeling giddy and weak. Every part of my body was bruised. My upper left leg was particularly painful. I wondered if I would be able to make it to the village. As if in answer to my need, the officer halted our small column, and we sat down in the grass along the side of the road. A soldier offered me his canteen; another gave me a thick slice of dark bread. The water was sweet and the bread had a rich, grainy flavor. After I finished eating and drinking, I took a cigarette from my pack. The men were watching me. I couldn't refuse them. I gave the officer one, and then gave what was left in the pack to the soldiers.

We sat there like comrades smoking our butts, taking our break in the sun and enjoying the gentle wind that blew across the land. The men laughed and talked. The officer sat alone, isolated by his responsibilities. His thin, young face was firm. No one could say he took his duty lightly. I did not wonder about the days ahead. I was in a strange new place, among different men, under a different sky. Each moment that would come would be met, and each day would pass. I threw my cigarette away. I was a prisoner.

Chapter XVIII

BULGARIA

I have grown tired of sorrow and human tears;
Life is a dream in the night, a fear among fears,
A naked runner lost in a storm of spears.

—ARTHUR SYMONS

I didn't feel like a prisoner; I didn't feel less free, and I chose to believe I was simply marching into a new camp. I was in a new circumstance where I would have little chance to do anything other than what I would be told I could do, and that would not be much of a change for me. In my three years of military duty, which I remembered as being much longer than that, I had learned to be at ease with what was imposed on me by the rituals of war and discipline. I had learned to isolate myself from the things I was required to do and the things that were done to me. I had acquired a certain durability, or at least a conditioned apathy, and I was rarely surprised when I was lost or confused. All men learn in some way to muddle through the wretchedness and terror of their lives. Some manage it with incredible grace; some blunder through it battered and bloody; but all find their way as best they can until at last they are cut down.

As I made one painful step after step toward the village, I needed to find something to carry me there, something to remind me I was not alone. I needed a joke of a comrade; I needed a friend to walk with me, to curse me if he must or to laugh at my labored progress, anything as long as he would whip my pride and not let me fall. My body was a throbbing burden to me, my head felt as though it were about to burst. My left leg was a hot, searing iron attached to my hip, and I could barely control its trembling weakness. My mind was wandering in a wilderness of fearful images. I had to find my way out. I

heard Sandy's voice; I grasped at the memory of my brother, and I
held it. I could see his mocking smile. ". . . you must believe in God.
You must never venture west of Dedham or east of Nantucket; if you
do, you'll fall off the face of the earth." The Bulgarian officer was
watching me curiously, wondering what the hell I had to smile about.
Sandy was right. I had gone too far from home. I had fallen off the
face of the earth.

When we entered the village, which was a modest collection of
small, shabby houses cringing in the shadows of three larger brick
buildings, I was brought to a large open square. There was no pavement; it was all hard-packed earth, and dust drifted across it and under
the legs of an old horse tethered to a rail in front of one of the houses.
A group of civilians were standing in the center of the square. They
were looking at something on the ground, and they were talking quietly. One woman had both her hands against her mouth; she was
weeping. Six members of my crew were being held at the far end of
the square by three soldiers armed with rifles.

The officer waved his automatic in the direction of my comrades,
motioning me to join them. The crew watched me approach. They
were all smiling in a sheepish, self-conscious way, except Tom. He
wasn't smiling; he was angry. He was the first to speak. "What the
hell did you kick me for?" he asked.

I was startled by his question. The picture of him crouched in the
nose hatch waiting to dive out of the burning plane came to my mind
like something that had happened a long time ago. I didn't think he
would ever want to speak of it.

I mumbled a reply. "Gee, Tom, I thought you were frozen in the
hatch—for a minute there anyway."

"I was waiting for you, for Christ's sake! I wasn't frozen in any
fuckin' hatch!" he stormed. And then his voice changed to one of
concern. "What the hell happened to you? You look like you been
run over by a truck."

I told Tom about landing in the tree, and then tumbling down the
side of the gorge.

Willy was grinning as he listened. "Jeez, that must have been somethin'," he said. "You coulda' sold tickets of that and made a bundle."

I was beginning to feel better. My head was clearing, and the company of my comrades cheered me. And then Willy's view of things
had to be considered. He had a hard street wisdom that could twist
the arm of any disadvantage to make it work for him.

"What do you think, Willy?" I asked.

"Oh, this is going to be good for me," he said. "I need to dry out. I've been on the sauce real hard. And lookit all the dough you'll save. Yeah, this'll be good for all of us, you'll see. You're outa' the fuckin' war, and all you gotta do is sit around for a while."

Even Tom was smiling now. "You got it all figured out, Sarge. Right?"

"Yes, sir," Willy answered. "Just do the time easy—do it easy."

I turned to Tom. "Where's the other two men?" I asked.

"Well, the bombardier, Lieutenant Prairio, hasn't turned up yet. Maybe he got away. The left waist gunner, Sergeant Ramirez, was hit in the chest. He was probably killed, but Willy and Charlie here put his chute on him anyway and pulled it when they threw him out the waist door." Tom paused, and then he said, "And you know about the top turret."

"Yes," I said. "He was on the flight deck when I left. It was quick for him anyway, it was quick for him." My words were so fatuous I wished I hadn't said them.

"Lou Prairio was right behind me when I went out." It was George Hamilton, the navigator, talking more to himself than to any of us. "He was right there, ready to go."

"Yeah," Tom said. "When I went into the nose, Lou and George were both gone. There was nobody there." Tom looked at me, remembering his anger. "And then I waited for you, you bastard."

I smiled weakly at him. "Old buddy," I said. "Bootin' you in the ass seemed like the right thing to do at the time. I owe you one."

An old man had separated from the group in the center of the square, and he was talking with the three soldiers who were guarding us. He was a very small man with a brown weathered face. He was wearing a heavy gray sweater that was much too big for him. I could see his soiled undershirt poking through holes in the elbows and hanging out beyond the ragged unraveled ends of his sleeves. His legs were wrapped in dirty strips of pale blue cloth. The soldiers nodded as he spoke, listening intently to what he was saying. When he finished his conversation, he turned toward me and said, "It's all right. Don't be afraid. Please come with me."

His English was easy and natural; if there was a trace of an accent, it was one of urban America, perhaps one of the eastern cities. He led us through the villagers, gently pushing them aside to make a path for us.

What he had brought us to was on the ground. It was a human leg that had been torn away just below the knee. There was nothing else.

There were no marks on it and there was little blood; where it had been severed at the top of the calf, there were some jagged edges of red tissue, and I could see a white end of bone. It was bare, without a shoe or a sock. We stared at it. We didn't understand. The woman who had been weeping rubbed her eyes with her fist. She shook her head and began weeping again.

Tom spoke softly. He was the first to comprehend the meaning of this terrible evidence. "Christ, it must be the gunner's leg—the top turret. When she blew it must have been thrown all this way. . . . Jesus. I don't even know the poor bastard's name. God Almighty," he said in an awed voice. "God Almighty. . . ."

The old man stood silent for a time. After he heard Tom's words he murmured, "Ah, too bad, too bad." He took a bottle out of his back pocket and unscrewed the top. "Do you want a drink?" he asked. I nodded to indicate that I did. He shrugged and put the bottle to his lips, and then he screwed the cap back on and returned the bottle to his pocket.

He wasn't as friendly as I had supposed. He had put me down. It was later, when I came to know something more of Bulgaria, that I learned by their custom, by nodding my head the way I did, I had refused the drink. If I had nodded to the side, toward my shoulder, he would have passed me the damned bottle.

I was suddenly aware of a new presence. A man in a dark flight suit was standing beside me. He was not a man whom I could call young, although I supposed he was. He had dark brown hair, which was cut short; his face was pale, and I could see the pink impression around his mouth where his oxygen mask had pressed against it perhaps no more than an hour ago. His goggles and his flight cap were in his left hand. He didn't speak or look at me but glared down at the thing on the ground. Without moving, he finally muttered the question, "Comrade?" And then he turned for my answer.

I said, "Yes."

We looked at each other for what I remember as a long moment. I looked into the face of my enemy, a German fighter pilot. I looked into the dull, tired eyes of a man who seemed not unlike me. His stern expression never changed. He took my arm and drew me away from the civilians, who were regarding him closely, as though they feared something he might do. He pointed across the square to a pile of yellow fabric about ten yards from where we were standing. It was his parachute. He had been shot down too. He watched me, to observe my reaction, to see if I understood. He was smiling now. He was telling me in his mad way this wonderful joke that only he and I could share. You crazy bastard, I thought. What's so bloody funny?

He offered me a cigarette, and then he lit it for me. He pointed to the sky and said some heavily accented words that sounded more German than English, "Beautiful day, is it not?"

It was so absurd to be standing there with him. We had been trying hard to kill each other a little while ago, and now we were smoking cigarettes like two friends waiting for a bus. I was relieved when we were joined by a Bulgarian officer who had apparently arranged transportation for my brief companion. Before he walked away, the German pilot bowed and offered me his hand. To this day, and it will always be so, I cannot remember ever being so perplexed. Who were we? Why were we standing there? I shall never know. I shook his hand.

Two soldiers, accompanied by the old man who told us his name was Joseph, escorted us to the smallest of the three brick buildings. It looked like a school but there were no children about. We were taken to a room on the second floor, which was sparsely furnished with a desk and chair, and a long, sturdy table. There were no windows; there was one door; a naked light bulb that had died long ago hung from a frayed cord over the table. It was the first place where we would be closeted; it was the first of many such places we were to live in during our travels south.

Before the old man left us, he again assured us we would not be harmed. "If you have to take a leak or a crap, tap on the door," he said. "The guard will take you, one at a time. They'll bring you some bread and soup later on." He turned to leave. The two guards were standing by the open door.

"Hey, Uncle Joe, wait a minute." It was Sgt. Willy Balcom. "Where'd you pick up the English?" he asked.

The old man smiled. His teeth were yellow; there was one broken one in the front of his mouth that was beginning to turn black. "I lived in Chicago for a long time—about thirty years," he said. "Drove a cab there." He didn't volunteer any more information. He had said enough. It would be dangerous for him to be too friendly. He passed through the door, and the guard slammed it shut.

No one spoke. I could hear the guard outside, pacing back and forth. It was warm in the room; the air was very still. I took off my leather jacket and rolled it up to put under my head. I stretched out on the floor and began to do my time easy, as Willy had advised us to do.

Deep sleep was the consequence of the calamitous day; without dreams or care, I sank into unconsciousness, and it was no more than that. I did not move. I had no wonder about what had happened. I had no fear about what would happen tomorrow. My body and spirit turned away from all of it with contemptuous indifference, and sought the dark womb of sleep. If I could have chosen then, I would not have roused from it. I would have stayed forever in its peace, or I would have waited as long as I had to in time to find another way. . . .

There was a light shining in my eyes. Two soldiers with flashlights had entered the room; one of them held his light steady while he replaced the burned-out bulb. When the new bulb flickered on, it cast a pallid glow, and it swayed from the end of the long cord, making a moving shadow on the wall that looked like a fat man hanging from a rope.

A young boy struggled in carrying a large iron kettle. Tom helped him set it down on the table. The boy went out and immediately returned with metal bowls and spoons; he had a loaf of dark bread clutched to his side with his elbow. The soldiers paid little attention to us; the boy seemed nervous. The door closed, and we were alone again.

Willy lifted the cover off the soup. "It looks good," he said. He began to stir it with a large wooden spoon the boy had provided. The soup was thick and it had a strong smell of cabbage. Willy filled his bowl. We were all watching him, incredulous that he was going to eat it. "Come on," he said. "Come on, Lieutenant," he said to me.

"I'm not hungry, Sarge," I answered.

Willy put his bowl down. His thin face turned to each of us. He glared with impatience, considering how he could persuade us to eat. No devoted mother could have been more concerned. "Lookit," he growled. "You gotta' eat. This is good soup, and this is good bread. We won't get fed every day. You gotta' eat. Who knows how fuckin' long it'll be before we eat again. You gotta' keep yourself goin'. Come on, nobody's goin' to do it for you."

Willy Balcom was a man born of trouble. We knew he had been there before, and we knew he was right. We meekly filled our bowls. We ate the soup. We ate the bread. We would be ready for tomorrow.

In the morning, the seven of us were herded into a small black van that had become old and was worn from years of hard service. There were some Bulgarian words in faded white paint stenciled neatly on either side, probably to identify the vehicle's official status as a carrier of desperate men. There were no windows, but there was a small rectangular opening behind the driver and his companion that was made secure by six steel bars. As soon as we were seated on the benches inside, the two back doors were shut and locked. We waited to begin our journey to the prison camp where we would be held for the duration of the war. No one seemed to be in a hurry to get us there. I could hear the voices of the soldiers; I didn't have to understand the language to recognize their banter and their indifference to this routine duty. They had apparently made the trip before with other men. I felt chilled. I would have given anything for a mug of hot coffee and a cigarette.

We traveled until ten-thirty, when the van was stopped after a short, bumpy deceleration over rough ground. A few moments later the two rear doors were thrown open, and the guards were standing there with their rifles pointed at us, motioning with them that we were to step outside. When I came out of the dark interior of the van, I found myself in dappled sunlight in the center of a large stand of birch trees. We were about twenty yards off the highway. I could see our tire tracks on the grass leading from the narrow road that stretched away in either direction, completely empty of traffic. The hills around us were barren too, without a sign of life or habitation.

But there was a sound, a great roaring sound that had driven everything away. It was the thunder of hundreds of bombers far above us heading east. Looking north from under the cover of the trees, I could see the pale streams of their vapor trails. The seven of us were silent with wonder looking up toward them, more lost than ever now in this strange land. The sound of the bombers faded, and I could hear the wind stirring the birches, murmuring through the pavilion of small green leaves that swayed over my head and endlessly changed the jeweled sunlight cascading down through them.

The guard passed a canteen around, and rather than face Willy's disapproval, we drank deep though the water was tastelessly warm. We were put back in the van to continue our journey, which was halted again at one o'clock when the bombers were returning. On this second occasion, we parked under a viaduct in a shallow ravine until the two soldiers felt it was safe to travel on the open, narrow road. We continued our interminable trek in the old hard-riding van, and it was five o'clock when we arrived at our destination, a large weathered and beaten white house surrounded by fenced pastures that reeked of dung and offal.

All the armies of the world find such dreary backwaters where a few bored and listless men are required to be stationed. It is essential to the morbid intelligence of war. One must guard space occupied by rocks, lifeless barren earth, and drowsing bullocks covered by swarms of buzzing flies; communications posts must be manned where there is no reason to listen or to speak except to hear the tedious silence or to curse the fool who kept you there.

The officer in command of the hovel was a middle-aged man in a soiled, ill-fitting uniform who was drunk when we stood before him. He didn't look at us but stared at a piece of paper placed on his desk by one of our guards, a document I supposed that transferred us to his authority. While he continued to stare at the paper, he spoke sharply to one of his soldiers, and we were taken outside to a filthy latrine where we stood to add our bit to an overwhelming stench of urine and excrement. We were still trying to recover when we were taken back inside and were marched down a drafty corridor to our room, a small bare cell that was once occupied by goats. It was Willy who identified the pungent stink.

"Oh, yeah," he said, "that's goat piss."

Willy didn't look good: his face was ashen; he held himself in a bent position and seemed unable to straighten up. He was obviously in pain.

"What is it, Sarge?" I asked him. "What's the matter?"

"I'm okay," he said. "Just a little sore. It's nothin'."

Charlie Coffin, the right waist gunner, then told me what had happened. "A twenty millimeter exploded just in front of Willy's guns. You know that chunk of armor plate between the two barrels? Well, that blew off right into his gut. Knocked him all the way back into the waist. Come on, Sarge. Let's take a look at it."

"Why the hell didn't you say something?" I asked him. "We might have been able to get you a medic back there in the village."

"Fuck that," Willy growled. "They might have kept me there. I'm stayin' with you guys."

Over Willy's protestations, we stretched him on his back on the floor. Sergeant Coffin unzipped his flight suit and lifted his undershirt up to expose his stomach and lower chest.

Willy's whole torso, from his rib cage to a jagged line of ridged flesh just below his navel, was an awesome bruise. It hurt me to look at it. I couldn't understand why he hadn't said anything. He had taken a terrible blow.

"Sarge," I said, "for Christ's sake, why didn't you say something?" I was repeating myself in my usual banal way, trying to impose guilt on Willy because "he didn't say something." By such idiocy I implied

I would have made everything right if he had only told me about it.

"It's okay," Willy insisted. "It's okay. My flak vest took most of it. Nothing's broken. It'll be okay."

None of us knew what to do. We held his battered flesh with our eyes and our pity, as though we were old prophets who could heal by these things alone. But the obscene colors that ranged from bright red through hues of purple to yellow and brown did not change. Below his navel, the line of ridged flesh formed by dried blood and a crusting pale fluid still rose and fell with each painful breath.

He didn't try to get up. He pulled his undershirt down and primly closed the zipper of his flight suit. George Hamilton put his rolled jacket under the sergeant's head. "Thanks, Lieutenant," Willy said. "Don't worry about me. I'll be okay. It looks worse than it is. No kiddin', it does." He grinned and added, "I'm going to take a nap. Call me when chow's ready." He closed his eyes and was very still. He hadn't fallen asleep; he had passed out. We watched him for a while. Tom took off his sweater and gently placed it over the sergeant's chest.

There was no reason that night to disturb Willy. No food or water was brought to us. We talked in the quiet darkness before we slept, and we no longer smelled the goats. It was the end of our second day. We were not dead men; we would see the morning, and that was good.

We sat on the ground in the strong sunlight waiting for our transportation; when it came we knew it would take some time for us to reach our destination, unless our destination was no more than ten miles away. Two guards, who were older men than the ones we had yesterday, waved us up on our feet and pushed us toward a large wagon half full of hay. Hauling the wagon were two enormous bullocks whose bulk was sullen and ponderously indifferent to the prod the driver was using to control them. We climbed aboard. Willy looked better to me; his face had a little color, and he only grimaced slightly when Tom and I pulled him up over the tailboard. The wagon lurched forward; the day began.

It was a dirt road full of ruts, suitable only for our primitive wagon and the stolid beasts pulling it. A van, or any motor vehicle, would have hopelessly bottomed out in the first fifty yards of this tortuous trail. We moved slowly away from the sallow farmhouse. The stench of the wretched pastures faded too, and I began to catch a fragrance from the thick groves of pine that covered the lower slopes of the hills around us. It all seemed like Vermont, except the hills and mountains looked poor, if that can be said of hills and mountains. Whether they loomed in the distance or were near, I felt discomfited, oppressed by them, unlike Vermont where the mountains were a glory all around me when I used to drive my red Ford from Woodstock up the long climb through Killington, past Pico Peak and north to Round Mountain and Breadloaf. . . . For this was not my beloved New England; here the whole earth was prisoner and brooded over the bones of tyrants and long despair.

After an hour, we passed in our labored creaking way through a valley where the beginning of summer wild flowers' color was splashed across the land. Alone in a field and shading some of the flowers, a giant beech tree witnessed our passage; its red leaves trembled in the sunlight, calling to us to rest there. We didn't answer; we groped on through the dust . . . heading somewhere. Not here, but somewhere.

There was one thing, a small matter of two or three hours, an encounter I remember well from those lost, empty days that marked our journey south toward Sofia. I remember a room, a room something like a classroom. A Bulgarian officer was standing at a desk in front of us. There was a blackboard behind him half covered by a map of the United States. We were drinking delicious strong tea. We had a plate heaped with fresh bread and we had two jars of fig jam. I particularly remember we were trying not to wolf down the bread in an unseemly manner, or gulp the tea, or make a mess with the jam while he was talking, but it was a strain for us to behave well. We were very hungry.

He was a tall, gray-haired man dressed in an immaculate light blue uniform. He was much older than we were, in his late fifties I thought, and as he spoke to us it was in the manner of a man skilled in drawing out what he could from men of inferior gifts and less fortunate circumstances. His eyes waited on us patiently, and he often smiled as a teacher might smile to encourage the attention of a dull student. His English was extraordinarily good, with only a slight accent that sounded more French than Bulgarian, which did not surprise me. I could not imagine such a man speaking, in a coarse Russian-like way; if there were to be any accent at all, it would have to be French.

Our predicament seemed to amuse him, and he sought to entertain himself by talking with us. "I am Colonel Raychev," he stated. He smiled at our response, which was a collective close-mouthed stare from seven faces trying to appear courteous and attentive though full of bread and tea. "This is such a delightful opportunity to speak English again; I cannot tell you how agreeable it is for me." He chose to ignore our gulping efforts to swallow our food and clear our throats. "Now please go on with your tea," he said. He turned to the map. "Some of these names puzzle me. Here for instance," and he tapped the map with his hand. "Mississippi, now that is an Indian name, is it not?"

I managed to be able to speak first. "Yes, Colonel," I said. "It means Father of Waters. The name comes from a tribe called the Algonquin."

"Ah, fascinating," the colonel responded. "Now let me see what else I would like to ask. The Mississippi is a large river?"

I pressed on with my geography recitation. "Yes," I said. "It's our largest river and drains most of the central plains between the Rockies and the Alleghenies."

"Now you are speaking of your mountains—east and west?"

I nodded. The colonel rubbed his hands together, and he seemed pleased with the progress of our conversation. We continued to talk about places and names. In a few minutes the seven of us were standing with him in front of the map. We talked of French names, of Indian and Spanish names, Italian names, English, Scotch, and Irish names; and not least of all, we talked of the names left by the stubborn wanderers who had pushed their way west, names that told their story: Lucky Boy Pass, Lost Hope, Last Chance, Fort Despair, Deadhorse Wells, Skull Valley, Farewell. . . .

I turned away, surprised by emotion that tightened my throat. The map threatened me; I could not bear to look at it any longer. I found my cup and I pretended to drain it so I would not have to speak, but the colonel caught me. He watched me with concern before he, too, turned away from the map.

"Well, gentlemen, thank you," he said. "I have other duties; dull ones, but duties. I must say good-bye." He started for the door to call our guards, and then he paused. He appeared to be considering whether he should speak or not. He smiled, as though he were amused at his hesitation. "You are young men," he said. "This will pass. Be patient. The Russians are knocking on our door, and it will be over for us soon. Who knows? Perhaps, if I have good luck, I shall be your guest one day soon. Yes, perhaps I shall." He waved his hand as if to dismiss the folly between us, and he walked through the door. I heard him speak again as he left, not to us but to himself. "Farewell, what an astonishing name for a town. How appropriate. . . ."

The colonel was an aristocrat, and a Fascist for the moment. He probably cared little for the causes of freedom or equality or justice, and if there must be such things, I was sure he would have preferred to administer them as matters subject to his indulgence. He was worldly; he was patient in a cynical, effete way; he probably treated dogs and horses well; in the company of women, I was sure he was gallant. I imagined that long ago he had decided that the time of history he lived in was untidy and boorish, not worth the trouble to seek to change or oppose it. He was of another world, another time, and he seemed to me to have chosen to remain there. In his tradition, we were brother officers who were to be treated with courtesy and consideration. Our causes meant nothing, for they were ephemeral, wistful things that passed. I would like to believe the Communists didn't kill him. I would like to believe the colonel lived for a long time.

Chapter XIX

THE PRISON IN SOFIA

But if a man live many years,
and rejoice in them all; yet let him
remember the days of darkness; for
they shall be many.

—ECCLESIASTES

We arrived in Sofia, where we disembarked from the van and stood waiting for our next transport. We were outside of a small streetcar station. It was a pleasant day; the sun was warm. My left leg was feeling better, and it was a relief to be able to move about after being cramped in the van for six hours. Our three guards moved us off to the side, away from the few civilians who were watching us curiously. A thin, middle-aged woman seemed particularly agitated by our presence. She spoke excitedly to her companion, a stout elderly man who kept puffing on his pipe as he listened, nodding his head again and again, apparently agreeing with everything she was saying. Suddenly, she moved away from him and approached us. Without warning she pushed past the guards, spitting at us as she began a hysterical harangue accented by blows with her handbag and her bony fist, which she rained on our heads and shoulders. Other civilians quickly gathered behind her, at first amused by her rage; but then, becoming caught up in it, they joined her, cursing at us with increasing anger.

Our three guards, who I thought were country boys with little experience in this kind of madness, seemed confused by the sudden violence. The civilians pushed against them; the soldiers yielded, putting us behind them. My eyes became fixed on one soldier's unbuttoned holster. The handle of the Luger was nearly within my reach. It would take only an instant to grab it, to cock it to put a shell in the chamber, and then fire. The woman would be first, the screeching bitch with the spittle running down from the corners of her mouth, she would be first. How many rounds in a Luger? How long would I last?

A streetcar clanged into the station and squealed to a halt. The door opened; six soldiers led by an officer brandishing a revolver leaped out. The soldiers charged into the civilians swinging their rifles like clubs. The officer grabbed the screaming woman and drove his fist into her face. She put her hand to her bleeding mouth; then she wrenched herself fiercely away from his grasp and fled. The melee could not

have lasted more than a minute. We and the soldiers were now the only ones in the station, except for the companion of the woman, the stout man who had been listening to her before she had abandoned herself to her rage and turned on us. He was lying on his back on the pavement; blood was streaming from a gash on his forehead, and he was moaning. His pipe lay beside him, still smoldering. One of the soldiers kicked it away; the soldier did not look at the stunned and bleeding man.

One of our guards handed the officer some papers, and then he and his two companions returned to the van. We were put into the streetcar. I could see the officer who now was inside the station talking on the telephone; he was probably giving a report of the incident to his superior. Through the reflecting glass that held the image of our orange trolley, I could see him posturing and laughing. When he came out he lit a cigarette. He stared casually at the man on the pavement.

George Hamilton was the first to speak. "Look at the bastard," he said. "He doesn't care whether that guy is alive or dead. Christ—those civilians scared the shit out of me. . . . I got a feelin' about this damn country. It's going to be rough."

Sergeant Keisacher, the radio operator, sat quietly, looking straight ahead. He was very pale. The others were nervous and wary. Only Tom seemed unconcerned. "The civilians are always bad," he said. "No discipline. But hell, if you'd been bombed five or six times, you'd like to get your hands on the guys that did it. Maybe that woman's kid was killed. Who knows?"

The six soldiers and the officer came inside and motioned for us to move to the rear of the compartment. One of the soldiers sat in the operator's chair; the others sat near the front, half turned in their seats so they could watch us. We began to move out of the station. The officer took a position on the step near the door. We traveled for about thirty or forty minutes away from the center of the city. After we reached what must have been the end of the line, we left the streetcar to finish our day's journey on foot. We marched for what seemed to me to be a long time. My leg was throbbing with pain; the dried cuts and scratches on my face were burning in my sweat. Willy was in a bad way, and grimly silent.

"Hang on, Sarge," I said. "It can't be much farther."

"It better not be," Willy grunted. "I'm fuckin' near done."

And then we came to the place.

The building before us was oppressive. We had come as far as the flat, dull expanse of earth it stood upon, and we were considering its sulfurous façade, its unrelenting ugliness. It was a long, rectangular structure three stories high, and the worst architect in the world could not have designed it. It must have been made by brutes to crush the spirits of the poor souls it held. Its silent, uncaring monotony loomed over us in the afternoon sunlight, challenging us to find one redeeming flaw of beauty. There was none. This was the political prison in Sofia.

·   ·   ·

We were taken inside where the light immediately died and objects could only be perceived as indistinct shapes made even less visible by a rank, stinking odor that distracted our senses, or occupied them so fully we were aware of nothing but the smell. We climbed a staircase to the third floor, prodded by the rifles of two guards behind us. A third guard preceded us with a large revolver in his hand. No one spoke; there was only the sound of our boots echoing in the stairwell.

A long corridor with guards posted about every thirty feet led us to our cell, which was a large one in the center of the building. When the guards left us and locked the heavy door, I thought we were alone, but then I saw two men on the far side of the room crouched in the shadows. One of them came toward us. He was a strongly built young man, a Bulgarian in the torn rags of what had been a uniform.

We talked, and it seems strange to say now that we did; but with George's limited French and the soldier's gift of both French and pantomime, we were able to understand. He told us we were in a political prison that was also the interrogation center for Allied prisoners of war. He told us the prison was holding hundreds of Bulgarian men and women for crimes against the state: some for being Communists, some for being Socialists, some for hiding or aiding Communists or Socialists, some for being Jews, some for teaching the wrong thing, some for listening to the wrong thing, some for committing sabotage, some for thinking of committing sabotage, and some, as in his own case, he claimed, for simply being suspect.

The soldier's companion, whom we could see now in the dim light slumped half-conscious on a small wooden pallet, had been a professor of English in one of Sofia's universities. He had been beaten regularly during the year he had been in prison, and he was near death. The professor had been unable to speak for a long time; he did not know where he was, or who he was; he knew neither day nor night; the soldier had to feed him with a spoon as he would an infant. The soldier's eyes were suddenly filled with tears, and he was pleading about something, saying the same French words over and over.

"What is he saying?" I asked George.

"He's asking us to pray for the professor's death. He says if we all pray maybe it will happen." George's voice was tight when he added, "He says it's enough. He says God must have mercy. It's enough."

Heroics, or acts of rashness, are more often manifestations of fatigue, or of frustration, or of contempt, or of desperate indifference, rather than incidents of courage. One forgets, or chooses to not think of consequences. If a dog is kicked often enough, he will snarl and bite. Our small rebellion, which was an imperative gesture of contempt on our part, was more comic than brave, but what we did gave us some satisfaction.

We had not had anything to eat for two days except a slab of stale bread. Our guards who had brought us to Sofia had given us water, but little else. Our desire to piss had become urgent, and we were determined to satisfy our needs, at least on that score. We began to pound on the cell door and yell for the guard.

In a few moments we heard shouts from the corridor, then our door burst open and two guards stood there, both of them tense and careful. They had bayonets fixed on their rifles. They didn't venture into the room. The Bulgarian prisoner translated George's halting French while the guards listened with growing impatience, incredulous that we dared to make demands of any kind. When the prisoner finished talking, the guards responded with a stream of loud, angry words and then withdrew, slamming the door behind them. George spoke with the Bulgarian again before he turned to tell us what the guard had said.

"We'll be taken to the toilets in the morning. We'll be fed in the afternoon, after we've completed our interrogations. We're to keep quiet and not cause any trouble. That's it."

But we were not to be put off. Whether we were goaded by the tortured man on the pallet, or by the concerned alarm of the Bulgarian soldier, or whether it was simply our compelling need to strike at something, I could not say. We were agitated and restless. We had to do something . . . something.

It was Jimmy MacNaught, the ball turret gunner, who was inspired when he took two white condoms out of the knee pocket of his flight suit, though when I saw them I wondered where he thought he might have an opportunity to use them. When I prepared for a mission, I sometimes remembered to pack one full of wooden matches and put it in my escape purse, but it was puzzling to me why Jimmy had them in their natural state sans matches. My wondering and my doubts were not valid; his plan for the condoms confirmed his foresight, even if they were not to be joyfully employed.

"We can piss in them." He grinned. "Then we can squeeze them between the bars in the window and bomb the fuckin' sentry."

As Jim pointed out, the small barred window in our cell was directly over the building's entrance. The sentry would be a perfect target. "C'mon," he urged, "load 'em up."

It was incredible; I could not believe they would stretch as they did.

The two condoms became two long amber balloons. We handled them very carefully as we edged our way to the window. Some of the urine sloshed out during the maneuver of squeezing them through the narrow openings, which were about five inches apart. Four of us had our hands through the bars holding our latex bombs that were now in position. We were laughing; the Bulgarian soldier was beside himself with excitement, and he kept running over to the poor, wretched figure on the pallet, pointing back at us as he told him about the mad thing we were doing. The professor didn't move or respond. His eyes were as sightless as before, and he remained in his hell.

Tom took over as bombardier. "Okay," he said, "bombs away." We released the two urine-filled condoms.

Two loud splats broke the silence of the early evening. Shouts from the sentry, which I knew were curses, assured us if we hadn't hit him we had come very close. There were other voices shouting now, and the sound of men running. We gathered in the center of the cell to wait for them. We could hear them rushing up the stairs. I was surprised that the door was opened quietly. An officer entered holding a Luger in his hand; he was followed by six soldiers with rifles.

They were rough with the rifles as they pushed us into a corner of the cell. They went over us one at a time, and their hands slammed hard into our stomachs and groins as they made their search for anything else we might have to annoy them. A soldier standing close to me had his bayonet pointed at my chest. I was desperately wishing I had a weapon when my hand touched a lump of dried bread in my pocket, a piece I had saved for an emergency ration. On an impulse, I took it out and impaled it on the point of the bayonet.

When the officer saw me do it, he roared with anger, and to my amazement he struck the soldier in the face. I could only guess he hit him because he was enraged at the soldier's stupidity; I should never have been allowed to touch his rifle. The officer continued to gesture at us in a threatening way and bellowed in a loud voice until he seemed to become weary of our indifferent stares. He muttered a few more words, which were probably warnings, and he turned for the door, motioning to his men to follow him. The last soldier to leave was the one I had offended. He glared at me, and suddenly he drove the butt of his rifle at my groin. I tried to turn away, but the blow caught me on the left thigh. An exploding pain collapsed my leg, and as I was falling to the floor I had the comforting thought that he had wasted the blow on my already injured leg. The dumb bastard should have hit the other one.

I yelled at the soldier before he went through the door, "Screw you, you stupid asshole!" He didn't turn. The door slammed shut.

In the morning we found good reason to irritate the Bulgarians again. The opportunity occurred when we were taken to the toilet facilities, which were in a small stone building near the prison. There was a high wire fence around the structure, and we were waiting impatiently for the gate to be opened. Four soldiers were guarding us with an NCO in charge who was much older than the rankers. I guessed he was a sergeant, and he appeared quite comfortable with his authority. He kept puffing on a foul-smelling cigarette, holding it with his thumb and forefinger in the European fashion, while he looked us over. He seemed to want to impress us by regarding our presence as a matter of small account; we Americans were nothing to get excited about.

Two guards were bringing a group of twelve women toward us. As they came closer, I could see that some of them had bruises on their faces; three were lame, and all were silent. It was a shameful silence, so unlike women. I wanted to hear their voices; I wanted to hear their laughter. When they joined us at the gate, they didn't look at us but kept their heads down. They stared at the ground, not daring to look up, at the sky, at the seven of us standing there watching them, or at the faces of their captors. It was not possible to know their ages; they all looked old, worn half to death, but most painful was their silence.

The NCO opened the gate to allow the women to move through. As they shuffled toward the small building, he motioned for us to follow them. We didn't move. He motioned again while we stood fast.

I spoke to George. "Tell that ignorant bastard we don't go in until the women come out."

George relayed the message in French to our Bulgarian fellow prisoner, whose name we decided would be Pete. Pete smiled when George gave him our message. He spoke quietly to the NCO, who responded in a predictable way. He did nothing. He was an old hand, and he wasn't going to lose his stripes by being any part of an incident, certainly not if he could avoid it. He repeated his command, through Pete, for us to move toward the toilets. His eyes were carefully appraising me as he spoke, trying to gauge my reaction to see just how determined I was, to see how far I would be willing to go.

"George," I said, "tell the sergeant that we are officers and noncommissioned officers of the United States. We are not peasants. We will wait here until the women come out."

The sergeant, I was sure, assessed my moderate tone, and my appeal to him as a gentleman. If he could have, he probably would have preferred to shoot me, but such an extreme confrontation would make things difficult for him and destroy his anonymity, which was essential to his survival as a noncommissioned officer. He turned away and spoke sharply to his men.

The soldiers advanced toward us with their rifles held across their chests. They pushed us back away from the gate. George and Pete were both smiling.

"What the hell's going on, George?" I asked.

George was still smiling when he answered me. "You got away with it. The sergeant says that men are not allowed in the toilets when women are there. It's regulations. We will have to wait until they come out."

It was a small victory; it would be one of the few we would have. To endure we sought to win such trifles to measure the day. We had become aliens of the poorest kind, and we had to find more than bits of bread to live on. We were in our early, awkward stage, in the adolescent years of our captivity. We were not the casual, day-by-day adventurers we would become, nor were we the arrogant young men we had been, who had lived with praise and honor. For now we were changed by fortune. We were in some middle ground, a desolate land where we were lost, abandoned like children, and like children longing to be found. We would have to learn to weather the days, to wear them down; and when they would not pass, we would have to burn them away with our curses. Time . . . time held us in this place, in this damned place. We would have to wait upon it. The last hour, the last minute, the last second of the last day, would come to pass, opening the way for us. That would be the moment of our glory, our long-remembered glory.

In the afternoon, I was taken from the cell down the staircase to a room on the first floor. Before I left the cell, with two guards escorting me, Sergeant Balcom gave me my instructions.

"Name, rank, and serial number, Lieutenant—and fuck 'em. Good luck."

The room did not seem threatening. A German officer was sitting at a large desk talking with a Bulgarian civilian, an older man with gray hair who was wearing thick, dark-rimmed glasses. A younger man, a Bulgarian officer, was standing beside the two seated men with his right hand resting on the back of the older man's chair. There were no windows, but the dim light was brightened by a small, shaded lamp

that sat on a round table in the center of the room. There was a
straight-backed chair in the front of the desk where presumably I was
to sit during my interrogation.

When I entered, the two seated men ignored me, and continued
their conversation. The Bulgarian officer dismissed my two guards.
He, too, ignored me as he pretended to be engrossed in what was
being said by the men leaning over the desk. He lit a cigarette and
blew the smoke at me in an insolent manner; I was sure he practiced
in front of a mirror. I wondered whether I should sit down or remain
standing; I decided to sit down, and I made a point of being noisy
about it. The German looked distressed; the older man smiled. The
Bulgarian officer then spoke to me in English. "Your name and rank,
please."

"John Muirhead. First lieutenant. Zero, seven, five, one, zero, two,
three."

"Do you wish to make a statement?"

"No."

"Your group and squadron?"

I responded by repeating my name, rank, and serial number.

The interrogation proceeded. I was asked question after question by
the Bulgarian while he paced back and forth behind me. Where was
I based? At Foggia? What was our target? How many aircraft were in
our formation? How many tons of bombs were we carrying? What
types? Where was my home? What state? Where did I train? How
many months? How many missions had I flown? What were the targets?
What were my feelings about the war? Why did I murder defenseless
women and children? Why did I fight for that Communist Jew, Roo-
sevelt. . . .

It was endlessly banal, and I kept giving my name, rank, and serial
number as each question was asked, which did not appear to elicit
any reaction from my inquisitor. The four of us seemed to be performing a familiar ritual, a tedious routine to confirm my apostasy,
and the sooner it was done with, the better.

The questioning suddenly ceased. The room became quiet. The
German officer was thumbing through some papers on the desk; the
civilian appeared to be dozing. I could no longer hear the man pacing
behind me, but his hand appeared by my side holding a lighted cigarette. I took it, and immediately felt that I should not have. What
the hell, I thought, so I'm compromised. Once a whore, always a
whore. Paul would not have taken it. He would have sat here stiff and

proud, his eyes straight ahead. I was surprised I had thought of him, my old comrade, my dear, old comrade. I wondered if he were still alive. I wondered if he had remembered to grab my air mattress. It was comfortable, and there were only a few of them around.

Their discussion was being carried on in French, and as they talked, the Bulgarian civilian, the older man, kept writing notes on forms that were neatly arranged on the desk, precisely arranged, I was sure, to satisfy the German's exquisite sense of order. Occasionally, as he worked, the Bulgarian looked toward me with a disturbed expression, no doubt considering my needless recalcitrance about the modest bits of information he required to fill out the empty spaces on the papers before him. Even if I were inclined to help him, I could not have told him very much. I was a dedicated know-nothing about the progress of the war, and had been concerned only with my pilgrimage through thirty-five missions. Beyond my little parish in the squadron, I had been blithely unconcerned for anyone else's troubles.

But I was changing. There were things I would have liked to have told him had I dared, or had I thought they would move his country's conscience by as much as a hairbreadth: about the tortured man on the third floor dying on his pallet, about the silent, beaten women, about the stink of the floor I slept on, about the misery of this prison, this soulless hole without hope or light. I was changing. I was beginning to see the land and the people around me. For the first time, I was beginning to see the countenance of repression, the brutal, cruel face of tyranny. I wished now, on that first day when I was captured, when I was asked if I had bombed Bulgaria, I wished now I could have said yes. By God, if I had bombed this place I would have put my heart and soul into it.

After the three men concluded their French conversation and finished marking papers, they seemed relieved and anxious to be rid of me. The German officer yawned, drumming his fingers on the desk. The civilian took out a pipe and put it in his mouth without lighting it. The Bulgarian officer turned to me. "Well," he said, "I think that will be all for now. Do you have anything further you wish to say?"

"No," I said.

"Very well, Lieutenant." He smiled in a patronizing way. "It's all over for you now. The luck of the game. Is that not so?"

I shrugged and said, *"C'est la guerre."*

He struck me hard with the back of his hand, and he began screaming at me, first in a torrent of French and then in English. "You bastard!

You American bastard! You were listening, listening to every word! You speak French! Don't you? Don't you? You'll pay for it! You'll pay for it, you gangster!"

I was astonished, not hurt. The blow was no more than an angry cuff, a reflex of anger common to mothers, to someone impatient with a dog. What the hell was going on? Was my interrogation phony and this the beginning of the real one? But the civilian and the German were as startled as I was. They were on their feet, wide-eyed and confused by the officer's outburst. They both shouted at the man, perhaps commanding him to control himself, for he quieted down and walked away from me. He stood with his back to the three of us trying to regain his composure.

The room was quiet, except for the sound of two very fat flies buzzing around the lamp. After a long moment, the officer turned and began speaking in a calm voice. He didn't look at me but directed his words to the German and the civilian; my deceit, which he had brilliantly perceived, was about to be exposed. I waited. Their heads were close together over the desk. Their hushed, secret voices were accompanied by the noisy hum of the fat flies that kept bumping against the lamp-shade with comic persistence. My use of the one French phrase I knew had destroyed the interrogator's poise, and had driven him into a frenzy of concern. I tried to remember other French words so I could plague him again, but I had exhausted my linguistic skills.

After discussing the matter at length with his superiors, the young officer turned back to me, being careful this time not to display any shred of the hysterical rage that had possessed him moments before. "Do you speak French, Lieutenant?" he asked.

"No," I answered. "No, I don't."

"You spoke French to me? Quite clearly."

"*C'est la guerre* is a universal expression, for God's sake," I said. "Everyone uses it. It is suitable for any situation—especially when one can't sensibly respond. One shrugs and says *C'est la guerre*. Do you understand?"

"I'm not sure that I do."

"It's an absurdity," I explained patiently. "The war's to blame for everything. Your wife runs off with your best friend—*C'est la guerre*. The cow doesn't give milk—*C'est la guerre*. I'm a prisoner in Bulgaria—*C'est la* fuckin' *guerre*. You see, there is nothing devious about it. That's all the bloody French I know."

"I see," the officer said. He was angry at my deliberate insolence, but he was determined not to give in to his anger. "I'll give them your explanation," he said, nodding toward the two men behind the desk. "If they're satisfied, that will be the end of the matter." He went to the door to call my guards. While I waited, I was subject to the curious stare of the German, who seemed to be amused by the incident. When I stood to leave, he was smiling. The bastard understood English; he understood every word I said. Before I followed the two guards out through the door, I spoke to him. "Good afternoon, Captain."

He replied with only a slight accent, "Good afternoon, Lieutenant."

Back in the cell, the dark, stinking cell, I warned Lieutenant Hamilton, telling him the details of my interrogation, including the squall of anger I had raised by saying *c'est la guerre*. "They know you speak French, George. They've heard you talk to Pete," and I nodded toward the Bulgarian prisoner. "Don't wait for them to ask you; tell them straight out. Don't be clever. I don't know how far they dare to go, but let's not find out. We may not be winning the goddamned war tomorrow. Let's get through the interrogations, and get the hell out of this hole. Watch out for the German, he's a cute son of a bitch."

George put his hand on my shoulder. "Don't worry, chum. I'll be all right." Then he said, "They've taken the professor again—for another session. They'll pound the shit out of him. Jesus, what bastards."

I could not respond to what George told me. There was nothing I could say. The man had been beaten senseless, and he would be beaten again. As Pete had implored us to do, I could only pray for the professor's death. What a pitiful testament to carry through one's life, to have witnessed such a thing . . . and to have done nothing.

Late in the afternoon, when we were through with the mindless questions, when we were through with our equally mindless answers of name, rank, and serial number, we were given soup, such as it was: a foul-smelling liquid with thick pieces of cabbage floating on top and with some other objects floating in it, which we optimistically identified as beans. We ate it, not with relish—not even Willy could manage that—but we ate it.

We had never eaten anything worse, and it was impossible for us to imagine that it did us any good, except it increased our worth in Willy's eyes. When we finished the last scrap of moldy bread and the last drop of the sour liquid, he told us with a proud grin, "You guys are doin' all right. In a couple of weeks you'll like the stuff. It'll grow on you."

"It'll grow on anything," Tom Connors growled.

Jim MacNaught moaned, "Jesus, forget it, will you? I'm trying to keep it down."

We were able to recover an hour later when we were taken from the cell out into the yard where we were allowed to walk about in the fresh air for a few moments before we were herded toward the latrines. There were no sad women to confront us this time; we were not required to be gallant. But without their presence touching us, even from their circumstances of worn despair and degradation, we were made to feel our loneliness. We longed to be reminded of what had happened to them so we would remember; we longed to find something before we left, just a fragment of what they were before. Each of us wished for them to come to us. Perhaps one would have smiled; perhaps one would have murmured a timid greeting.

We were taken away in the morning, which freed us at last from this odious place. I feared it. I feared the repulsive generation of misery that crept out of its stones and slouched down the dark corridors through every room and every cell. I feared the cries muffled by its walls, and I feared what I had not seen. From the back of the truck, I steadied myself with my hand on the tailgate, and I looked back toward the building until it was taken from my sight. We turned down a narrow street lined by trees. I watched the dust stream behind us.

Sergeant Keisacher spoke for all of us. "Christ, I'm glad to get out of that rathole."

Charlie Coffin put it to bed. "Amen to that, Mike," he said. "Wherever we're goin' has gotta be better than that."

I looked at the crew, the six of them, and I felt the surging pleasure of pride. By God, they were good men. They'll make it, I thought, they'll make it. Willy's massive bruise was getting better, and there were no signs of infection. Sgt. Mike Keisacher was coming around, emerging from a shocked silence that had held him for three days; Lt. George Hamilton, our tall, aristocratic navigator, seemed to be regarding the experience as a holiday, one he had particularly chosen, an arcane adventure to be shared later with a friend over an ice-cold martini. Sgt. Charlie Coffin, the waist gunner and a tough man like Willy who had seen hard times, was taking it all in stride. He and Willy had buddied up, and they shared a querulous view of everything Bulgarian, which they expressed in a hilarious torrent of obscenities. Jimmy MacNaught, the ball turret, was a slender boy with the quickness of a cat, and now he was sniffing around in a new backyard. He was always wary. Nothing escaped him.

And Tom Connors, the copilot, was our rock of dispassionate objectivity. He would walk through hell for a friend, but you had to earn his friendship. I wasn't sure that I had. He had waited gamely for me in the nose hatch when we were going down, and I knew if I hadn't made it, he would have come back for me. I really couldn't blame him if he were still holding a grudge because I had kicked him. It would take him some time to forget, not the blow to his backside but the blow to his honor. How could I have thought for a moment that he was frozen in the hatch?

Their loyalty to me was generously given, but more each day as a courtesy rather than a duty. I was no longer the pilot, their plane commander. My aura of infallibility, if not entirely faded, was considerably dimmed. None of the six men hesitated to let me know when they were troubled or when they thought I was wrong. We were each beginning to hear the wisdom of the other man. We were each beginning to learn of our need for one another in simpler and more direct ways than we had known before. It had no meaning now to be a pilot, a gunner, a navigator, a radio operator, a bombardier; these comfortably precise disciplines belonged to another world. Our vanity, our isolation as individuals, was being worn down by a new reality, and we were being changed. There was a peace and comradeship between us that strengthened as each day passed. Even Tom, my unrelenting copilot, made his gesture to make me whole again by finally forgiving me for my almost unpardonable offense.

We were about an hour away from Sofia prison, still rumbling along in the ancient truck, when he put his arm around my shoulder, and in a backhanded joking reconciliation, he let me know he understood my misdeed.

". . . well, you must have been in one helluva hurry to get out. Right? And there I was, between you and all that nice, blue sky. You were in such a goddamned hurry—now I'm not saying you were scared shitless, or anything like that—but you just didn't think of your buddy. You know that's a helluva thing to do, kickin' me in the ass like that."

"I know it was, Tom," I said meekly. "I won't do it again."

Tom was grinning at my servile apology. "Look," he said, "In the next war when we get shot down, you go first, then I'll come down and kick your ass out of the hatch. How's that?"

"Fair enough, Tommy," I said. "Fair enough."

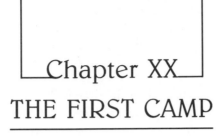

Chapter XX

THE FIRST CAMP

In adverse days it is easy to despise death; more courageous is he who can be wretched.

—MONTAIGNE

I can't remember whether we traveled a day, or for more than a day; it was not important, but it has plagued me for years: my inability to put the events of the first seven or ten days, or for that matter any subsequent days, into a sensible sequence of time. Perhaps it was because time took a different turn for me and I was conscious of it, not as day followed day, but as a gathering of small things. There were no minutes or hours or days or weeks. There were empty spaces, long emptiness; there was a rush of occurrences, one after the other; there was idleness and listless talk; there was sickness and the specter of typhus; there were wounds to be washed, and burns; there was always hunger, lust for coffee and strangely for candy; there was rarely fear; there was an inward searching, an ineffable purity of being. I suppose it was the kind of time an outcast knows, time passed carelessly with little concern for the familiar certainties of struggle by which other men mark the days and years.

We left the truck at the main road, and we walked down a wide dirt path toward the camp. There were three drunken Bulgarian soldiers sitting in the grass near the highway torturing a cat. Screams cut through the sunlight and through the moody silence of our march, so piercing, so horrifyingly sudden, we could not comprehend what was being done until we saw one of the soldiers hold the creature up in his hand. My God! He was laughing! The drunken fool was laughing!

I cannot describe, I will not attempt to describe, what I saw. It was a hideous cruelty, a vision seared into my soul forever of man, of noble, divine man, with his legs spread in triumph holding the agony of a small, blood-drenched cat high over his head.

Tom Connors was yelling at the top of his voice, "Kill it! You son of a bitch, kill it!"

Sergeant Keisacher was being held back by George Hamilton and Jimmy MacNaught, and he was yelling louder than Tom. "Oh, you bastards! You filthy bastards! I'll get you! I swear to Christ, I'll get you!"

Our two guards, who had been quietly escorting us from the truck down to the camp, now put themselves between us and the drunken soldiers, at the same time barking commands at them, apparently telling them to get the hell away, for two of the men turned and ran. The third man, the one who held the cat, threw the pitiful creature to the ground, stomping it with his boot before he, too, ran down the road. The screaming stopped.

It was so quiet; it was so unbelievably quiet. Then I heard the rustle of the wind moving up over the gently sloping land, seeking the trees and the long grass. I heard the guards' voices speaking strange words with no meaning. The seven of us were silent. The guards motioned to us to move on, and we began walking down the path again toward the camp. Mike Keisacher was staring up at the sky; his lips were moving but there was no sound. If he's railing at heaven about the soul of the little cat, I thought, it's a waste of time, a fuckin' waste of time. Who cares? Who cares about a cat? We can think about it later, Mike. We can dream about it later. . . .

At the gate we were met by a crowd of American prisoners, all of them dirty and cheerfully loud, rallying us through the barbed wire as though we were returning heroes. All of them looked wretchedly thin. Only the unlined leather jackets many of the men were wearing were reminders that this ragged band was air crew. The officers' suntans were soiled like mine. The men who were wearing olive-drab flight suits looked better; the dirt didn't show as much. The gunners who had worn heated suits were comically childlike in their blue woolens. Shining fine wire crisscrossed their garments, giving them a quilted appearance, and with their felt slippers, which were also laced with fine heating wires, the gunners looked for all the world like oversize three-year-olds ready for bed on a cold night.

Gifts were pressed upon us. I was given a cigarette and an egg. They threw their arms over our shoulders, and we were asked a thousand questions we were unable to answer because they were fired at us so fast: When were you shot down? Where? How many got out? What group were you with? How near are the Russians? Someone gave me a thin stick to poke holes in the ends of my egg, which I did and sucked the soft yolk into my mouth. There was only a light taste of egg; it would have been grand fried. I was grateful for it, very grateful. It was the first bit of food I had received in two days. I wanted to light my cigarette after my feast, but I didn't have any matches. I stood there grinning like a fool, surrounded by comrades, surrounded by countrymen. I was happy in the midst of their tumult. I was home.

The camp was situated on the side of a long slope of grassland; it included a low, rambling building that had once been white, and nearby there was a small barn. There were two areas surrounding the structures that were separated by barbed wire. The inner area, where we were allowed to gather, was about twenty yards wide. The outer area was of the same width and was patrolled by guards. Two vintage water-cooled machine guns were set up at the ends of the outer strip, and two ferocious guard dogs occupied the end boundaries of our inner strip. The dogs were tethered to a heavy wire stretched across the twenty yards that allowed them to move freely back and forth. They were large, mean beasts; it was impossible to approach them.

The latrine, which was a filthy pesthole, was located on the lower slope near the main building; it was always occupied by sick, white-faced men who, when not in it trying to ease the cramping pains in their bellies, were waiting along the high-fenced path that led down to it. Violent diarrhea and the weakening distress of dysentery were common plagues for which the only treatment was one recommended by the Bulgarian guards, that of ingesting charcoal-saturated water, and they were decent about providing us with a stock of small ends of charred wood for making this coarse, gritty remedy. It tasted vile, but it seemed to reduce the symptoms. It was common for many of the sick men to carry small pails, also provided by the guards, to use when they couldn't make it to the latrine. With their pails, their chunks of charcoal, and with their tired words of self-mockery, these wasted, gentle young men shuffled through each day until, by strength of will alone it seemed, they became well again. I had the honor of sharing their misfortune after a few days in camp when I came down with stomach cramps and extreme diarrhea. I also discovered, to my disgust, I had come to share something else: I was completely lousy.

The crew and I were assigned to quarters in the barn where we joined the overflow of other new arrivals; we were barely able to fit in. When we stretched out to sleep, we took up the last floor space available, leaving only a narrow path in the center for access to the waste and urine bucket that was placed under our one small window at the end of the room.

On the first night, I couldn't sleep. I stood up and moved out from between the still forms on either side of me. I began to pace up and down in the open area, trying to be careful not to step on anyone's legs or feet. I paced for perhaps five minutes when I heard a voice coming it seemed from the wall across from me. "Sit down, for God's sake. My head's killing me. Your boots sound like freight trains."

I remembered the man as soon as he spoke. We had shared the reeking tedium of the line to the latrine; we had shared some hours in the sun. His name was Dan Wylie, a P-38 pilot with a bad wound in the back of his left shoulder. "Sorry, Dan," I whispered, and I found my way back to my spot on the floor. Through the window, I could see the shadow of the sentry slowly pass; I waited, then he passed again. The sleeping men were very quiet. My mind still paced, futilely, desperately searching, back and forth. I've got to get out. . . . I've got to get out. . . .

When daylight came, the flies took over; I could not believe the swarming, damned hordes of them. Someone yelled, "Okay, fly drive! Time for fly drive!" One man opened the small window, the others gathered at the opposite end of the barn as close together as they could stand, and then they began to advance waving their hands violently over their heads. They drove the black cloud of flies in front of them toward the window where the flies, buzzing much louder now, swirled in a torrent into the sunlight. The window was slammed shut. The men yelled their cry of victory, but it was not a victory for long. In less than half an hour, and as the sun became warmer, the flies were back in greater numbers than before. We rallied again. "Fly drive! Time for fly drive!" Before we were entirely overwhelmed, we were rescued by the guards who opened the doors so we could go to the main house for our breakfast of watery, ersatz tea and a slice of hard bread.

We spent all the time we could outside, regardless of the weather, pleased to be away from the stench and the close confinement of the barn. There was little to occupy us except gossip, and most of it was about the exotics, as George Hamilton called them, who were a fascinating minority in our community.

Maj. Richard Sheldon was one of the exotics. He was a British officer, a ruddy-faced man, I would guess in his mid-forties, who was of medium height and build, sported a thick mustache, and had an irrepressible penchant for bad jokes. He never told a straight story. We could never learn for certain how he had been captured or why he was in Bulgaria. When we confronted him with questions, he always answered us with entertaining lies. "Well, there I was, you see, out for a bit of a stroll, minding my own affairs—you know, thinking about having a pint, tits, and all that sort of thing, when these bloody buggers pick me up. Bulgaria they say—I'm in bloody Bulgaria! Now how did that come about? What?"

The old-timers in the camp told us when the major had been brought in, months ago, he had been in bad shape, and had been tortured and beaten. His recovery had been doubtful for many weeks. Rumors had it he was with British Intelligence, and that he had been their liaison with Tito in Yugoslavia. The rumors went on to suggest his presence in Bulgaria was a mistake. He was supposed to have rendezvoused with Tito's staff somewhere near the border, and, among other duties, hand over a large sum of money he was carrying to bolster the partisans' war effort. But either his jumpmaster, or the Wellington's pilot, screwed up, for when he parachuted on his fateful night, he drifted into Bulgaria.

We were all fond of the major. On the fourth of July, we asked him to join our celebration. To affirm our victory over the British, we demanded that he serve our soup, which he did, cheerfully ladling it out while he muttered, "Colonials, bloody, damned Colonials, every one of you. Gad, what cheek."

If the major were reticent, sworn to secrecy as we presumed he was, Andreas, our Greek paratrooper, was not. He also wore a British uniform, but he did not share the major's obligation to be silent. Andreas was a powerfully built young man with black hair and dark brown eyes that blazed with passion when he talked about his specialty, which was sabotage. He had been dropped many times, for missions in Bulgaria, in Greece, and in Yugoslavia. He always operated behind the German lines, and he said he usually carried, along with his heavy bag of explosives, food for three or four days, a rifle or a semiautomatic, three knives, a revolver, ammunition, at least six grenades, and occasionally a portable bicycle. Blowing bridges was the greatest joy he could imagine, except when he could consummate his hate and kill a German. When he talked of it, of cutting a sentry's throat, his voice softened as he caressed the death, savoring it like a man remembering love. He told us how to drive a knife into a German's back or chest— not a man's back or chest, but a German's—and twist it in such a way the victim's lungs would fill with blood and he would be unable to cry out. He described, with smiling intimacy, the sound of a German's skull—not a man's skull, but a German's—being crushed by a blow from a short length of iron bar.

Andreas was an obsessed man, a doomed, pathological man, and I could not endure being with him for long. He was destroyed by the cruelties he had seen in his village, and he lived only to kill every German he could confront. There was nothing else for him. He was near madness . . . very near.

When I could free myself for any length of time from long, painful vigils in the latrine where I squatted in weak, sweating misery eight or ten times a day, I usually sought the company of the Dutchmen. They were brothers, Hugh and Lou, and both were lithe, tall men with the long-muscled bodies of athletes. The amusing assonance of their names, which reminded me of the riotous nephews of Donald Duck, belied their reserved manner and their thoughtful, measured way of speaking. They were at ease with the English language, as they seemed to be with French and German, but they used it in a stilted, laconic style. I suspected this was deliberate and manifested a reluctance to indulge in careless, thoughtless words that might be misunderstood or unnecessarily revealing. Of the few slang expressions they used, their favorites were "pissed off" and occasionally a reference to someone brash and stupid as "having a large pair of balls." They were cautious men, always wary, and if they were not literally looking over their shoulders, I sensed they were certainly aware of everything going on around them. They watched each other's back, and they were always together.

They didn't lie as blatantly as the major: the story they stuck to we knew was not altogether true, but it did account in a general way for the many months of their incredible walk from Amsterdam to the Turkish border, where they were taken captive by the Bulgarians. They insisted they were innocent of any wrongdoing, or any covert games against the Germans, though they did admit they were on a Gestapo list and were wanted by the Nazis. When we asked them why they hadn't made their escape from Holland by way of the channel to England, they shrugged and said, "It was not possible. We had to head east."

Lou told us he had been a police officer in Amsterdam; Hugh, the older one, claimed to have been the owner of a small appliance store. We knew this was nonsense. The men were agents; we were certain of it. There were rumors, of course, and some I thought were probably near the mark. The one I favored as nearest the truth was that they had been setting up a communications network across southern Europe and establishing escape routes for downed airmen through southern France, Italy, and the Balkans. We were never to know any of this for sure, and our interest waned after a time. Hugh and Louis were blandly noncommittal, so beyond the entertainment our speculation provided, there was not much point in pressing them.

I was healing, thanks to the charcoal remedy and to the long naps I was taking stretched out on the grassy slope between the two barbed-wire enclosures. My trembling weakness had passed, and I felt blessed not to have to spend the better part of every day in that foul latrine.

My curiosity about the exotics had been brief, as I knew it would be. Andreas, the vengeful paratrooper, the whimsical Major Sheldon, and the silent Dutchmen were men I decided I would never understand, men whose impenetrable commitment to isolation and peril seemed to me to be a perverse and ill-chosen way to fight a war. I could only wonder at their lonely courage. They were strange soldiers, I thought, but so were we in many ways. We all had secrets we didn't share.

Sgt. Tiny Culhane, a top turret gunner from one of the B-24 crews, appeared to be acting in a secretive way. Or was I becoming paranoid, imagining secrecy all around me? But it wasn't like Tiny to sit off by himself; he was one of the most companionable men in the group. He was never a loner; every man in the camp was his friend. It was puzzling each day why he chose to sit alone, very quietly near the far boundary of our narrow area; I was becoming concerned. My God, if Tiny went bonkers who the hell could manage a mountain like him? When I asked Willy what he thought of Sergeant Culhane's behavior, he laughed at me.

"Naw," he said. "Tiny's just trying to make up to the dog."

"The dog?"

"Yeah, the guard dog—that fuckin' elephant down there with all the teeth. Tiny thinks he can get to him."

I should have known; I should have been able to figure it out. It was the kind of challenge Tiny couldn't resist. Sure, that's why he's sitting there, every day moving closer to the dog.

None of us interfered, nor did anyone want to; the dog was big, vicious, and he was agitated by Tiny's nearness. If we were quiet and the wind was still, we could hear Tiny's voice crooning to the beast.

"That's a good boy, that's a good, old boy. You're a good baby—a good baby. You're goin' to be Tiny's dog. Yes, sir, you're Tiny's dog. . . ."

The encounter went on, and each day the two were closer until the distance between the snarling, straining animal and Tiny's outstretched hand was no more than six inches. On the final day, when Tiny won the dog over, the end was sudden, and those of us who had watched the entire courtship could not see clearly.

The quiet scene of man and dog together on the hillside had become a familiar tableau. A fair blue sky stretched over them, and it seemed that nothing would change. The confrontation would go no further. Tiny was sitting in his usual position near the dog; his back was to me. For a moment he blocked my view. Then the dog was free! He was running around Tiny! My God! He was charging into the man—he was attacking him! I gasped with relief when I saw Tiny embrace the shaggy monster around the chest, trying to hold him to quiet him down. I could hear Tiny's voice soothing the dog. "Take it easy, boy. There's a good boy . . . good old boy."

The damned dog would have none of it. He was wild with joy, and there then ensued a celebration of freedom, a declaration of love, a raucous ballet, a joyful *pas de deux* as inelegant as I had ever seen. The two tumbled over and over in the grass, and when Tiny managed to stand, the great dog kept leaping on him and knocking him down again. They ran around in circles, they grappled in desperate combat, the dog yipped and growled as Tiny challenged him back into the fray again and again. This joining of man and beast, this ritual of play, went on for almost an hour until both were exhausted and lay spent on the grass, the man puffing and laughing, the dog panting heavily with his pink tongue hanging out of the side of his mouth.

Major Sheldon was standing beside me watching with an approving smile. He spoke quietly, to no one in particular. "Well done, Sergeant. Bloody well done indeed."

If there was a meaning to it, a meaning known to Tiny during his patient four-day vigil, and a meaning he felt he must share with the savage dog, it was one he could not share with us. It was a secret between them, this mysterious need between dog and man that sent each searching for the other until the world of one was yielded and everlasting trust was finally given.

The guards, who had watched Tiny's intrusion into their security system with only mild and puzzled curiosity, made no attempt to return the dog to his wire run, and this surprised me. I thought there would be hell to pay, but nothing happened. Tiny was not punished; there was no effort to reclaim the dog. I supposed the guards might have thought if the animal could not be relied on for consistent ferocity, he was of little use to them. As it turned out, the guards' indifference was not a matter of casual, good-humored indulgence; they knew we were to be moved out in a day or two, so someone else could worry about Tiny. They would deal with the dog's betrayal later, and shoot him at their leisure—if the poor beast was lucky.

After a night in the fetid barn, where in our sweat and dirt we renewed our quarrel with the lice and with the pestilent swarms of flies and with vermin rustling in the darkness, we roused to the first light of a new day. We emptied the foul waste bucket; we had our tea, and then joined the slow procession in the fenced path that led to the latrine.

Tom Connors was standing beside me. "I hear we're moving out," he said.

"Where are we supposed to be going?" I asked him. "Not that it makes a helluva lot of difference."

Tom smiled. "Beats the hell out of me," he said. "I don't give a shit where we go as long as we get out of that fuckin' barn. Ain't it a pisshole?"

"Well," I said, "it isn't exactly the Parker House, but it's home, Tom. You know, we could burn it down."

Tom laughed. "Now that's the best idea I've heard today, but no kidding, I hear we're getting out. I mean we're getting out of this place."

Tom was right. At nine o'clock about fifty of us were lined up in a long column to begin another journey. I can't remember whether all the men in the camp were taken out at this time. Some were very weak from dysentery, and our few walking wounded could not have possibly made the march. If there were others who remained, I cannot say.

We walked out to the main road in shambling disarray. It was a hot July day, and I thought if Paul were with me we could have talked about Gettysburg—not talked exactly, but we could have yelled at each other about Lee and Longstreet and Meade. It would have passed the time. Let's see, just about now eighty-one years ago Lee was making his way, slowly and painfully, out of Pennsylvania heading south. Meade was sitting on his ass, doing nothing . . . Funny how it turned out.

After twenty minutes, my leg began to act up. It was not intolerable, but it was a tormenting pain. I tried very hard not to limp. When we neared the end of the first hour, we stopped for a short rest. The guards shouted something at us, which loosely translated I supposed was, "Take ten! Smoke if you got 'em!" I didn't sit down. I was afraid my leg would stiffen. My belly and my groin were burning from the feverish activity of the lice. I was very thirsty. Someone handed me a canteen. The tepid water tasted delicious, though like a true hypochondriac, I was fretful because there was no charcoal in it.

The guards shouted again, and we continued our march. They were trying to set a fairly brisk pace. The second hour dragged on. I began to wonder how long I could keep up. I tried to concentrate, to find a comfortable rhythm. I counted steps; I counted minutes, and I tried not to look at my watch. I grunted and hummed. All armies are the same—always walking to some goddamned place no different from the one you just left. Why couldn't they let you die and rot in one spot? What the hell difference did it make? The sun was getting higher and hotter. Jesus, where were they taking us? To Berlin. They were going to march us all the way to fuckin' Berlin. I was sure of it.

Where had Willy come from? He was walking beside me. "You okay, Lieutenant?" he asked.

"Yeah, I'm okay, Sarge. How about you?"

"I'm doin' pretty good. Yeah, I'm doin' pretty good. How's the leg?"

"Lousy."

"Where do you think they're taking us, Lieutenant?"

"Berlin."

"Berlin, huh. Hey, that's great. We'll be there for the October Festival—you know, when all the krauts sit around and slop up beer."

"Sarge, how about one right now—a nice, cold pint in one of those big steins."

"Jesus, Lieutenant, cut it out, will ya?"

We walked together in silence, both dreaming of the cool taste of beer. After a while, Willy looked at me with concern. "Did you shit yourself, Lieutenant?" he asked.

"Yeah, twice so far."

"You sure you're okay?"

"Yeah, it's just brown water. You get a pain in your gut, and you can't do anything about it."

"The Dutchmen have been talking with the guards," Willy said. "If there's a stream or somethin' up ahead, we'll stop for ten minutes, and you guys can wash."

"That's great, Sarge. Many of the other guys sick?"

"Yeah, I guess a third of the column is. They're either pukin', sweatin', shiverin', or shittin'; we're worried about you guys dryin' out—you know, dehydration. Tommy—I mean Lieutenant Connors is in kinda' tough shape. He and a few others have dropped back quite a bit. The Dutchmen think we got about an hour to go, maybe less, then we're supposed to take a train to wherever the hell it is we're goin'. Can you make it okay?"

"No sweat, Sarge. No sweat."

"Jesus, don't sweat, Lieutenant." Willy continued in his best motherly style, "You can't afford to lose any more water. Look, Jack," he said, "I'm going to drop back." He was grinning at his boldness, knowing I would not reprove him for not addressing me properly. Why should I? He was my friend, my comrade. "I might be able to help back there," he said.

"Yeah, good, Sarge. Tell Tommy love and kisses."

Willy laughed and stepped to the side of the road to wait for the stragglers. As he waved me along, he yelled, "Try and scrounge some water!"

By God, he was a good fellow. Short, skinny, ugly as sin, and as tough as nails, as good a man as I would ever know. His company had cheered me. I was pleased with myself now, and I was moving along quite well. I was keeping my place in the column. The aching pain in my leg had leveled off to no more than a tolerable nuisance. My stomach gurgled loudly from time to time in response to convulsive spasms in my bowels, but there was nothing left. I was as empty as a drum. If the Dutchmen were right, it would be a three-hour march. All we had to do was forty minutes more, only forty minutes.

It must have been nearly ninety degrees, a perfect summer day for the sound of tennis balls, for the sound of a girl's voice, or for the murmuring sound of cool water and the hiss of a dry fly reaching out to touch the gleaming pool. A soft wind drove a pageant of white clouds across the sky, and there, from that wide azure plain, I felt some presence and serene and indifferent eyes fixed upon our march, watching. I looked up. The sky revealed nothing but the procession of the white clouds passing over us. Why should we be watched, by old gods or new? We were alien, uncaring men soiled and worn to slovenry. We would not give them homage.

I could hear something, the sound of engines . . . unfamiliar . . . single engine. There they were! Four ME-109s to our right at about two thousand feet were heading north. Another flight of three roared almost directly over our heads. They were beginning to climb; I watched them until they were dark spots high over the mountains. I watched them until the sky was empty. But my mind held them, and I knew the old fear again. I could see them framed in my windshield, the blinking wing guns and the black bursts of cannon shells . . . I could see them.

The column marched on. The sound of our boots echoed down the empty road. Dust drifted around us, then moved away, borne by the wind in thin streams like mist. I could hear someone singing. The great bulk of Sgt. Tiny Culhane's back, stained with sweat, loomed in front of me. The fighters hadn't killed me, and now they passed over as though I were not here. The flak hadn't killed me. It could not possibly have been that way. I was alive. I was bloody well alive. The last half-hour of that weary walk long ago in the sun was sublime. I was happy on that road with my comrades, tasting the sweetness of the air, dreaming of freedom.

Chapter XXI

THE HILL

Alone he goes where no wind blows
Unto the land which no one knows.

—EBENEZER ELLIOTT
Plaint

We walked through the outskirts of a village. The few citizens who were about seemed poor, and they scarcely looked at us as we passed; only one or two were brazen enough to glance in our direction in a quick, furtive way. Either they were afraid of the soldiers guarding us, or perhaps they believed the German propaganda that described American airmen as gangsters, destroyers of schools and hospitals, pathological brutes who would rape any woman, old or young, given the slightest chance, and that they were fiends who dropped tiny delayed-action explosives hidden in lollipops for the children. One little girl in a brightly colored dress stared at me, resisting the pull of her mother's hand for just a moment. I smiled at her and winked my eye. She giggled, putting her small closed fist to her mouth as she continued to stare. The mother shouted at the child and raised her hand as if to strike her. Yes, love, I thought, you must learn from your mother. I am your enemy.

The Dutchmen were right. There was a train waiting for us at the village station. Like many of the others, I was coming to accept what Hugh and Louis told us as gospel, but there was a minority reluctant to put their expectations wholly into the hands of the adventurers from Holland. Tom Connors was one who was marginal, and he chose to question the Dutchmen. Looking pale and wobbly, he gamely challenged Hugh as Hugh offered to help him board the train.

"You and Louis said there'd be some water so we could wash. How come no water?"

"I'm sorry you misunderstood, Lieutenant. If we had come upon a stream, we had an agreement with the guards to stop for ten minutes." Hugh's tone was mild and patient. "Unfortunately," he added, "we didn't have any luck. If there's enough water on the train, maybe we can get some cleaning done. We'll be on the train for three or four hours, perhaps longer."

"How do you know?" Tom asked. He was belligerent, very weak, and trying hard not to fall.

"Just a guess, Lieutenant. Just a guess." Hugh was watching Tom closely as he spoke. "I think you've got a touch of malaria, Lieutenant," he said. "How long has it been since you've had your Atabrine?"

"Three weeks—four weeks. Something like that."

"Come on, let me help you," Hugh said. He put his arm around Tom, and with an easy, sweeping motion, he lifted him up over the three steps into the car. It was such an extraordinary act of strength so casually performed, I could hardly believe what I had seen. Tom was not a small man. He must have weighed a hundred and seventy pounds. Hugh, the mild, gentle shopkeeper from Amsterdam, selling toasters and electric irons? Not likely. No, his reserve and self-control seemed to me a kind of vigilant cunning, a practiced deception. Like his brother, Louis, he hid his strength. I wondered what the Gestapo wanted them for. I wondered how many Germans they had killed.

We were crammed into two cars, and most of us stood in the passageway. The Bulgarian soldiers took the compartments, sharing them with prisoners who were ill and with men who were lucky enough to be the first to load and were able to find empty seats. There was water, but only a cup for each man. The prisoners who had to use the toilet, and there were many who did, were accompanied by a guard. The men were confined to the hopper; the wash basin was off-limits. It was not a true hopper, very few in southern Europe were; it was a hole in the stained tile with slightly raised footstands on either side. It was a demeaning accommodation, hellishly uncomfortable, and in my mind, an absolute manifestation of Bulgarian inferiority. One of our favorite fantasies was to dream of a clean, warm bathroom, with a real throne where one could sit, a book or a magazine in one's hand, a pack of cigarettes in one's pocket, and time, plenty of time.

Late in the afternoon we arrived at our destination. The town was called Shumen. There were tired wrecks of trucks waiting for us that had seen long, hard service and little maintenance. Their idling engines gasped for air; clattering pistons, leaking valves, and the chatter of worn tappets, all wrapped in poisonous fumes spewing from grievous wounds in the exhaust systems, were evidence of the pitiful state of these veteran machines. We could not possibly be traveling far; the trucks were dotards trembling at death's door.

We climbed over the battered tailgates, chose a place to sit where we would not be lacerated by exposed rusted rivets or the torn shreds of metal around them, and we waited. The guards hurried the loading, shouting and prodding the laggards with their rifles. Our small convoy at last began to move, not with purpose but more in the manner of old men rising slowly and painfully in the morning.

The two trucks made their careful passage out of the railroad station and proceeded along a narrow road that bordered the town. We passed three horse-drawn wagons, a large warehouse where two men were sitting on a loading platform smoking cigarettes, and in a field I saw two antiaircraft batteries. I could hear the voices of the soldiers, for the wind was blowing toward me. I could hear the wind-caught music of bagpipes. And then I saw the piper. He was walking toward the guns with a squad of six soldiers following him. The pipes looked the same as Scottish pipes except the bag was made of skin, and the music was different, strangely different. Its reedy cry swept across the long meadow plaintively singing, filling the air and sky with its longing.

Beyond the town were hills, and beyond the hills rugged mountain terrain stretched in every direction. George Hamilton, who was sitting next to me in the truck, said we had been traveling east all day, and we were probably near the Black Sea. He pointed away from the sun. "The coast is over in that direction," he said. "Probably about a hundred miles or so. Down there," he added, pointing south, "is Turkey, and a corner of Greece." He grinned. "It's a long walk, but if we were lucky, we might make the coast. What do you say? One day soon, what do you say?"

"I'll keep it in mind, George," I said. "I'll sleep on it. How are you at navigating over mountains?" I asked him.

"Oh, absolutely wizard, chum. Piece of cake." George was enjoying himself considering all the adventurous aspects of our predicament. He wrapped his arms around his knees pulling them close to his chest. He sat there coiled in happy contemplation, no doubt thinking of the romance of wandering through the mountains, of all the wonderful things that might happen.

Our trucks were heading for a high hill whose deep, long shadow reached out from the precipitous slope to shield us from the sun. Tom Connors was huddled in sleep not far from George and me; sergeants Willy Balcom and Coffin were beside him, watching his rest with ferocious concern and softly cursing the driver for every lurching bump. Sergeant Keisacher and Sergeant MacNaught were in the truck ahead, which was leading us up the long incline that crossed the face of the hill.

We made our way slowly; the trucks labored; the gears whined, and I felt sorry for their torment. I wondered if these damned Bulgarians knew they were supposed to put oil in the engines once in a while— the dumb bastards. We'll never make it, I thought. We're going to break down on this goddamned hill.

We didn't break down, which surprised me. I was amazed, as I always am at the faithful durability of machines that so willingly serve the undeserving. The trucks struggled in low gear, winding now around the side of the hill, clawing their way up the rock-strewn road. Near the top, the grade became less steep, and we were able to accelerate. As we approached the plateau, the gears shifted into second, then into third; we roared triumphantly across the uneven ground at the top of the hill, braking to a stop ten yards from the outer fence of barbed wire that enclosed our new prison. We had scattered a small herd of goats, and three horses nearby raised their heads from the sparse grass to look at us.

After unloading, we were assembled at the outer gate, beyond which I could see groups of prisoners inside the compound sitting in the sun. There was only one prisoner waiting to greet us; he was standing behind the inner barbed wire watching us with an amused smile. He was a slender young man with thick blond hair that strikingly contrasted with his body, which was bronzed and weathered, and completely unclothed. His nakedness was not unreasonable, for it was a pleasant afternoon and the sun was warm, but there was something unusual about him. I could not recall ever seeing a mature man with hairless genitals, and sun-tanned at that. When our column was brought through the second gate and we came near him, he greeted us in a curious, ribald way.

"Good afternoon, gentlemen. Lt. Harry Winston Jones extends greetings. Welcome to Shumen Heights, the garden spot of Bulgaria. You'll never get out alive, boys. Believe me, you'll never get out alive. Remember, old Harry told you. You got the straight scoop."

The men responded to Lieutenant Jones as they passed by him, laughing and calling out, "Hey, Lieutenant, where's the chow line? . . ." "Where's the broads? . . ." "How come you're bare-ass, Lieutenant? You hiding something? . . ."

George, whose tall figure was striding a few steps ahead of me, stopped in front of Lieutenant Jones, and with rude concentration, he stared at the naked man's privates; then he slowly looked up and spoke in a solemn, melancholy voice, "My, Lieutenant, you're so young."

Harry laughed and put his hand out toward George. "Glad to meet you, pal," he said. "What you see is a sure cure for lice. Stay out of your clothes when you can; clean the nits out of your seams, or better still, pop them with your cigarette—if you can get a cigarette, and shave yourself where the buggers like to nest, which is mostly around your balls. Courtesy of old Dr. Harry Jones, and I'm not shittin' you, pal."

"Ah," George said, shaking Harry's hand. "My name is Hamilton, George Hamilton." Pointing back to me he added, "This is my friend, Lieutenant Muirhead. We might just stay here in this charming place for a week or two."

"Yeah, you do that, George," Harry said. "You stick around. You'll love it—the asshole of the world. Good guys here, though—all good guys." As George and I walked away, he called after us. "Don't forget what I told you! You'll never get out alive!"

The hill was higher than Big Blue, where my brother Sandy and I used to walk on Sunday morning. Big Blue was about six hundred and thirty feet; this hill must have been over seven hundred. The top was nearly flat, sloping gently down from the escarpment from which we could have viewed the town and the land below if we could have gone beyond the barbed wire. The lower slope was open to the outer perimeter of wire and to about thirty yards beyond it, where thick shrubs and trees defined the boundary of the plateau. The width from the escarpment to the trees was perhaps five hundred yards; the length of the hilltop was no more than nine hundred or a thousand. We shared this place with goats, a small herd of horses, two jackasses, a gun emplacement, a few soldiers, lice, bedbugs, rats, an old dog, and with a muezzin whom we could not see but whose cry from the mosque in the town below drifted with the wind over the hill. "There is no God but God. . . ." For all the time I was there, on that wretched, peaceful hill, and when the wind would carry his high, mournful voice to me, I wondered at his folly, and mine. I wondered who in all the world could find his way past the right hand of God? Who in all the world could enter paradise?

There was a low stone building in the center of the compound that looked like it might have been a military barracks a long time ago. Its bleached and stained walls did not promise comfort, not a shred of it, but it was not as forbidding as the prison in Sofia had been, and sitting in the clear air of the hilltop, it could not possibly be as foul as the barn I had slept in the night before. It might not be too bad. I stood there considering the place, as though I need not stay and could go on to find another accommodation. It helped to pretend one had a choice. Like a weary traveler, I chose to stay; this would have to do for today; there would would be something better tomorrow, or the day after. I watched two goats nibbling grass near the entrance of the building. I remembered I was very hungry. I wondered if I would be given any food . . . anything would do. My legs were trembling; my bowels were churning, and the activity of the lice on my belly was a torment. I wanted to lie down . . . anyplace would do.

Two officers came through the open double doors of the entrance and stood looking down at our small company from four steps above us. The senior officer was a major, a slender, self-assured fellow who inspected us with a wry smile before he spoke. He had a slight southern accent. "My name is Smith," he said, "Major Smith. You boys look about done in. The gentleman with me is Lt. J. P. Darlington. We've got some bean soup being dished out in the back, and some water. If you go through the entrance here and down the corridor to the rear doors, Sergeant Dogget will provide utensils and a bowl. Any wounded or sick, please report your situation to Lieutenant Darlington. Tomorrow I'll be asking about the status of your shots, particularly typhoid, tetanus, and typhus. I want you to try to remember when you had them. Think about it. After we eat, we'll see about assigning you a place to sack out. Okay, boys, if you'll just follow J.P. and me."

A young officer, who obviously was not Sergeant Dogget, gave each of us a small metal bowl about the size used for breakfast cereal. He also gave each of us a spoon and a short-bladed knife with the point broken off. We then took our place in line and proceeded in a shuffling approach toward an iron kettle steaming on an old wood-fired stove where a red-faced Sergeant Dogget scowled in sullen silence as he served the pale brown broth.

I was sitting in the shade under the rear wall of the building finishing my soup and wishing I had more, when a man spoke to me. "Have a bit of this," he said, handing me a piece of bread. "I've got some more I saved from this morning." I looked up at a dark-faced man with bright, gleaming dark eyes. There were burn scars on his throat, and he had one leg. He supported himself on a crude crutch with the casual confidence of an athlete whose strength commanded the piece of wood he used for a leg as though it were flesh and blood. His good-hearted vigor admonished me, diminishing the distractions of my weakness, my churning bowels, and my itching belly to precisely what they were—nothing.

I mumbled my thanks for the bread, and then stupidly blurted out, "That's just like Long John Silver's crutch."

To my immense relief, my new friend laughed. "Hey, yeah, that's right. Did you see Wallace Beery in that movie? Wasn't he great? I saw it three times. I read the book, too. Great story. I wish we had some goddamned books around here." He dropped his crutch to the ground and sat down beside me. He grabbed my hand in a strong grip. "Sergeant Blackwell," he said. "Call me Blackie. Everyone does."

"Muirhead," I said. "Lieutenant Muirhead. Call me Jack. And thanks again for the bread. I was pretty hungry."

"Yeah, I could tell. I've been there myself, buddy." Blackie laughed, and then he went on in a confidential, serious tone. "You gotta keep your strength up. J.P. says we're going to be getting out soon, so you gotta watch yourself. You gotta' make it. You know what I mean?"

"J.P.?" I asked.

"Yeah, Darlington, Lieutenant Darlington—J.P. He's my pilot." Sergeant Blackwell seemed astonished that I did not know J.P. "Yeah, we went down on the first Ploesti raid—from North Africa. I've been here since August of '43. If it hadn't been for old J.P., I'd have never made it. Where did you get it?"

"Ploesti—a few weeks ago."

"No shit. Fighters?"

"Yeah, and engine trouble, lagged—you know. And I think I fucked up."

"Everybody thinks they fucked up. Over three hundred fuck-ups, that's what we got here."

"Were you and J.P. the only ones that made it?" I asked Blackie.

"Naw, there's another one-legged guy around—Sergeant Dobson. We think the rest of the crew made it into Turkey. We were near the border when we crashed. J.P. stayed with me and Dobson."

"J.P. must be quite a guy," I said.

Sergeant Blackwell reflected for a moment. "I just don't know how it is with men like J.P.," he finally said. "They're different—I don't know. They're a cut above the rest of us. They've got somethin' in them—somethin' you can't put a finger on. He's one in a million, I'll tell you that. He's one in a fuckin' million." And then the sergeant abandoned his attempt to tell me of his love for his friend, who was more noble in his eyes than any man who had ever lived. "Hey," he said, "we gotta get inside. They lock us up at six." He grabbed his crutch and jabbed the staff against the ground, pulling himself up with one hand. "Take is easy, Jack," he said. "I'll see you tomorrow." As he swung away from me, he turned back laughing, "Just like Long John Silver. Right? Avast there, me hearties!" he cried, and he waved an imaginary cutlass over his head, putting fear into the hearts of those of us who watched him before he began in earnest to cut a bloody path to the rear door of the prison.

The corridor divided the building into two large rooms: one was assigned to the enlisted men, the other to the officers. The rooms were of the same size, but since there were more enlisted men—over twice the number of officers—their room was crowded, certainly more crowded than ours. The building was not intended to accommodate more than one hundred and eighty men. All in all, we were a total of three hundred and thirty-five.

Many of the men were sick, many more were recovering from burns, and there were about thirty wounded men who had been released from Bulgarian hospitals along with the burned men after only a brief and indifferent period of treatment. There were no medical facilities; there was no medicine of any kind. The only bandages available were the ones the exhausted convalescents were wearing when they were sent from the hospitals to the prison camp. Their recovery was challenged every day by filth, by overcrowding, and by the pestilent presence of lice and vermin. Food was another matter: the scarcity of it in an odd way provided a preoccupation for the sick and wounded. Their yearning for bacon and eggs, steak, heaps of steaming mashed potatoes, pots of coffee, hot biscuits and creamy butter took precedence over their pain, and fortunately our meager, tasteless rations never allowed them to put aside their obsessive hunger.

Making the best of it is a tired phrase, an insulting platitude that plagues the souls of the abandoned, the sick, and the poor, yet this is what these men were able to do—they made the best of it, and they did it with such élan that they swept my spirit along with them, convincing me there was no better place in all the world to be than in their company on this damned hill in Bulgaria. And they were right, although on that first day I would not have said so.

I was lucky. I was assigned a space near a large window—barred, of course—in the front of the building. I was given a bed, the lower bunk of a flimsy two-tiered affair that included a straw mattress and a thin gray blanket. Lieutenant Hamilton was in the bunk over me. Most of the men were spared the embarrassing luxury of a bed, and they simply found a space for their straw mattresses on the stone floor. A few stoics were without mattresses of any kind, though they were promised that some would be available in a few days. I suppose it was a discriminatory arrangement consistent with the military way of doing things, but no one spoke of it or seemed to care. I would have preferred to have given my place to someone else; however, it would have been considered bad form for me to raise such an issue. One did not offer a small advantage of comfort to men who lived in contempt of it.

In the days following our arrival in Shumen, I moved into the pattern of my new circumstances with the ease of a seasoned traveler. To get money for cigarettes, I sold my Hamilton watch to one of the guards, who was supposed to pay me twelve hundred leva; he ended up giving me eight hundred but did throw in a half kilo of cheese. My new comrades had been surprised that I still had my watch, suspecting, I thought, some deceitful cleverness on my part by which I had frustrated the interrogators in Sofia who were infamous for their acquisitive ways. The fact that I also had my ring, a cameo Jean had given me, doubly assured my prestige, and I was encouraged to play cards with the clique around my bunk and exchange great lies with them about our past valor in combat.

When I wasn't playing cards, I spent hours following Harry Jones's advice, sitting naked in the sun while I closely studied my shirt and pants to learn about lice eggs. I found their hiding places, and I was fascinated by the hundreds of small white beads draped in delicate, graceful chains in the seams of my clothes. Harry was right about using a cigarette: it was most satisfying to hear the faint crackle of exploding clusters of nits when I ran the glowing tip of my butt over them, killing the devils before they could feast on me. That it was a squalid life did not occur to me; I ate my bean soup twice a day, I talked with my friends, I watched the frisky young goats play. From day to day I moved in the narrow freedom I was allowed, not remembering I had lived in any other way. It was too long ago to remember . . . too long ago.

I had become one of a chaste community dedicated to poverty, comradeship, and obedience. We were not required to take vows, and our self-abnegation was not freely chosen; it was thrust upon us, the last of many lessons. Our first lesson had been discipline, the seemingly absurd rite of military life that harshly punished any taint of heresy, any inclination or willfulness toward imagined prerogatives. We had learned the purity of submission to a cause, and we had learned to accept the infallibility of command. In combat our strength was measured; our faith was measured, and we were sent out again and again to impose a will, which was not ours, on an enemy we did not know, to burden him with blood and ruin. We were culled by death, some were lost, and some were put upon a hill in the wilderness. For me it was a perplexing end, to be abandoned on a hill. I waited. I waited for someone to find me, to tell me it was over. I would learn no more.

The days of waiting were not all the same; there were things we found to make each day different, not significantly so, but enough to tell us whether it had been good or bad. In the morning, our hunger always made us apprehensive: How much bread would we get? Would it be as moldy as yesterday's? It had been a week since we had our last teaspoon ration of fig jam. Would we have some this morning? If a dollop were not put on our bread, should we complain to Major Smith? If our portion of bean soup at noon were thinner than usual, or worse, if it were cabbage broth instead, this made the day as sour as the stinking soup, and friends became testy bitching about trifles they would not remember tomorrow. If a man's suppurating wound began to dry, showing clean flesh where it had been festering before, the word would spread around the camp. "Charley's doin' good. The leg's gettin' better. . . . No shit, it's really a lot better." This kind of news raised our spirits, and we marked the hour of the wounded man's progress as a gain toward the time when all the men would be well again.

Tom Connors's recovery from his brief bout with malaria was a special occasion for the crew and me, a special day. We celebrated by giving Tom a gift of two packs of Bulgarian cigarettes from our precious supply, and he convinced us he was moving toward a full recovery when he grumbled and complained because the cigarettes weren't Chesterfields.

He was resting on a straw mattress, which had been placed on the floor against the rear wall of the building. I watched him examine one of the packs before he opened it. His face was streaked with white blotches where sweat had furrowed through the dirt. I thought his eyes looked wider and darker than before. He opened the pack and pulled out a cigarette, looking at it skeptically before he put it in his mouth. I held a match for him.

"Thomosins," he said. "What the hell kind of a butt is that?"

"Bulgarian, Tom—they're not bad."

He took a puff. "It's sweet," he mumbled. "It tastes like horseshit."

"Well, Tommy," I said, "why don't you get off your ass and go down to the PX and get a carton of your goddamned Chesterfields. And save the backs of the packs. We use them to make our playing cards."

Tom looked up at me, indignant and feigning shock. "That's a nice way to talk to your buddy," he said. "When I'm dead and gone you'll be sorry you gave me this lousy butt." And then he sighed and took a long drag from the cigarette, watching the smoke swirl up away from his face before he spoke again. His voice was raspy, and his words were slurred with fatigue. "Well, that's how things are, I guess. Your buddy kicks you in the ass, and then when you get sick, he gives you a stinking Bulgarian butt. *C'est la guerre.* Right, Jacko? *C'est la guerre.*"

"That's the way it is, Tommy," I said.

Tom handed me his cigarette. "I think I'll snooze now," he said. "Don't worry, I'll be up and around in a couple of days. Thanks for the smokes." He was asleep when we left him.

We wandered through our listless idyll with little thought of what might occupy us, for an instant or for an hour. We did not feel time a thing of consequence, as a passage that might lead us somewhere. We could not change the monotony of days blending into days. We were caught in a stillness. It didn't matter. The sun was warm. Beyond the barbed wire, sleek golden and dark-coated horses grazed; the muezzin called from his tower, and when his shrill passion came over the hill, the pale-eyed goats paused in their feeding and raised their heads, but only for a moment. The weaver who held the colored threads of our lives was quiet at his loom, rapt in silence and dreaming of patterns. When he chose to begin again, the shuttle would clatter, and we would move on.

July had passed; the long days of summer were gone, and the angles of the sunlight were changing. The sky was changing, and the wind seemed to be blowing more from the west. I probably wouldn't have thought about it if Sergeant Corelli hadn't told me it was his birthday, the seventh day of August. The sergeant wasn't doing well; his hair was falling out, and he didn't know why. His burns looked as bad as the day he had come into camp. Under his buttocks, where his smoldering chute harness had burned into his flesh, I could have put the width of three fingers into the deep crusted wounds.

Lt. Dan Wylie, the P-38 pilot who had complained about the sound of my boots when I had paced between the sleeping forms of my comrades in the foul barn at Ruschuck, was not making any better progress than Sergeant Corelli. The steel fragments in Dan's back and shoulder had not been totally removed or cleaned, and he needed treatment for the infection that was now ravaging him with fever and weakness. Lt. J. P. Darlington and Major Smith had been nagging the commandant for days to try to get Dan and the sergeant down to the hospital in Shumen, and they finally succeeded. The two men were to be moved in the morning.

Tom Connors had recovered from his bout with malaria, but there were four new cases. An Australian crew, who had crash-landed a Wellington in the marshes along the Black Sea coast a week ago, and had spent two nights hiding in the deep, wet grass before they were captured, were now down with the fever. When they were brought into our camp, their faces, hands, and ankles were bloated and discolored from hundreds of mosquito bites. In a matter of hours, they were shaking with chills. We had nothing to give them but four thin blankets that J.P. was able to scrounge. I was sure that one of the blankets belonged to J.P. He would give away anything if he thought another man was in need of it.

There were about thirty nationals other than Americans in the camp: a South African crew, the Australians, Major Sheldon, Andreas the Greek paratrooper, the Dutchmen, and two Yugoslav B-24 crews who were flying under British command. They were all good fellows except for the two idiots in Captain Korsha's crew, a Croatian and a Slovene, who won the contempt of every man by getting into a bloody fight with their bread knives over an old hatred about a piece of dirt in Yugoslavia. Hugh and Louis broke up the fight with violent efficiency, and managed to keep the two fools from bleeding to death. I don't know why the good Dutchmen bothered; I would have left the bastards on the ground and walked away.

The conditions of other prisoners beyond the pale of my small group, I could only surmise as being marginal at best. There was a constant problem with infections. The slightest bruise or scratch turned into a swollen festering mess within days of the injury. And a new problem was beginning to plague many of the men; it seemed to be a kind of scurvy, a debilitating outbreak of running sores that appeared on a man's arms and thighs, and sometimes on his buttocks. Within a week or ten days, the sores usually dried out, leaving scaly pockets in the victim's flesh. But the sores were only a nuisance symptom; more disturbing to us was the extreme fatigue and apathy that overcame the men who were afflicted.

The coming end of summer promised nothing but shorter days, longer, colder nights, and the bleak prospect of winter. It was not the best of times; the days ahead seemed to assure the attrition of our company in this poor and ravaged country. The insatiable maw of the German military machine had devoured the grain of Bulgaria's fields; German soldiers had crushed the soil, stripped the orchards, slaughtered the lambs and the pigs; they had taken the cattle; they had slaked their thirst with Bulgarian wine; they had taken the bread; they had taken wood and fuel; they had taken cloth and the wool from the sheep. They had taken everything they wanted, and they wanted everything. They had raped the land. In the months of winter, the Bulgarian people would go hungry, and it was more than likely we would starve, growing leaner and leaner until, in the tradition of good soldiers, we would slowly fade away. It would be a different kind of battle for us, a drawn-out, hopeless siege against an enemy we could not see, a specter without banners or trumpets coming among us with the silent weapons of cold and hunger.

If there were reasons to dread the future, there was little evidence of it in the camp. The men were cheerful; they rarely complained, and if they did curse, it was never against their fate but against the malevolence of small things: bad luck at cards, a rainstorm that kept them inside, moldy bread, their failure to kill a rat that stole their small hoard of cheese. J.P.'s one-legged sergeants were always about stirring us up with rumors and bits of gossip. Their closeness to J.P. gave them credibility; even the skeptics listened.

"We got the straight scoop from J.P. The Russians are pushin' the krauts out of Rumania. They're up in the northwest corner right now. They're pushin' them right into Hungary. They'll be down here in Bulgaria in no time."

"How the hell do you know, you one-legged asshole?"

"Lieutenant Radeoff said so. He told J.P. He said the Bulgarians are scared shitless."

"Bullshit."

And there would be the usual mournful observation from Lieutenant Jones. "You'll never get out alive, Sarge. Take it from old Harry, you'll never get out alive."

The source of Sergeant Blackwell's information, the Bulgarian officer, Lieutenant Radeoff, visited our camp once a week. We did not

have the slightest idea what the lieutenant's assignment was or how
he could so brazenly ignore the protocol between prisoners and captors.
He was a dashing, handsome fellow who made no attempt to disguise
the ease and familiarity he shared with J.P. and Major Smith, and he
always talked with Lt. Tom Judd for a while before he left the hill,
which was usually in the late afternoon. Some of the bolder prisoners
skulked about near Judd and Radeoff as they talked, trying to pick up
bits of what was being said, but it was a waste of time. The conversation
was always in French. To those of us outside the trinity of J.P., Smith,
and Judd, Lieutenant Radeoff was a mystery, albeit a benign one. It
was always after his visits that J.P.'s pirate sergeants, and occasionally
J.P. himself, filled us in on the progress of the war, and in particular
on the progress of the Russian South Ukraine army, which was now,
according to our informants, on the outskirts of Bucharest and pushing
south toward the Bulgarian border.

It was a sunny morning in late August. George Hamilton, my once-
upon-a-time navigator, had joined me in the compound with a few
other men to witness a breeding. Beyond the barbed wire, the horses
were coupled; the Bulgarian soldiers looked relieved that the violent
task of handling the crazed stallion was over. The mare was standing
quietly under the burden of her mate; her ears were laid back and her
great soft eyes bulged as she endured the thrusting phallus.

George, of course, had to comment on the performance. "You
know, chum," he said, "sex is a bad business. All that terrible urgency.
It's a wonder that damn stud didn't kill someone. You know, God
should have made it simpler. Wouldn't you have thought He would
have? Even with us, all that grunting and thrashing about. The ridiculous mechanics of the whole thing. So absurd."

I was only half listening to George. I had changed my attention to
a flock of large birds that were flying very high over us. They seemed
to be caught in an upper wind, a slow vortex that kept them turning
as they drifted toward the south.

"What kind of birds are they, George?" I asked him.

"I think they're storks, probably what they call black storks, *Ciconia
nigra*, which are indigenous to this part of the world."

"Good God, how do you remember such stuff?"

George smiled. "I don't know," he said. "I remember odds and
ends. I've got a couple of degrees that make me master of nothing at
all—different kinds of junk. I studied a bit of ornithology for fun. I
just happened to remember about the storks."

"Where do you think they're heading?" I asked.

"Maybe Turkey. Maybe Greece. Migrating to North Africa maybe. They like marshy land—like the Nile delta."

I could hear the quiet voices of the soldiers soothing the horses while I kept my gaze fixed on the sky. I envied the birds. I imagined the serene patterns of earth they saw from their great height. I felt the rush of air they felt against their wings. I felt the pulse of their blood, and I felt the surging joy of their journey. I wondered if they could see me . . . they must be able to see me standing here. Look down! Tell someone! Can't you see me? I'm here! Tell someone I'm here!

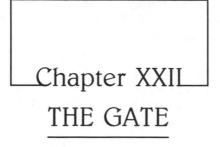

Chapter XXII
THE GATE

What candles may be held to speed them all?
Not in the hands of boys, but in their eyes
Shall shine the holy glimmer of good-bys.

—WILFRED OWEN

During the first week of September, two months after our arrival at the prison camp in Shumen, the Russians were massed on the Bulgarian border. The Bulgarians were given an ultimatum: capitulate and declare war on the Germans, or be overwhelmed and slaughtered. Until that moment of resolute confrontation, the Bulgarians had held the tenuous position of being at war with the Allied forces, but not with Russia. The Bulgarians had declared that they were nonaggressors against their northern neighbor, the Great Bear whom every Balkan country feared. Now the Russians were pounding on the door; the Germans were in full retreat. It was Hobson's choice. Bulgaria surrendered.

All Allied prisoners were to be set free. All political prisoners were to be set free. Major Smith was flown to Bulgarian headquarters in Sofia so he could provide details of our situation and contribute to decisions regarding our evacuation. When he returned, he told us we would be taken by train to Istanbul. From there, after a brief internment, we would travel, again by train, to a British base in Aleppo. From Aleppo, we would be flown to another British base in Cairo. At the time, the major did not know who would take us across the Mediterranean to Italy. We hardly cared. We would begin our journey sometime within the next forty-eight hours.

I have never forgotten that last day on the hill. We were happy but subdued; there was a strange ambivalence in our mood, and I could not understand, nor could any of the other men I suppose, the sensation of faint regret that our bond of common misery was being loosened. It did not seem possible, but I did not want to leave these men; I did not want to leave the place where I had come to know them, where I had come to know myself. . . .

No, I cannot say for sure it was that way. I cannot say for sure there was any subtle ambivalence distracting me. It may be nearer the truth that I am an old man now, and I like to think there was regret. The memory of Shumen has not left me; I have recalled so many things, so many, many times, and perhaps my constant recall has burnished the memory, giving it different hues. It may even be the time of day, a shadow moving in the night, or a breath of wind, that stirs and changes the ghostly fragments I remember. I cannot say for sure.

The prison commandant was particularly visible. He wandered among the prisoners smiling in an encouraging way as though he wanted to remind us he was a good fellow who had always done the best he could. He seemed to be imploring us, asking for our understanding. After all, he was not a senior officer, only a mere captain. He had to do what he was told; there was policy he could not impugn. If the prisoners were half starved, if the sick and wounded were not taken down to the hospital in Shumen, if there were no medicines, not even a damned aspirin, it was not his fault. If the prisoners had been beaten, it was done to them before they arrived in Shumen. He could not have prevented it. Of course, there were cases when we had to maintain discipline. When Lieutenant Judd and those other officers tried to escape, they had to be punished. Didn't they? If there were only one keg of water a day for three hundred and thirty men—well, what could he do? He had his orders. The poor wretch, I thought. I wondered how long he would be alive after the Communists took over his country. It must have been the first sweet drops of freedom I felt washing away my hate, for I pitied the commandant.

He persisted in making amends, and arranged for forty or fifty prisoners at a time to be taken from the compound to a stream about a half mile away where they might bathe. His sudden concern for us was amusing, so pathetically transparent, so hopelessly unredeeming.

We knew our being sent out to the stream was a matter of trying to eliminate the reeking evidence of neglect we might present. It would be very bad for him if we were seen, or smelled, in our present state. The hapless man even went so far as to present Major Smith with a written statement to the effect that he, the commandant, had treated the prisoners well, within the constraints imposed on him by his superiors. The major, who was a man who did not find it difficult to punish his enemies, of course refused to sign the document.

Each group was sent out under guard, and the commandant tried to assuage the major's irritation by telling him the guards were only escorts for our protection. He implied there might be German patrols still in the area; apparently he had chosen to forget we had heard the German armor crashing through Shumen three nights ago heading west. We had listened to them all night long with great apprehension, fearing they might come up on the hill to take us. But now they were gone. I was sure the Russians would fill the void left by the Germans, and would maintain the vigorous climate of oppressive brutality. The Bulgarians would hardly be aware of the difference, for after a time the despairing faces of the victims would look the same. One would not know if they were Fascists or Communists. One would not know who they were.

At one o'clock my group, which was the next to last, was marched out of the compound. At the gate, we were each given a small bar of soap by a grinning guard who then with two companions followed our slovenly parade. We were led by Sergeant Dogget, and he was very familiar with the path; he had traveled it every day for months with a small gentle donkey pulling a two-wheeled cart with a keg, our daily ration of water, secured behind a single seat, which the sergeant never used. He always walked by the donkey's head and talked to the good little beast as he made his way to the stream and back. I thought the sergeant enjoyed his brief freedom from us every day and preferred the company of his donkey. He was a lonely man who kept to himself. He rarely smiled, and he was rarely idle. He cooked the soup; he made our tea; he washed the soiled bandages, draping them like scarfs over the bare scrubs of brush left by the hungry goats; he ordered us about when the wounded were moved into the sun; he cursed and labored every day. He was a good man, and I wished I could have earned a word from him, but I never did.

The stream was fast-running water, splashing over smooth black rocks, and unbelievably cold; it was impossible to stay in it for more than a few moments; it was equally impossible to wash in it. The soap could have been a flat stone. I rubbed it as hard as I could over my skin, and there was not a trace of lather. The determined ritual of bathing with the intent to become clean again was doing no more than putting a greasy, wet sheen over my weathered patina of grime and dirt, so I forgot about washing and enjoyed wallowing in the cold water for as long as I could stand it. When I came out of the stream to sit shivering on the bank, I joined in the chatter about how cold the water was and about our aching balls. I was astonished when I saw my shrunken penis, which was now blue and no larger than a young boy's. This brief thrall of innocence pleased me, for it sent me back remembering a summer day and a river. . . .

"Come on, Jack, I'll race you to the bridge! Come on!" . . . There were white gulls over us then, wheeling and soaring in the sunlight. And when we swam under the bridge, quiet in the deep, cool shadowed water, we heard cars and trucks rattling over us and the sounds of footsteps brisk with purpose, not knowing we secret, naked warriors were beneath them, raging and fierce, ready to strike. . . .

We met the last group coming out of the compound as we were returning. There were the usual obscene exchanges, and we were surprised at the pleasure we felt to be greeting someone as though we were truly free, speaking to old friends whom we could meet anytime or anywhere we chose. The last to pass by was J.P. and his two sergeants, whose torn brown jackets flapped about them like the tired wings of two large earthbound birds, and their crude crutches drove them forward, bouncing up and down beside their friend.

I had not come to know J.P. well; I had spoken with him only a few times. Of course I had heard stories about the legendary man, how he had devoted himself to the two men he had pulled from the flaming wreckage of his B-24, how he had cut the bloody shreds of one man's leg with his pocketknife to free him, how he had ordered the others in the crew to make their escape while he stayed with his bleeding gunners. There were stories how the three of them had lived alone as captives through the hard winter of '43 and '44, how they had endured their misery and the cruel arrogance of Fascist Bulgaria, then so assured of victory. All the stories were probably true. I was never to really know, for J.P.'s memories of that terrible mission from North Africa to Ploesti, and the bitter days after it, were his memories. He never spoke of them; at least he never spoke of them to me or to any of the men I knew.

J.P. was not prepossessing; there was nothing in his appearance or in his manner to encourage inquiry into his epic story. He was a modest man of medium height, quiet, slender, and sometimes he appeared frail to me. His head was bald with just a few wisps of fair hair; he had a slightly receding chin and clear, pale eyes. His countenance was pleasing, but not more than that. When I had talked with him I thought at first he was diffident and shy, although I soon began to feel the substance of the man. He preferred to listen rather than to speak, and I found myself guarding my words, fearing his disapproval. But I did not need to be concerned, for J.P. listened to what I told him as a matter of routine. Everything was routine to him, as he assumed it to be for each of us: my story or his, pain, fear, valor or despair, death and duty—all were matters of war's routine. One did not have to speak too much about them.

When we entered the compound the gates were shut behind us. I looked back but I could not see J.P. and his sergeants. They had gone over the crown of the hill and had entered the stand of young trees that grew along the banks of the stream.

The commandant was pacing nervously back and forth. His head was down; his hands were clasped behind his back. He seemed agitated, as though he were pondering some inspired action, some gesture to persuade us he could do the right thing if he were given a chance. Suddenly he stopped and shouted to the nearest sentry, who responded by quickly slinging his rifle over his shoulder and running toward the gate. The soldier fumbled with the lock for a moment, then hurriedly pushed the gate open. The commandant shouted again. The harassed soldier pushed harder, opening the gate as wide as it would go. The commandant, who appeared satisfied at this point, now turned toward us and made what seemed to be an appeal for us to do something. His Bulgarian words, of course, were incomprehensible to us. He was smiling; he was making urgent motions with his hands. He was trying to tell us to go outside, to leave the narrow compound and go out to enjoy the freedom of the hilltop.

No one moved toward the open gate. The commandant looked puzzled, and then dismayed. Perhaps he thought we suspected some kind of trap. He renewed his pleading gestures; his voice was gentle and assuring. I did not understand the words he said, but I guessed with reasonable certainty he was telling us he would not betray us. How could we think he would do such a thing? The war was over between us; we could be friends now.

A small goat was pushing against my leg, trying to plague me into rubbing the coarse knobs of his horns, which were just beginning to grow. I ignored him while he repeatedly demanded my attention, ramming his small head into my knee with furious persistence because I would not give him the pleasure I gave him yesterday, and the day before. . . . But I wanted to be rid of him. I didn't want to pet him.

I wanted to stand at the edge of the hill to look down into the town. What was holding me?

I wondered if it could have been a matter of ceremony. How could we take our first step toward freedom without it? There should have been colors, our standards bravely curling in the wind. There should have been a band with sunlight dazzling the brass and cymbals. Shouting adjutants with spit-shined boots, grim-faced and concerned, should have been forming the parade. . . .

George Hamilton broke my reverie. "Why doesn't someone tell that damn fool commandant we have to wait for the others?" he demanded.

"Oh, he'll figure it out after a while, George," I said. "The boys will be back in a few minutes anyway. There's no rush. We've got plenty of time." After I said it, I thought how strange it was, to say one had plenty of time. I shouldn't have said it; I didn't want to confront it, it was unfamiliar . . . the vast, forbidding future.

George was staring down at my small, stubborn friend, who was still pushing his head against my leg. "Your pal stinks, chum," he said.

"He's a goat," I said. "He's supposed to stink."

George grinned. "Yeah, I guess you're right," he agreed. He crouched down to rub the small beast's horns. The goat's eyes glazed with ecstasy.

"Here they come!" The loud cry startled the commandant; he was apprehensive, perhaps fearing we were about to attack him. He relaxed and resumed his idiotic smile when he saw we were looking beyond him toward the group of prisoners who were emerging from the trees near the stream.

George was standing now, trying to fend off the insistent goat and at the same time watch the returning prisoners. He began to laugh. "Isn't that the raunchiest mob you ever saw in your life?" he asked. "The heroes of Ploesti! My God, what a sight!" George's words were full of pride, for who could have contempt for such men?

"You're right, chum," I said. "They're beautiful—as long as you stay upwind of them."

Indeed, as George had said, the men looked wretched: some were barefoot; some were half naked, carrying their rags; some were leaning on their friends; two men were kicking a stone between them, intent on bringing it through the gate as if they were scoring a goal; three men had drifted behind the group like reluctant schoolboys; and some walked staring at the ground, indifferent to the day as though it were for them the same as any other day and nothing had changed.

Before the last man was inside the compound, the commandant hurried toward Major Smith. Pointing to the open gate, he began to repeat the pleas he had made to us. In French, in Bulgarian, and in pantomime, he begged the major to understand his gesture. We must accept him he seemed to ask; we must accept this small freedom he could give us. Major Smith nodded to the Bulgarian captain, indicating that he understood, but he did not smile. He turned away instead, dismissing the commandant's importunate presence as a tedious nuisance. He knew, as we all did, who would be the first to stand on the hill. Not one of us would go before them.

A group of prisoners were pushing J.P. toward the gate; his two sergeants were being pushed along with him. Men were shouting and cheering. The friendly melee floundered to the boundary of barbed wire that defined the end of our narrow compound; there the open gate beckoned the three banished men; there they accepted their fate and the modest honor we could give them; there they turned their backs to us and walked alone to where they could stand to look down on the town.

As parades go, it wasn't much, I suppose. There were just three ragged men walking across the hilltop, undistinguished men except for the lack of two legs and a certain enduring spirit that burned from them, and burned from them in me. There were no colors or standards; there was no band or sounding brass or cymbals; there were no shouts of adjutants echoing over the field. But there was glory, and I have remembered it. I shall always remember.

ABOUT THE AUTHOR

JOHN MUIRHEAD was born in East Braintree, Massachusetts, the son of a chief engineer of a large ore carrier. At eighteen he entered an apprenticeship at the Fore River Shipyard as a structural draftsman and also trained in marine engineering and naval architecture. Later he was accepted into the aviation cadet program and became a bomber pilot. Discharged in 1945, John Muirhead returned to the shipyard in supervisory positions until 1983.